Scaling up integrated Community Case Management

Lessons from the Rapid Access Expansion (RAcE) Programme in 5 sub-Saharan African countries

Edited by
Salim Sadruddin

Published in the United Kingdom by Inishmore Laser Scientific Publishing Ltd.

Inishmore Laser Scientific Publishing Ltd
Caledonian Exchange, 19a Canning Street, Edinburgh
United Kingdom, EH3 8HE

Printed in Croatia by LaserPlus, Ltd

ISBN: 978-1-9999564-2-4

Cover photograph: A relais communautaire near Kalemie, Tanganyika province,
Democratic Republic of Congo administering a malaria rapid diagnostic test on
a child presenting with fever (from the collection of Salim Sadruddin, used with
permission).

Scaling up integrated Community Case Management

Lessons from the Rapid Access Expansion (RAcE) Programme in 5 sub-Saharan African countries

Edited by
Salim Sadruddin

2019

Contents

PREFACE

The World Health Organization's (WHO) integrated community case management (iCCM) Rapid Access Expansion (RAcE) Programme was a continuation of excellent work done over the years by the WHO's Department of Maternal, Newborn, Child and Adolescent Health, UNICEF, USAID, and other international organizations in promoting iCCM as key strategy to improve access to life saving interventions for communities with poor access to health facilities. Their work on development of training materials, job aids, monitoring tools and support to Ministries of Health (MOH) facilitated introduction of iCCM in sub-Saharan African countries.

The RAcE Programme was the first operational initiative for the Global Malaria Programme led by a dedicated team of technical and management staff at headquarters with technical support from the Africa Regional Office, West Africa Inter-country support team, and the WHO Country Offices in Democratic Republic of Congo, Malawi, Mozambique, Niger and Nigeria. The global and country level staff of International Rescue Committee, Malaria Consortium, Save the Children, Society for Family Health, and World Vision facilitated MOH's to implement and scale-up iCCM in RAcE supported countries. The ICF staff provided technical support for programme monitoring, data quality assessment and evaluation. The MOH leadership and support by abovementioned organizations lead to policy changes, quality implementation, improved access to care, and provision of treatment to millions of children under five years of age in the 5 sub-Saharan African countries. In addition, the country level implementation, research on implementation issues, and results of the household surveys produced rich learning.

In this publication, staff from non-governmental organizations, ICF and MOH have documented key learnings in a series of articles. This work has built capacity at multiple levels and will increase the knowledge basis to inform and influence national policies and programmes.

The Global Affairs Canada funding of the RAcE Programme, is deeply appreciated. It has facilitated the scale-up of iCCM in the 5 countries, training of thousands of health workers, and provided life-saving treatment to millions of children under five years of age. The RAcE collection is also the fruit of the financial support received from the Global Affairs Canada.

Salim Sadruddin, July 2019
Global Malaria Programme, World Health Organization
Geneva, Switzerland

Lessons from the integrated community case management (iCCM) Rapid Access Expansion Programme

Salim Sadruddin[1], Franco Pagnoni[2], Gunther Baugh[3]

[1] Global Malaria Programme, World Health Organization, Geneva Switzerland
[2] Director, TIPTOP Project, Barcelona Institute for Global Health, Barcelona, Spain
[3] Independent Consultant, Geneva, Switzerland (formerly with Global Malaria Programme, World Health Organization)

In 2012, the Government of Canada awarded a grant to the World Health Organization's Global Malaria Programme (GMP) to support the scale-up of integrated community case management (iCCM) of pneumonia, diarrhoea and malaria among children under 5 in sub-Saharan Africa under the Rapid Access Expansion Programme (RAcE). The two main objectives of the programme were to: (1) Contribute to the reduction of child mortality due to malaria, pneumonia and diarrhoea by increasing access to diagnostics, treatment and referral services, and (1) Stimulate policy updates in participating countries and catalyze scale-up of integrated community case management (iCCM) through documentation and dissemination of best practices. Based on the results of the implementation research and programmatic lessons, this collection provides evidence on impact and improving coverage of iCCM in routine health systems, and opportunities and challenges of implementing and sustaining delivery of iCCM at scale.

After the publication of the WHO and UNICEF joint statement on iCCM, countries started implementing small scale iCCM projects funded by global funding agencies [1]. The American Journal of Tropical Medicine and Hygiene 2013 supplement on "Evidence for the implementation, effects, and impact of the integrated community case management strategy to treat childhood infection" and the iCCM evidence symposium and subsequent publications of articles in the Journal of Global Health 2014 supplement provided an impetus for scaling up iCCM [2,3]. However, the donor supported initiatives to introduce iCCM through NGOs in many countries, oftentimes bypassing the Ministries of Health, raise questions on continuity and sustainability of service delivery by community health workers. According to Daelmans et al., a persistent challenge to scaling up iCCM has been understanding prerequisites for successful iCCM implementation at national scale [4]. The multi-country RAcE Programme was thus set up to strengthen the evidence base for iCCM best practices and sustainability and to generate knowledge for policy-makers and practitioners to accelerate access to care [5].

The WHO's RAcE Programme governed by an International Steering Group selected civil society organizations (CSO) to receive grants to support implementation of iCCM in the Democratic Republic of Congo, Malawi, Mozambique, Niger and two States in Nigeria. The CSOs were selected through a transparent review process by an independent body, the Project Review Panel (PRP), consisting of members with expertise on iCCM and health systems strengthening . In each country RAcE initiative was implemented under the leadership of Ministry of Health, with iCCM technical committees chaired by the MOH providing technical support and programme oversight.

Over 1.49 million children were provided access to life saving treatments for malaria, pneumonia and diarrhoea through training and equipping of more than 8,200 Community Health Workers (CHWs) in the 5 countries. In each country the programme was at scale, covering all of Tanganyika Province in DRC, 8 Districts in Malawi, 4 Provinces in Mozambique, 4 Districts in Niger, and two States in Nigeria. Four years of implementation resulted in diagnosis and treatment of over 8.24 million clinical cases of malaria, pneumonia and diarrhoea by community health workers.

The implementing partners were encouraged to include implementation research in their proposals. Implementation research studies were embedded in the programmes, and placed under the overall strategic guidance of the country level steering committee headed by the Ministry of Health. WHO undertook the role of technical support and oversight. A dissemination meeting to share the results of implementation research and best practices with policy-makers and implementers was organized in Abuja, Nigeria in 2014. Following the Abuja meeting the study investigators, and CSO and MOH technical staff were encouraged to develop manuscripts for sharing the research results and programmatic lessons with neighboring countries and globally.

This supplement presents results of the implementation research and programmatic learning in the context of the RAcE programme in the five countries. The articles are structured around five themes: **Impact of iCCM on care seeking and treatment and child mortality; sustainability; monitoring and health information systems; challenges in mature iCCM programmes; and tools and approaches to improve quality of care.**

With regards to impact om mortality, Prosnitz et al. present the results of RAcE programme evaluation to demonstrate plausible contribution of RAcE to any changes in treatment coverage and mortality in RAcE supported programme areas. The Lives Saved Tool was used to estimate changes in child mortality in RAcE sites. Under-five mortality declined in all six RAcE sites, with an overall average decline of 10 percent.

Oresanya et al. and Isiguzo et al. in their articles demonstrate the effect of introducing iCCM in increasing care seeking and treatment from CHWs in two geographically and culturally diverse states in Nigeria. Their analysis demonstrates how bringing quality care closer to home improves overall care seeking and also shifts care seeking from public sector facilities that are not accessible or provide poor quality care, as well as from for-profit retail drug outlets. Maintaining the improvements in health outcomes beyond the introductory phase requires a structured, participatory planning approach. Yourkavitch et al describe a facilitated sustainability planning process to identify and address health systems factors that influence the sustainability of iCCM services, along with planning for transition from an externally supported implementation to a national system. While, Alegbeleye et al describe the process of community engagement and mobilization in Niger State, and how it fostered ownership and service uptake.

With regards to monitoring and health information systems, Moonzwe Davis et al. and Yourkavitch et al. in their articles describe a unique approach to assess iCCM reporting systems and data quality and how iCCM data quality assessments can serve as a collaborative and evidence-based activity to influence discussions of data quality and stimulate HMIS strengthening efforts.

Two articles from Malawi and one from Mozambique highlight the challenges faced by mature programmes implemented at scale. Zalisk et al. present the findings from the household surveys in Malawi. The article highlights factors that influence communities' trust and confidence in CHWs and resulting effect on care seeking from CHWs. The article by Guenther et al. on introduction of home visits for newborn and pregnant women in the CHW service delivery package in Malawi demonstrates the need for thorough assessment of CHW capacity and workload, and community acceptability before introduction of a new intervention or delivery strategy. Källander et al. present the limitations of CHW training and deployment on child mortality. This has to be accompanied by increasing community awareness to seek care promptly, improved referral linkages and availability of CHWs when a child falls ill. The challenges faced by the multi-purpose CHWs in Malawi and Mozambique, who service multiple villages with a variety of curative, preventive and promotive activities, or spending significant amount of time in the facility demonstrates the limits of this cadre. These CHWs are overloaded, and programmes keep identifying more interventions and tasks for them as part of an expanding community platform. Interventions to be delivered by CHWs must be prioritized based on an objective evaluation in terms of positive or negative synergistic effects at the CHW level.

With regards to tools and approaches for improving quality of care delivered by CHWs, Langston et al. demonstrate the improvements that can be made through streamlining existing tools and CHW training strategy. Peart Boyce et al. and Zakus et al. present results of studies assessing effect of smart phones with mHealth applications on quality of care delivered by the CHWs in Malawi and Niger respectively. Both studies observed that mHealth applications improved adherence to the iCCM protocol for assessing sick children and classifying illness by CHWs, with limited or no effect on treatment. Considering additional costs, logistics and national capacity to manage the mHealth system, questions around its viability remain.

The diverse set of articles in the supplement along the spectrum of implementation and different health systems provide valuable lessons for implementing iCCM and important reflections for scale-up within the health system. They also highlight the importance of carrying out implementation research as part of program implementation in order to maximize gains in public health knowledge.

References

1 World Health Organization and UNICEF. Integrated community case management: an equity–focused strategy to improve access to essential treatment services for children. Geneva and New York: WHO and UNICEF; 2012. Available: http://www.unicef.org/health/files/iCCM_Joint_Statement_2012.pdf. Accessed: 16 November 2015.

2 Marsh DR, Hamer DH, Pagnoni F, Peterson S. Introduction to a special supplement: Evidence for the implementation, effects, and impact of the integrated community case management strategy to treat childhood infection. Am J Trop Med Hyg. 2012;87(5 Suppl):2-5.

3 Diaz Y, Aboubaker D, Young M. Current scientific evidence for integrated community case management (iCCM) in Africa: Findings from the iCCM. J Glob Health. 2014;4;020101.

4 Daelmans B, Seck A, Nsona H, Wilson S, Young M. Integrated Community Case Management of Childhood Illness: What Have We Learned? Am J Trop Med Hyg. 2016;94:571–3.

5 Rapid Access Expansion Programme (RAcE). Global Malaria Programme, World Health Organization. Geneva: WHO; 2015.

Evidence of Impact: iCCM as a strategy to save lives of children under five

Debra Prosnitz[1], Samantha Herrera[1,2], Helen Coelho[1], Lwendo Moonzwe Davis[1], Kirsten Zalisk[1], Jennifer Yourkavitch[1]

[1] ICF, Rockville, Maryland, USA
[2] Save the Children, Washington, D.C., USA

Background In 2013, the World Health Organization (WHO) launched the Rapid Access Expansion (RAcE) programme in the Democratic Republic of the Congo, Malawi, Mozambique, Niger, and Nigeria to increase coverage of diagnostic, treatment, and referral services for malaria, pneumonia, and diarrhea among children ages 2-59 months. In 2017, a final evaluation of the six RAcE sites was conducted to determine whether the programme goal was reached. A key evaluation objective was to estimate the reduction in childhood mortality and the number of under-five lives saved over the project period in the RAcE project areas.

Methods The Lives Saved Tool (LiST) was used to estimate reductions in all-cause child mortality due to changes in coverage of treatment for the integrated community case management (iCCM) illnesses – malaria, pneumonia, and diarrhea – while accounting for other changes in maternal and child health interventions in each RAcE project area. Data from RAcE baseline and endline household surveys, Demographic and Health Surveys, and routine health service data were used in each LiST model. The models yielded estimated change in under-five mortality rates, and estimated number of lives saved per year by malaria, pneumonia and diarrhea treatment. We adjusted the results to estimate the number of lives saved by community health workers (CHW)-provided treatment.

Results The LiST model accounts for coverage changes in iCCM intervention coverage and other health trends in each project area to estimate mortality reduction and child lives saved. Under five mortality declined in all six RAcE sites, with an average decline of 10 percent. An estimated 6200 under-five lives were saved by malaria, pneumonia, and diarrhea treatment in the DRC, Malawi, Niger, and Nigeria, of which approximately 4940 (75 percent) were saved by treatment provided by CHWs. This total excludes Mozambique, where there were no estimated under-five lives saved likely due to widespread stockouts of key medications. In all other project areas, lives saved by CHW-provided treatment contributed substantially to the estimated decline in under-five mortality.

Conclusions Our results suggest that iCCM is a strategy that can save lives and measurably decrease child mortality in settings where access to health facility services is low and adequate resources for iCCM implementation are provided for CHW services.

Integrated community case management (iCCM) is an equity-focused strategy to provide timely treatment for common childhood illness at the community level by community health workers (CHWs) [1]. The iCCM strategy targets hard-to reach-areas where access to care is typically a challenge, defined in most contexts as communities more than five kilometers from a functional health facility. iCCM targets three common, treatable, and curable childhood illnesses that account for high rates of mortality and morbidity and exert a significant burden on the health system: malaria, pneumonia, and diarrhea. iCCM interventions include diagnostic, treatment, and referral services for malaria, pneumonia, and diarrhea. The implementation of iCCM interventions has been demonstrated to increase prompt and appropriate treatment in children under five years of age [2-5].

In 2013, the World Health Organization (WHO) launched the Rapid Access Expansion (RAcE) programme in the Democratic Republic of the Congo (DRC), Malawi, Mozambique, Niger, and Nigeria to increase coverage of iCCM interventions among children ages 2-59 months. Two projects were implemented in Nigeria; one in Abia State and one in Niger State. Through training, deploying, equipping, and supervising CHWs, RAcE aimed to achieve universal iCCM coverage in designated hard-to-reach areas supported by the programme. iCCM-trained CHWs in RAcE project areas assessed, diagnosed, and treated or referred as appropriate, children with malaria, pneumonia, and diarrhea. Malaria was diagnosed using rapid diagnostic tests (RDTs) and treated with artemisinin combination therapy (ACT); pneumonia was diagnosed by counting respiratory rate and classified as having fast breathing pneumonia using WHO age–specific cut–off points for age and treated with amoxicillin; diarrhea was treated with oral rehydration solution (ORS) and zinc. iCCM protocols aligned with the national policy in each country supported this case management by CHWs. While RDTs were used to diagnose malaria in most project areas for the duration of RAcE implementation, in Malawi RDTs were rolled out mid-project, resulting in a change in malaria treatment protocol from presumptive treatment to confirmed treatment.

RAcE projects were implemented by international non-governmental organizations (NGOs) under the leadership of Ministries of Health (MOH) and WHO technical support. Each project's area of implementation, target population,

Table 1. *RAcE project areas of implementation, target populations, implementing partners, and period of performance*

RAcE Project	Area of Implementation	Target Population	Implementing Partners	Period of Performance
DRC	7 health zones in Tanganyika Province in 2013; expanded to 11 health zones by 2016	Estimated total population of 1 000 000 including 150 000 children under 5 years of age	International Rescue Committee, DRC Ministry of Public Health (MOPH), WHO	September 2013 – November 2017
Malawi	Dedza, Mzimba North, Ntcheu, and Ntchisi districts in 2013; expanded to Likoma, Lilongwe Rural, Nhkata Bay, and Rumphi districts in 2014	Estimated total population of 1 625 036 including 276 256 children under five years of age	Save the Children, Malawi Ministry of Health (MOH), D-Tree International, Medical Care Development International, WHO	April 2013 – September 2017
Mozambique	Inhambane, Manica, Nampula, and Zambezia provinces	Estimated total population of 4 196 074 including 719 444 children under 5 years of age	Save the Children, Malaria Consortium, Mozambique Ministry of Health (*MISAU*), WHO, UNICEF, World Bank	April 2013 – December 2016
Niger	3 health districts in Dosso Region (Boboye, Dogondoutchi, and Dosso) and 1 health district in Tahoua region (Keita)	Estimated total population of 994 904, including 230 833 children under five years of age	World Vision, Niger Ministry of Public Health (MSP), WHO	July 2013 – September 2017
Nigeria – Abia State	15 local government areas (LGAs): Arochukwu, Bende, Ikwuano, Isialangwa North, Isialangwa South, Isuikwuato, Nneochi, Obingwa, Ohafia, Osisioma, Ugwunagbo, Ukwa East, Ukwa West, Umuahia North, and Umuahia South	Estimated total population of 1 268 738, including 202 998 are children under 5 years of age	Society for Family Health (SFH), Abia State Primary Health Care Development Agency (PHCDA), Abia State MOH, Grassroots Community Development Initiative, Population Services International, and the Institute of Tropical Diseases Research and Prevention at the University of Calabar, Nigeria, WHO	November 2013 – December 2017
Nigeria – Niger State	Six LGAs: Edati, Lapai, Mariga, Paikoro, Rafi, and Rijau	Estimated total population of 814 845 including 161 973 children under 5 years of age	Malaria Consortium, Niger State MOH, Niger State PHCDA	November 2013 – December 2017

RAcE – Rapid Access Expansion, LGA – local government area, DRC – the Democratic Republic of the Congo implementing partners, and period of performance are shown in **Table 1**. In RAcE project areas in the DRC, Niger, and Nigeria (Abia and Niger States), iCCM was introduced through the RAcE projects and operated in an environment with few other child health interventions.

In 2017, ICF conducted final evaluations of each of the six RAcE project areas to determine whether the programme goal of increased coverage of diagnostic, treatment, and referral services for malaria, pneumonia, and diarrhea to decrease overall child mortality was reached. One of the main evaluation objectives was to estimate the reduction in childhood mortality, and number of under-five lives saved over the project period in the RAcE project areas.

METHODS

We used the Lives Saved Tool (LiST) to estimate the impact of changes in coverage of treatment for the three illnesses targeted by iCCM – malaria, pneumonia, and diarrhea – while accounting for other changes in maternal and child health interventions in each RAcE project area.

LiST is computer-based software for modeling maternal and child mortality that runs through Spectrum. Spectrum is a suite of eleven integrated modules built and maintained by Avenir Health under guidance of a team at Johns Hopkins Bloomberg School of Public Health's Institute for International Programs [6-8]. Included in the Spectrum suite of modules are DemProj (demography), AIM (AIDS impact model), FamPlan (family planning), and LiST (child survival). LiST estimates the impact of scaling up of maternal, newborn, and child health and nutrition intervention coverage. Specifically, LiST estimates all-cause child mortality and the number of child lives saved by intervention and by cause. To produce these estimates, LiST incorporates detailed demographic information through automated linkages with the DemProj and FamPlan modules; country-specific cause of death information for newborns, children under five, and mothers; health and nutrition status, including through linkage with the AIM module; coverage of key health interventions; and effectiveness measures for each intervention determined by scientific review [9-11]. LiST Version 5.55 was used for this study.

We created six LiST models, one for each RAcE project area. Each LiST model was built from the country's DemProj data and national mortality profiles in Spectrum. The under-five cause of death information for each country, which includes the three iCCM focus illnesses, is shown in **Table 2**.

Using LiST's subnational projection module, we adjusted each model to reflect the RAcE project area population, baseline subnational mortality rates

Table 2. *Cause-specific mortality for under-five (ages 1-59 months) mortality by country, from Spectrum*

Country	Diar-rhea	Pneu-monia	Ma-laria	Men-ingitis	Mea-sles	Per-tussis	AIDS	Injury	Other
DRC	14.1%	22.8%	17.9%	4.1%	7.1%	1.6%	0.7%	6.6%	25.2%
Malawi	13.1%	18.8%	19.5%	3.7%	4.1%	1.9%	7.9%	6.7%	24.4%
Mozambique	11.6%	25.3%	13.4%	7.4%	0.3%	2.3%	4.5%	8.3%	27.0%
Niger	14.6%	31.5%	10.9%	7.8%	0.04%	1.2%	0.2%	8.8%	25.1%
Nigeria	14.3%	29.1%	18.3%	3.8%	2.5%	0.5%	1.0%	7.0%	23.6%

DRC –the Democratic Republic of the Congo

(as available), and baseline intervention coverage estimates. This adjustment relies on a comparison between national (default data in Spectrum modules) and subnational data [12]. To accurately make this comparative adjustment, national data must be comparable to subnational data. If data were from the same source, then the data were comparable, and the subnational data point was input into the model. If subnational data were from a different data source than the source of national data in LiST, we adjusted these by creating a ratio between the subnational coverage rate and the national coverage rate, and then applying this ratio to the national coverage rate given in the subnational LiST module [12].

We used data from RAcE baseline and endline household surveys, Demographic and Health Surveys (DHS), WHO-UNICEF, and routine health service data as inputs for each LiST model.

Baseline years were set to 2013 for the DRC, Mozambique, Niger, and the two Nigeria models. For Malawi, the baseline year was set to 2010 in concurrence with the available baseline DHS. The subnational baseline files were used to create the full models in LiST.

Data for treatment of pneumonia with amoxicillin, treatment of fever with ACT within 48 hours, treatment of diarrhea with ORS, and treatment of diarrhea with zinc from the RAcE baseline and endline household surveys were input into each LiST model for baseline and endline data points, respectively. For Malawi, 2010 DHS data for treatment of pneumonia with amoxicillin, fever with ACT, and diarrhea with ORS and zinc were held constant to 2013 values, and 2013 RAcE baseline household survey data points were input for 2013. iCCM intervention coverage modeled is summarized in **Table 3**.

Baseline and endline data points for other maternal, newborn, and child health (MNCH) interventions input into the model were sub-national DHS data,

Table 3. iCCM intervention coverage in RAcE Project areas

iCCM INTERVENTION COVERAGE	DRC		MALAWI		MOZAMBIQUE		NIGER		NIGERIA – ABIA STATE		NIGERIA – NIGER STATE	
	Baseline	Endline	Baseline	Endline	Baseline	Endline	Baseline	Endline	Baseline	Endline	Baseline	Endline
ORS for diarrhea	48.9 (40.9-57.0)	71.7 (63.1-79.0)	72.3 (64.9-78.7)	72.6 (65.3-78.9)	69.8 (60.9-77.5)	69.9 (62.5-76.5)	61.7 (53.8-68.9)	78.4 (69.3-85.4)	31.4 (25.7-37.8)	55.4 (46.6-63.9)	68.2 (59.5-75.7)	88.3 (81.9-92.7)
Zinc for diarrhea	2.9 (1.5-5.5)	58.8 (48.6-68.3)	23.8 (17.4-31.5)	28.3 (21.2-36.6)	9.9 (6.1-15.6)	35.0 (25.2-46.4)	30.4 (24.3-37.2)	72.6 (65.7-78.5)	7.2 (4.2-12.2)	42.0 (34.7-49.6)	15.0 (10.5-20.9)	77.0 (66.8-84.8)
Careseeking for pneumonia	17.9 (13.1-23.8)	53.0 (42.8-63.0)	56.5 (48.2-64.3)	66.8 (59.0-73.8)	69.6 (61.1-76.9)	58.8 (50.9-66.2)	44.6 (36.5-52.9)	46.2 (36.3-56.5)	8.6 (5.3-13.6)	35.5 (28.3-43.5)	28.6 (21.6-36.7)	60.5 (50.2-69.9)
ACTs for fever within 48 h	5.2 (3.0-8.7)	49.6 (41.5-57.8)	43.5 (36.4-50.9)	-*	55.0 (48.4-61.4)	39.7 (33.5-46.3)	41.9 (34.1-50.1)	58.4 (47.4-68.5)	15.3 (11.9-19.4)	38.3 (33.5-43.3)	27.4 (22.1-33.3)	64.5 (56.3-71.9)

iCCM – integrated community case management, DRC – Democratic Republic of the Congo, ACT – artemisinin combination therapy, ORS – oral rehydration solution
*Due to the change in Malawi's iCCM treatment policy, from presumptive treatment to confirmed treatment of malaria, the percentage of cases of fever treated with ACT within 48 hours measured at baseline was held constant in the model to avoid an artificial decrease in treatment coverage resulting in lives lost.

where available. The lowest administrative level (eg, state, province, or district) of DHS data available comprising the project area was used. WHO and UNICEF estimates of immunization coverage were used in all countries except Malawi, for which DHS estimates were used. No llarge-scale national-level survey data for 2016 were available for the DRC, Mozambique, Niger, and Nigeria at the time of the RAcE final evaluation. Routine health service data for Mozambique project areas in 2016 were used for that model's endline; if data were unavailable, values were held constant. For the DRC and Nigeria, we projected 2016 estimates for MNCH indicators by applying linear interpolation to continue the trend as measured by DHS for the time period preceding the 2013 baseline. For Niger, available routine health service data were used for 2016 and linear interpolation of DHS data was used to estimate other indicator values. Thus, the models assumed that the same trends measured for the preceding time period continued through 2016.

Values for all indicators were linearly interpolated from 2013 to 2016 in each model, except where otherwise noted. If projected values were over 100 percent, these were determined unrealistic and consequently baseline values were held constant. Due to the change in

Malawi's iCCM treatment policy, from presumptive treatment to confirmed treatment of malaria, the percentage of cases of fever treated with ACT within 48 hours measured at baseline was held constant in the model to avoid an artificial decrease in treatment coverage resulting in lives lost. A summary of data sources for the LiST models is provided in **Table 4**.The data, and their sources, used to create each project's LiST model are detailed in Tables S1-S6 in the **Online Supplementary Document.**

Table 4. *Summary of data sources for Lives Saved Tool (LiST) models*

	LiST DATA SOURCES		
	LiST default	**Baseline**	**Endline**
DemProj			
Population	United Nations Population Division	Estimated by RAcE grantee adjusted with ratio	Calculated by model
Total fertility rate	DHS	DHS adjusted with ratio	Calculated by model
AIM			
HIV incidence or prevalence	DHS	LiST default or DHS adjusted with ratio	Calculated by model
FamPlan			
Contraceptive prevalence rate	DHS	DHS adjusted with ratio	Calculated by model
LiST			
Baseline child mortality			
Neonatal mortality rate	DHS	DHS	Calculated by model
Infant mortality rate	DHS	DHS	Calculated by model
Under-five mortality rate	DHS	DHS	Calculated by model
Pregnancy			
Antenatal care	DHS	DHS or routine health service data	DHS* or routine health service data
Tetanus toxoid vaccine	WHO-UNICEF	DHS or routine health service data adjusted with ratio	DHS* or routine health service data
Intermittent preventive treatment of malaria during pregnancy	DHS	DHS or routine health service data	DHS* or routine health service data
Multiple micronutrition supplementation (iron folate 90+)	DHS	DHS or routine health service data	DHS* or routine health service data
Childbirth			
Skilled birth attendance	DHS	DHS†	DHS* or routine health service data †
Institutional delivery	DHS	DHS or routine health service data	DHS* or routine health service data

Table 4. *Continued*

	LiST DATA SOURCES		
	LiST default	**Baseline**	**Endline**
Preventive			
Chlorohexadine for post-natal	N/A	LiST default, routine health service data, or N/A	DHS, routine health service data, or N/A
Postnatal care ("clean postnatal practices")	DHS	LiST default	N/A
Vitamin A supplementation	DHS	DHS	DHS*
Improved water source	WHO-UNICEF	DHS	DHS* or N/A
Water connection in home	WHO-UNICEF	LiST default or DHS	DHS* or N/A
Improved sanitation	WHO-UNICEF	DHS	DHS* or N/A
Hygienic disposal of child's stools	DHS	DHS or N/A	DHS* or N/A
Insecticide-treated net ownership	DHS	DHS	DHS*, MIS, or N/A
Vaccines			
Bacille Calmette-Guerin (BCG) vaccine	WHO-UNICEF	WHO-UNICEF or DHS	WHO-UNICEF or DHS
Diphtheria, pertussis, and tetanus (DPT) vaccine	WHO-UNICEF	WHO-UNICEF or DHS	WHO-UNICEF or DHS
Haemophilus influenza type b (Hib) vaccine	WHO-UNICEF	WHO-UNICEF or DHS	WHO-UNICEF or DHS
Hepatitis B vaccine	WHO-UNICEF	DHS or N/A	DHS or N/A
Measles vaccine	WHO-UNICEF	WHO-UNICEF or DHS	WHO-UNICEF or DHS
Polio vaccine	WHO-UNICEF	WHO-UNICEF or DHS	WHO-UNICEF or DHS
Pneumococcal vaccine	WHO-UNICEF	WHO-UNICEF or DHS	WHO-UNICEF or DHS
Rotavirus vaccine	WHO-UNICEF	WHO-UNICEF or DHS	WHO-UNICEF or DHS
Curative			
ORS for diarrhea	DHS	RAcE baseline survey	RAcE endline survey
Antibiotics for diarrhea	DHS	DHS, routine health service data, or N/A	DHS*, routine health service data, or N/A
Zinc for diarrhea	DHS	RAcE baseline survey	RAcE endline survey
Antibiotics for cough with fast or difficult breathing	DHS	RAcE baseline survey	RAcE endline survey
ACT for fever same or next day	DHS	RAcE baseline survey	RAcE endline survey

ACT – artemisinin combination therapy; DHS – Demographic Health Survey; MIS – Malaria Indicator Survey; ORS – oral rehydration solution, N/A – not available; when endline data was not available, the baseline value was held constant over time

*DHS data point input or obtained by extrapolating pre-baseline DHS trend.

†Set to same value as institutional delivery.

Each LiST model yielded three outputs: 1) Under-five mortality rates for each year, to estimate the change in all-cause child mortality from baseline to endline (estimated impact); 2) Number of lives saved per year, among children under five years of age; and 3) Number of lives saved per year by intervention, including malaria treatment, pneumonia treatment, diarrhea treatment with zinc, and diarrhea treatment with ORS. The number of lives saved by malaria treatment, pneumonia treatment, and diarrhea treatment in each RAcE project area model were then adjusted proportionally to the percentage of cases treated by CHWs as measured in the respective RAcE endline household surveys to provide an estimate of the lives saved due to iCCM services in the project areas. Because the LiST model uses the coverage estimates for the baseline year to estimate lives saved for the model's projection period, the estimated lives saved for the baseline year is, by default, zero.

RESULTS

Under-five mortality declined in all six RAcE sites over the course of the programme, with an average decline of 10 percent. An estimated 6200 under-five lives were saved by malaria, pneumonia, and diarrhea treatment in the DRC, Malawi, Niger, and Nigeria. Approximately 4940 (75 percent) of under-five lives were saved by treatment provided by CHWs. This total excludes Mozambique, where there were no estimated under-five lives saved. The total estimated lives saved – lives saved by pneumonia, diarrhea, and malaria treatment – in each project area are shown in **Table 5**. The proportion of estimated

Table 5. *Estimated lives saved by pneumonia, diarrhea, and malaria treatment by all providers, estimated under-five mortality decrease in RAcE project areas, and estimated under-five mortality decrease*

RAcE Project	Estimated U5 lives saved (net)	Estimated U5 lives saved by pneumonia treatment	Estimated U5 lives saved by diarrhea treatment (ORS and zinc)	Estimated U5 lives saved by malaria treatment	Estimated % decrease in U5MR
DRC	1855	493	579	743	15.2
Malawi	3161	508	64	0†	4.6
Mozambique	-95	-912	268	-1675	0.2
Niger	1931	54	747	327	12.6
Nigeria – Abia State	1573	472	455	480	12.1
Nigeria – Niger State	1298	407	361	506	14.5
Total	**723**	**1022**	**2474**	**381**	**Average: 9.9**

N/A – not applicable, U5 – under-five, iCCM – integrated community case management, ORS – oral rehydration solution, U5MR – under-five mortality rate, the DRC – Democratic Republic of the Congo, RAcE – Rapid Access Expansion
†Malaria treatment coverage was not modeled for Malawi.

lives saved by iCCM treatment from CHWs in each RAcE project area are shown in **Table 6**. Estimates of lives saved in each project area by year and by treatment intervention are provided in Tables S7-S12 in the **Online Supplementary Document**.

In the DRC, there was an estimated 15.2 percent decrease in under-five mortality over the course of the project. An estimated total of 1820 deaths were prevented (lives saved) by pneumonia, diarrhea, and malaria treatment interventions in children under 5 years of age over the course of the project. Based on the coverage of treatment by CHWs, an estimated 1730 (95 percent) of these lives were saved due to treatment provided by CHWs.

In Malawi, there was an estimated 4.6 percent decrease in under-five mortality over the course of the project. An estimated 570 deaths were prevented by pneumonia and diarrhea treatment interventions in children under 5 years of age over the course of the project. There were no estimated deaths prevented by malaria treatment. Based on the coverage of treatment by CHWs, an estimated 220 (38 percent) of these lives were saved due to treatment provided by CHWs.

In Mozambique, there was an estimated 0.2 percent decrease in under-five mortality over the course of the project. An estimated 100 child lives were lost in RAcE project areas over the project period. This estimate accounts for significant numbers of lives saved by increases in some interventions and lives lost due to decreases in coverage of others. An estimated 250 lives were saved due to the increase in diarrhea treatment coverage of zinc, and 20 lives due to the increase in ORS treatment coverage. An estimated 910 lives were lost due to a decrease in treatment coverage of pneumonia with oral antibiotics, and 1680 due to a decrease in treatment coverage of malaria with ACTs.

In Niger, there was an estimated 12.6 percent decrease in under-five mortality over the course of the project. An estimated 1130 deaths were prevented by

Table 6. *Estimated lives saved by CHW-provided treatment in RAcE project areas*

RAcE PROJECT	ESTIMATED U5 LIVES SAVED BY CHW-PROVIDED PNEUMONIA, DIARRHEA, AND MALARIA TREATMENT (iCCM)
DRC	1728
Malawi	216
Mozambique	N/A
Niger	965
Nigeria – Abia State	967
Nigeria – Niger State	1062
Total	4938

N/A – not applicable, U5 – under-five, CHW – community health worker, iCCM – integrated community case management, DRC – the Democratic Republic of the Congo, RAcE – Rapid Access Expansion pneumonia, diarrhea, and malaria treatment interventions in children under five years of age over the course of the project. Based on the coverage of treatment by CHWs, an estimated 970 (86 percent) of these lives were saved by treatments provided by CHWs.

In Abia State, Nigeria there was an estimated 12.1 percent decrease in under-five mortality over the course of the project. An estimated 1400 deaths were prevented by pneumonia, diarrhea, and malaria treatment interventions in children under five years of age over the course of the project. Based on the coverage of treatment by CHWs, an estimated 970 (69 percent) of these lives were saved by treatments provided by CHWs.

In Niger State, Nigeria there was an estimated 14.5 percent decrease in under-five mortality over the course of the project. An estimated 1280 deaths were prevented by pneumonia, diarrhea, and malaria treatment interventions in children under five years of age over the course of the project. Based on the coverage of treatment by CHWs, an estimated 1100 (83 percent) of these lives were saved by treatments provided by CHWs.

DISCUSSION

Our results reflect the observed coverage changes measured in each project area and, with LiST, show estimated mortality reductions in a way that can be adjusted to explain the impact of each iCCM project amidst other ongoing health trends [13]. We found an average estimated decline in under-five mortality of 9.9 percent across the six project areas, ranging from a 0.2 percent decline in Mozambique to a 15.2 percent decline in the DRC. An estimated 1020 child lives were saved from pneumonia treatment; an estimated 2470 child lives saved from diarrhea treatment; and an estimated 380 child lives saved from malaria treatment across the six project areas. Our findings show that when adjusted to reflect the proportion of treatment coverage provided by CHWs vis-à-vis treatment coverage by all providers, a substantial number of estimated child lives were saved by CHW-provided treatment. In the DRC, approximately 95 percent of the child lives were saved by CHW-provided treatment. In Niger and Niger State, Nigeria CHW-provided treatment accounted for over 80 percent of the child lives saved, and in Abia State nearly 70 percent. In Malawi, less than 50 percent of child lives were saved by CHW-provided treatment; the percentage in Mozambique is unclear because it could not be accounted for in the model.

Previous studies have used LiST to retrospectively evaluate changes in mortality and deaths averted by high-impact child health interventions [14-17]. LiST has also been used to demonstrate decreases in mortality by NGO-facilitated projects that used community-based intervention packages to contribute to improved coverage of child health interventions [18], as well as to demonstrate the potential impact of expanding coverage of such interventions through scaling up CHW-delivered interventions at the population level [19]. An evaluation of iCCM in Burkina Faso also used LiST to model mortality changes, and, similar to our study, used program data to inform the interpretations of both changes in mortality and changes in coverage measured through household surveys [17]. Two evaluations of the Catalytic Initiative in Malawi demonstrated the impact of iCCM, one using LiST. The first used population-based survey data with results showing a significant decrease in child mortality over the period of implementation, and that the majority of deaths averted were due to interventions that could be delivered at the community level by CHWs [14]. In contrast to our analysis, this study did not examine the proportion of these interventions actually delivered by CHWs. The second drew conclusions about a decrease in mortality using national level changes in mortality estimates from DHS and Multiple Indicator Cluster Survey (MICS), but did not find evidence that these increases in intervention coverage were due to iCCM [15]. Similar to our findings, contextual information suggested that, for a number of reasons, only a small proportion of treatment of malaria, pneumonia, and diarrhea is provided by CHWs in Malawi [15]. A similar evaluation of iCCM in Uganda that utilized household survey data in LiST found that iCCM increased treatment coverage for diarrhea and fever, mitigated effects of amoxicillin stockouts for pneumonia treatment, and saved lives [16]. While that study supports the potential impact of iCCM, it did not account for changes in other MNCH interventions during the study period, as our analysis did.

Substantial increases in the iCCM intervention coverage were measured from baseline to endline in the DRC, Niger, and Nigeria project areas, with high proportions of cases treated by CHWs. Small, non-significant increases were measured in diarrhea and pneumonia treatment in Malawi project areas. Holding the percentage of cases of fever treated with ACT within 48 hours measured at baseline constant in the Malawi model, to account for the change in iCCM treatment policy and to avoid an artificial decrease in treatment coverage resulting in lives lost, resulted in the model showing no estimated impact from malaria treatment. The Malawi model likely underestimated the number of child lives saved due to iCCM intervention coverage, because it does not account for lives saved by the improvement in malaria case management following the introduction of RDTs.

With the exception of Mozambique, overall coverage of pneumonia, malaria, and diarrhea treatment increased in each RAcE project area, including measurable increases in treatments provided both at the facility level and by CHWs in communities. Unlike other RAcE project sites, there were measured decreases in overall malaria and pneumonia treatment coverage – treatment by any provider – in Mozambique. Diarrhea treatment with ORS did not significantly change, while diarrhea treatment with zinc increased significantly. Due to the decreases in pneumonia and malaria treatment coverage, the LiST model estimated that lives were lost. However, the source of treatment among pneumonia cases that received treatment shifted over time – with a larger proportion being treated by CHWs at endline; the model obscured this effect of pneumonia treatment provided by CHWs. There was not a statistically significant increase in the proportion of malaria cases treated by CHWs, likely because of widespread stockouts of malaria kits. Thus, there were likely not a significant number of lives saved due to CHW-provided malaria treatment in Mozambique. The largest decreases in mortality and numbers of lives saved (estimated impact) were in project areas in which iCCM was introduced through RAcE (the DRC, Niger, and Nigeria). Given that, in these contexts, RAcE operated in an environment with few other child health interventions that could have influenced the estimated decreases in under-five mortality, it is likely that iCCM contributed substantially to the estimated mortality decreases. In areas in which RAcE was supporting the continuation and expansion of a more a mature iCCM strategy (Malawi and Mozambique), there was less estimated impact. In Mozambique, widespread stockouts due to weaknesses in the health system limited the provision of life saving treatment and consequently, we observed negligible impact on mortality reduction.

The LiST model is a valuable tool for estimating the impact of maternal and child health intervention coverage on child mortality, though not without limitations [13,20]. Direct measurement of child mortality is a time and resource intensive effort, and thus typically done every 5 to 10 years at the national level and highest subnational administrative unit by large-scale surveys such as DHS and MICS. This is a common constraint of sub-national public health programmes, and why models such as LiST can be a useful proxy for estimating impact. Child mortality was not directly measured before or after RAcE project implementation in any country, and valid mortality data were not available for the project sites before or after RAcE.

Limitations

LiST does not account for the mode of delivery or source of care (with the exception of facility birth). Thus, the model estimates the impact of malaria, pneumonia, and diarrhea treatment based on RAcE project data measured in

RAcE household surveys. For all other interventions, except immunization, the model and results assume that project areas had projected intervention coverage according to the same trends measured by the DHS or national health information system. The areas represented by these estimates do not align exactly with the RAcE project areas. Additionally, there are potential quality issues with the routine health service data, due to challenges in health management information system reporting. Some models had missing data points, and had values held constant over time or used projected estimates for endline values. WHO and UNICEF national immunization coverage estimates likely overestimated coverage in the hard-to-reach RAcE project areas. Furthermore, the LiST model does not account for changes in diagnostics, the quality of care, timeliness of pneumonia and diarrhea treatment, or referrals made or completed. This study was not designed to directly attribute changes in outcomes or impact to the individual RAcE projects or to the RAcE programme. There are no valid counterfactuals for these analyses. However, RAcE-supported iCCM services delivered by CHWs were the only iCCM services provided in the project areas.

CONCLUSION

The results of the RAcE LiST models suggest that iCCM is a strategy that can save lives and measurably decrease child mortality in settings where access to health facility services is low and adequate resources, including trained and supported staff and supplies, are provided. The overall increases in child health intervention coverage in RAcE project areas demonstrate the added value of iCCM as an extension of the health system and as an equity-focused strategy.

In the context of this evidence and limited funding for child health, we advocate for continued investment in integrated child health programming. For greatest impact, iCCM should be implemented as an extension of the health system. It is not a strategy to replace health facility services, but rather to extend select, critical life-saving interventions directly to hard-to-reach communities. A successful iCCM programme should be part of a larger effort to strengthen health systems and facility services. The case of Mozambique emphasizes this point in the context of the adage 'no drugs, no service.' Without adequate commodities in hand, CHWs are unable to provide life-saving treatment to their communities, and risk losing community trust of their work and the programme.

Acknowledgements: *The authors would like to thank the implementing NGOs – The International Rescue Committee, Malaria Consortium, Save the Children, Society for Family Health, and World Vision – the Ministries of Health, and the WHO representatives in each of the RAcE countries for sharing their data, time, thoughts, and experiences. We would also like to thank Salim Sadruddin and Gunther Baugh of WHO for their inputs* and support. *Finally, we want to thank the community health workers who work hard to provide services to caregivers and children in communities, and the caregivers who give so much to ensure and improve the health of their children.*

Disclaimer: *The content of this publication is solely the responsibility of the authors and does not necessarily reflect the views or policies of World Health Organization or Global Affairs Canada.*

Ethics approval: *ICF obtained ethical approval from ICF's Institutional Review Board as well as from institutions in each country for each household survey. The Lives Saved Tool analyses which used household survey results do not constitute human subjects research.*

Funding: *The evaluations were conducted by ICF under a contract with the World Health Organization (WHO) through funding by Global Affairs Canada.*

Authorship Contributions: *DP conceptualized the study and drafted the manuscript. SH, HC, LM, KZ, and JY provided critical reviews and content edits on manuscript drafts.*

Competing Interests: *WHO contracted ICF to estimate the impact of the RAcE interventions on all-cause mortality in children ages 2-59 months using the Lives Saved Tool (LiST) and to estimate the number of lives saved in the intervention areas based on coverage changes shown by baseline and endline household surveys in RAcE project areas. ICF developed a protocol for this evaluation. WHO provided inputs to that protocol and then approved it. ICF conducted the assessments, interpreted the results, and wrote the conclusions. WHO provided information pertaining to the accuracy of the data and supporting information used to develop this manuscript. The authors completed the Unified Competing Interest form at www.icmje.org/coi_disclosure.pdf (available upon request from the corresponding author), and declare no further conflicts of interest.*

Additional Material
Online Supplementary Document

References

1 WHO, UNICEF. WHO/UNICEF Joint Statement. Integrated Community Case Management (iCCM): An equity-focused strategy to improve access to essential treatment services for children. 2012. https://www.unicef.org/health/files/iCCM_Joint_Statement_2012.pdf Accessed April 2018.

2 Kalyango JN, Alfven T, Peterson S, Mugenyi K, Karamagi C, Rutebemberwa E. Integrated community case management of malaria and pneumonia increases prompt and appropriate treatment for pneumonia symptoms in children under five years in Eastern Uganda. Malar J. 2013;12:340. Medline:24053172 doi:10.1186/1475-2875-12-340

3 Nsona H, Mtimuni A, Daelmans B, Callaghan-Koru JA, Gilroy K, Mgalula L, et al. Scaling up integrated community case management of childhood illness: update from Malawi. Am J Trop Med Hyg. 2012;87:54-60. Medline:23136278 doi:10.4269/ajtmh.2012.11-0759

4 Yeboah-Antwi K, Pilingana P, Macleod WB, Semrau K, Siazeele K, Kalesha P, et al. Community case management of fever due to malaria and pneumonia in children under five in Zambia: a cluster randomized controlled trial. PLoS Med. 2010;7:e1000340. Medline:20877714 doi:10.1371/journal.pmed.1000340

5   Miller NP, Amouzou A, Hazel E, Legesse H, Degefie T, Tafesse M, et al. Assessment of the impact of quality improvement interventions on the quality of sick child care provided by Health Extension Workers in Ethiopia. J Glob Health. 2016;6:020404. Medline:27606058 doi:10.7189/jogh.06.020404

6   Health A. Spectrum. 2018. Available: https://www.avenirhealth.org/software-spectrum.php. Accessed December 2018.

7   Stover J, McKinnon R, Winfrey B. Spectrum: a model platform for linking maternal and child survival interventions with AIDS, family planning and demographic projections. Int J Epidemiol. 2010;39:i7-10. Medline:20348129 doi:10.1093/ije/dyq016

8   Health JHUBSoP. Lives Saved Tool. 2016. https://www.livessavedtool.org/ Accessed April 2018.

9   Health JHBSoP. Lives Saved Tool Two-Pager (Overview of LiST). 2016. https://static1.squarespace.com/static/5bbba6574d8711a7dcafa92a/t/5bbbb7cf652dea0e585e9e7f/1539028944554/LiST+Brochure_21Sep.pdf Accessed April 2018.

10 Fox MJ, Martorell R, van den Broek N, Walker N. Assumptions and methods in the Lives Saved Tool (LiST). BMC Public Health. 2011;11:I1. Medline:21501425 doi:10.1186/1471-2458-11-S3-I1

11 Victora CG. Commentary: LiST: using epidemiology to guide child survival policymaking and programming. Int J Epidemiol. 2010;39:i1-2. Medline:20348111 doi:10.1093/ije/dyq044

12 Health JHUBSoP. Webinar: Subnational Projections in LiST 2016.

13 Friberg IK, Walker N. Using the Lives Saved Tool as part of evaluations of community case management programs. J Glob Health. 2014;4:020412. Medline:25520802 doi:10.7189/jogh.04.020412

14 Doherty T, Zembe W, Ngandu N, Kinney M, Manda S, Besada D, et al. Assessment of Malawi's success in child mortality reduction through the lens of the Catalytic Initiative Integrated Health Systems Strengthening programme: Retrospective evaluation. J Glob Health. 2015;5:020412. Medline:26649176 doi:10.7189/jogh.05.020412

15 Amouzou A, Kanyuka M, Hazel E, Heidkamp R, Marsh A, Mleme T, et al. Independent evaluation of the integrated community case management of childhood illness strategy in Malawi using a national evaluation platform design. Am J Trop Med Hyg. 2016;94:574-83. Medline:26787158 doi:10.4269/ajtmh.15-0584

16 Mubiru D, Byabasheija R, Bwanika JB, Meier JE, Magumba G, Kaggwa FM, et al. Evaluation of integrated community case management in eight districts of Central Uganda. PLoS One. 2015;10:e0134767. Medline:26267141 doi:10.1371/journal.pone.0134767

17 Munos M, Guiella G, Roberton T, Maïga A, Tiendrebeogo A, Tam Y, et al. Independent evaluation of the rapid scale-up program to reduce under-five mortality in Burkina Faso. Am J Trop Med Hyg. 2016;94:584-95. Medline:26787147 doi:10.4269/ajtmh.15-0585

18 Ricca J, Kureshy N, LeBan K, Prosnitz D, Ryan L. Community-based intervention packages facilitated by NGOs demonstrate plausible evidence for child mortality impact. Health Policy Plan. 2014;29:204-16. Medline:23434515 doi:10.1093/heapol/czt005

19 Chou VB, Friberg IK, Christian M, Walker N, Perry HB. Expanding the population coverage of evidence-based interventions with community health workers to save the lives of mothers and children: an analysis of potential global impact using the Lives Saved Tool (LiST). JOGH. 2017;7.

20 Hazel E, Gilroy K, Friberg IK, Black RE, Bryce J, Jones G. Comparing modelled to measured mortality reductions: applying the Lives Saved Tool to evaluation data from the Accelerated Child Survival Programme in West Africa. Int J Epidemiol. 2010;39:i32-9. Medline:20348124 doi:10.1093/ije/dyq019

Integrated community case management: planning for sustainability in five African countries

Jennifer Yourkavitch[1], Lwendo Moonzwe Davis[1], Reeti Hobson[1], Sharon Arscott-Mills[1], Daniel Anson[2], Gunther Baugh[3], Jean-Caurent Mantshumba[4], Bacary Sambou[5], Jean Tony Bakukulu[6], Pascal Ngoy Leya[7], Misheck Luhanga[8], Leslie Mgalula[9], Gomezgani Jenda[10], Humphreys Nsona[11], Santos Alfredo Nassivila[12], Eva de Carvalho[13], Marla Smith[14], Moumouni Absi[15], Fatima Aboubakar[16], Aminata Tinni Konate[17], Mariam Wahab[18], Joy Ufere[19], Chinwoke Isiguzo[20], Lynda Ozor[19], Patrick B Gimba[21], Ibrahim Ndaliman[22] Salim Sadruddin[23]

[1] ICF, Rockville, Maryland, USA

[2] Independent Consultant, Silver Spring, Maryland, USA; formerly ICF, Rockville, Maryland, USA

[3] Independent Consultant, formerly with World Health Organization, Geneva, Switzerland

[4] Independent consultant for ICF, Kinshasa, Democratic Republic of Congo

[5] World Health Organization, Kinshasa, Democratic Republic of Congo

[6] IMNMCI Program, Kinshasa, Democratic Republic of Congo

[7] Abt Associates; formerly International Rescue Committee, Kinshasa, Democratic Republic of Congo

[8] Independent consultant for ICF, Lilongwe, Malawi

[9] World Health Organization, Lilongwe, Malawi

[10] Save the Children, Lilongwe, Malawi

[11] Ministry of Health, Malawi

[12] Independent consultant for ICF, Maputo, Mozambique

[13] World Health Organization, Maputo, Mozambique

[14] Save the Children, Maputo, Mozambique

[15] Independent consultant for ICF, Niamey, Niger

[16] World Health Organization, Niamey, Niger

[17] Ministère de la Santé Publique, Niamey, Niger

[18] Independent consultant for ICF, Abuja, Nigeria

[19] World Health Organization, Abuja, Nigeria

[20] Society for Family Health, Abia State, Nigeria

[21] State Ministry of Health, Niger State, Nigeria

[22] Malaria Consortium, Niger State, Nigeria

[23] World Health Organization, Geneva, Switzerland

Background The World Health Organization (WHO) launched an initiative to plan for the sustainability of integrated community case management (iCCM) programs supported by the Rapid Access Expansion (RAcE) Programme in five African countries in 2016. WHO contracted experts to facilitate sustainability planning among Ministries of Health, WHO, nongovernmental organisation grantees, and other stakeholders.

Methods We designed an iterative and unique process for each RAcE project area which involved creating a sustainability framework to guide planning; convening meetings to identify and prioritize elements of the framework; forming technical working groups to build country ownership; and, ultimately, creating roadmaps to guide efforts to fully transfer ownership of the iCCM programmes to host countries. For this analysis, we compared priorities identified in roadmaps across RAcE project sites, examined progress against roadmaps via transition plans, and produced recommendations for short-term actions based on roadmap priorities that were unaddressed or needed further attention.

Results This article describes the sustainability planning process, roadmap priorities, progress against roadmaps, and recommendations made for each project area. We found a few patterns among the prioritized roadmap elements. Overall, every project area identified priorities related to policy and coordination of external stakeholders including funders; supply chain management; service delivery and referral system; and communication and social mobilization, indicating that these factors have persisted despite iCCM program maturity, and are also of concern to new programs. We also found that a facilitated process to identify and document programme priorities in roadmaps, along with deliberately planning for transition from an external implementer to a national system could support the sustainability of iCCM programs by facilitating teams of stakeholders to accomplish explicit tasks related to transitioning the program.

Conclusions Certain common elements are of concern for sustaining iCCM programs across countries, among them political leadership, supply chain management, data processes, human resources, and community engagement. Adapting and using a sustainability planning approach created an inclusive and comprehensive dialogue about systemic factors that influence the sustainability of iCCM services and facilitated changes to health systems in each country.

Sustainability, or "the extent to which an evidence-based intervention is able to deliver its intended benefits after external support from a donor agency is terminated" [1], should be the end goal of most donor-funded global health interventions. Sustainability planning aims to facilitate the transition and may employ a specific transition plan for that purpose, leading to the formal handover of a donor-funded programme to a local partner. Although sustainability planning has been promoted in global health programmes, and, more recently, incorporated into strategies to strengthen countries' self-reliance [2], it has historically received limited resources because funding is focused on programme planning, implementation, monitoring, and evaluation. Nonetheless, the sustainability of positive health outcomes continues to gain importance in the current global context, with reduced funding for development programs and increasing recognition of the need for processes to transition them to country ownership [3-5]. In addition, a drive towards universal health coverage means that capitalizing on integrated health services and decreasing redundant or parallel efforts in health programming is paramount.

Integrated community case management (iCCM) of childhood pneumonia, diarrhoea, and malaria has increased access to treatment for children under five years of age, and notably reduced mortality in areas of limited health services [6]. A hallmark feature of iCCM programs is the use of trained community health workers (CHWs) that can deliver diagnostic and treatment services for multiple childhood illnesses [7,8]. As a health care service delivery strategy, iCCM includes the training, supplying, and supervising of CHWs to treat children for diarrhoea using oral rehydration salts (ORS), to treat children for WHO-defined pneumonia using oral antibiotics, and to administer rapid diagnostic tests and treat children with malaria using artemisinin-based combination therapy [9].

Given the focus of the Sustainable Development Goals (SDG), particularly SDG 3.2 (ending preventable deaths of newborns and children under 5 years of age) and SDG 3.8 (achieving universal health coverage), more countries are scaling-up iCCM to strategically increase access to essential health services. Understanding how iCCM has been implemented is therefore imperative to sustain and scale achievements in iCCM service delivery [10,11]. Questions around feasibility of sustainability in the long-term persist, particularly in light of donor-funded programmes [11-16]. Except for a few countries, iCCM programmes have been mainly funded by donors, putting the sustainability of such programs at risk due to reliance on external funding.

Substantial research on the critical elements required for sustainable health programs already exist, in particular, for HIV/AIDS programs. The US President's Emergency Plan for AIDS Relief (known as PEPFAR) 3.0 presided over a shift in HIV/AIDS programming to a more sustainable and country-owned approach, with a focus on countries and key populations with high disease burden [17]. This focus on transition has provided examples of implementation of key elements required for sustainability, some of which are generalizable to other health areas, including: leadership and management capacity, political and economic factors, supportive policies, alternative funding sources, integration of programs into the wider health system, institutionalization of processes, the strength of procurement and supply chain management, and identification of staffing and training needs, amongst others [17]. Analyses have indicated that current spending on AIDS is not sufficient to sustain achievements, necessitating a strategic approach to program and sustainability planning, so that low-income countries can reliably manage HIV programming [18].

Lessons from transitioning large-scale HIV/AIDS programs parallel those derived from iCCM program research. George et al. [15] emphasizes the importance of iCCM policy analyses to identify and understand factors that pose challenges to achieving and sustaining scale, and others advocate for including local perspectives and evidence [19,20]. Government support and political will, stable funding of financial support, organisational and contextual factors, community support, commodities and supplies, and human resources including management capacity are also identified as critical elements of sustaining the health gains made through iCCM [12-14,21-23]. Like sustained health behavior change, program sustainability is multidimensional, with both internal and external factors affecting it [24].

WHO's Rapid Access Expansion (RAcE) Programme increased access to treatment for malaria, pneumonia, and diarrhoeal disease among children under five years of age through iCCM in five countries: the Democratic Republic of the Congo (DRC), Malawi, Mozambique, Niger, and Nigeria, with funding from Global Affairs Canada (**Table 1**). The RAcE programme also aimed to strengthen the capacity of national and local health authorities to manage and implement iCCM activities in all five countries. WHO recognized that a systematic and inclusive process to plan for the sustainability and transition of iCCM interventions was crucial to sustain the achievements in reducing child mortality in each of the RAcE project areas. WHO contracted experts in 2016 to facilitate a planning process by providing technical assistance to national, state, and local health authorities, communities, and other key stakeholders to develop a sustainability strategy. The main documents produced included a roadmap consistent with national priorities and the many guidelines for the health system, particularly child and community health, and a plan to transition management and service delivery of RAcE activities to national structures. The purpose of this article is to describe the sustainability planning process for the iCCM programs and its outputs, and to examine progress against the roadmap to transition iCCM programs in RAcE countries.

METHODS

This article describes a program planning process and examines progress made against that plan; it is not research involving human subjects, so we did not seek ethics approval. We approached the challenge of sustaining iCCM programmes by incorporating recommended themes of adaptation and a learning health care system [38] in an established dynamic sustainability planning

Table 1. RAcE programme grantees, local partners, region of implementation, and child health context

LOCAL PARTNER	IMPLEMENTATION REGION	CHILD HEALTH CONTEXT	iCCM CONTEXT
Democratic Republic of Congo, International Rescue Committee			
Ministère de la Santé Publique	11 health zones of Tanganyika Province	104 deaths per 1000 live births [25]	Introduced in 2003, but uneven progress [26]; RAcE brought renewed emphasis in 2013.
		Leading causes of death for children under five: diarrhoea (11%), malaria (15%) and pneumonia (16%) [27]	CHWs (called *Relais Communautaire*) are supported by a primary health care strategy and a three-level pyramid system—a central level (top of pyramid), an intermediate level (provinces and districts), and a peripheral level (health zones), which oversee health services. A national Ministry of Health (MOH)-led iCCM Task Force established during the RAcE programme provides overall guidance
		Treatment was sought for only about half of children under five who had fever in 2014; 6% of children with fever received artemisinin combination therapy; less than half of children under five who had diarrhea in the two weeks preceding the survey received oral rehydration therapy [25]	
Malawi, Save the Children			
Ministry of Health	Eight districts: Dedza, Likoma, Lilongwe, Mzimba North, Nkhata Bay, Ntcheu, Ntchisi, and Rumphi	63 deaths per 1000 live births [28]	Began in 2009, building on IMCI programme.
		Leading causes of death in children under five in 2015 included pneumonia, diarrhoeal diseases and malaria [29]	Focuses on hard-to-reach areas more than eight kilometres from a health facility
		In 2015/16, caregivers of 67% of children under five with fever sought advice or treatment, and 35% of those children received artemisinin combination therapy. Caregivers of 60% of children under five with diarrhoea sought treatment from a health facility, and 65% of those children received ORS [28]	CHWs (called Health Surveillance Assistants) are recruited and salaried by MOH [30]
			The MOH IMCI unit, in collaboration with the Community-based Primary Health Care Programme and district teams, is responsible for oversight and implementation.
Mozambique, Save the Children			

Table 1. Continued

Local partner	Implementation region	Child health context	iCCM context
Malaria Consortium and Ministério da Saúde	Four provinces: Inhambane, Manica, Nampula, and Zambezia	82 deaths per 1000 live births [31] Leading causes of child death: malaria (13%), pneumonia (14%), and diarrhoea (9%) [31] In 2011, caregivers of 56% of children under five with a fever sought treatment, and 18% of those children received artemisinin combination therapy;[33] Of the 56% of children under five for whom advice or treatment for diarrhoea was sought, 55% received ORS [33]	Since 1978, the MOH (MISAU) has trained CHWs (*Agentes Polivalentes Elementares de Saúde* (APEs)) to increase access to health care By the end of 2013, MISAU and its implementing partners had trained more than 2200 APEs in iCCM [32] MISAU oversees APEs who provide preventative, curative, and referral services to communities across the country.
Niger, World Vision			
Ministère de la Santé Publique	Dosso region: Boboye, Dosso, and Doutchi districts; Tahoua region: Keita district	104 deaths per 1000 live births [34] Main causes of death for children under five in 2015 included malaria (11%), pneumonia (21%), and diarrhoea (11%) [35] In 2012, caregivers of 64% of children with fever sought advice or treatment, but only 15% of those children received artemisinin combination therapy. 51% of children under five with diarrhoea were taken to a health facility, and 44% of those children received ORS [36]	iCCM was adopted in 2005 using *Agents de Santé Communautaire*, but implementation was limited Through the RAcE programme, more than 1200 CHWs called *Relais Communautaires* (RComs) have been trained to diagnose and treat or refer malaria, pneumonia, and diarrhoea cases among children under five The government oversees the iCCM programme
Abia State, Nigeria: Society for Family Health; Niger State, Nigeria: Malaria Consortium			
State Ministry of Health and the Abia State Primary Health Care Development Agency	Fifteen of 17 local government areas	128 deaths per 1000 live births in Nigeria [37] 58% of child deaths in Nigeria caused by malaria, pneumonia, and diarrhea [37] Caregivers in Abia and Niger States sought treatment for about one-third of fever cases for children under five [37]	iCCM was introduced by RAcE in 2012 CHWs (community-oriented resource persons (CORPs)) provide case management in communities The Federal Ministry of Health established the National iCCM Task Force and subcommittees and developed national guidelines on iCCM
State Ministry of Health and the Niger State Primary Health Care Development Agency	Six local government areas		

ORS – oral rehydration salts, iCCM – integrated community case management, CHW – community health worker, MISAU - Ministerio da Saude, APE – Agentes Polivalentes Elementares de Saúde, RComm – *Relais Communautaires* process [39]. We utilised a sustainability framework focused on six components, to facilitate a series of defined steps to coordinate the local system of people and institutions managing, providing, and influencing iCCM services in each RAcE programme area. This awareness of health system dynamics and interactions within a local system, where people and institutions naturally and strategically adapt to one another and change in capacity in a nonlinear fashion [40], underscores the importance of coordinating and collaborating with both national and local stakeholders.

Creating a sustainability framework for iCCM services

We drafted a sustainability framework to guide the planning, identifying themes and components incorporated in previous work with sustainability planning for maternal and child health programs [39] and literature pertinent to iCCM programs [41]. The framework draft depicted six components, each comprising several elements. We presented the draft framework for discussion and validation to key RAcE project stakeholders (MOH, WHO, and NGO grantee staff) from the DRC, Malawi, Mozambique, Niger, and Abia and Niger States, Nigeria at the June 2016 inception meeting held in Abuja, Nigeria and subsequently refined the framework with feedback obtained at that meeting. We validated this framework with a larger group of stakeholders at workshops in each RAcE project area to create the final guiding framework for this sustainability planning (**Figure 1** and Appendix S1 in **Online Supplementary Document**).

Sustainability workshops

We organized and facilitated sustainability planning workshops in each country with support from NGO grantees and WHO country offices. The three-day workshops had two objectives: to draft a roadmap for institutionalising iCCM, and to draft a transition plan in support of the roadmap to guide activities during the last year of RAcE support. During the workshops, key stakeholders, including MOH, WHO, and NGO grantee staff, along with other influential government, academic, donor, and civil society actors, created a statement describing the national vision for the iCCM program (Supplemental File S.2.). To create a vision statement, facilitators prompted participants to form small groups and create a narrative or picture of what a sustained iCCM program would look like two years after the end of the RAcE project, taking on the role of a post-project evaluation team conducting an evaluation on how well aspects of the iCCM program had been sustained. Small groups then presented their

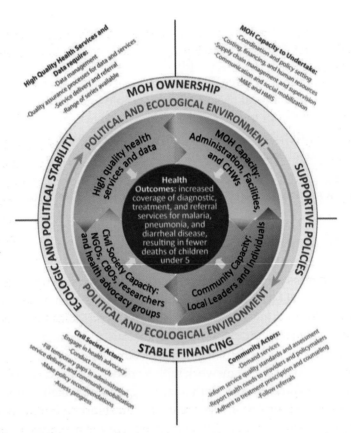

Figure 1. *Sustainability framework for integrated community case management (iCCM).*

visions to the full group. Facilitators and participants mapped commonalities and discussed differences to reach consensus on the vision statement.

At the workshop, participants also validated the sustainability framework and included points to contextualize it to their particular setting in the roadmap and transition plans (sample workshop agenda in Appendix S3 in **Online Supplementary Document**). For this purpose, roadmaps were conceptualized as documenting both the current state of sustainability of the iCCM programs and the milestones or benchmarks that, if achieved, would enhance sustainability. We created a roadmap template to guide participants' discussions and work. Participants worked in small groups to identify issues, next steps, and timelines related to one or more components of the sustainability framework. These groups also drafted detailed transition plans to guide activities during the next year. Transition plans typically aligned with the first year of activities articulated in the roadmaps. In each program area, state or national authorities approved the roadmaps.

Monitoring progress towards sustainability

We monitored the status of activities through progress update meetings with NGO grantees and related reports for three months for all project areas except Mozambique, where the project ended after the roadmap was completed, and then analyzed progress by synthesizing information from key informants and monitoring reports. We produced a synthesis report for each RAcE project area and co-facilitated dissemination meetings for participants to discuss the findings presented in the reports and to update the roadmaps.

For this analysis, we compared priorities identified in roadmaps across RAcE project sites and examined progress against roadmaps during the monitoring period and recommendations based on roadmap priorities that were unaddressed or needed further attention.

RESULTS

This section presents the main outputs of the processes undertaken: the sustainability framework for iCCM, vision statements, and roadmap priorities; and, synthesizes information about progress made against the roadmaps and future priorities for all RAcE sites. We present the planning process for Niger State, Nigeria as a detailed case study in Appendix S4 in **Online Supplementary Document**.

Sustainability framework for iCCM

The validated sustainability framework for iCCM comprises six components: health outcomes, high-quality health services and data, MOH capacity, civil society capacity, community capacity, and the political and ecological environment. Each component is supported by several elements (**Figure 1**). Health outcomes, at the center, are affected by interactions among high-quality health services and data, MOH capacity, community capacity and civil society capacity, which operate within a political and ecological environment that directly affects the iCCM program and its sustainability but is only indirectly affected by it. The same framework guided planning in all of the project areas except Malawi, where the team proposed minor adaptations (Appendix S1 in **Online**

Supplementary Document). Stakeholders in Malawi wanted to encircle the health outcomes with high-quality health services, supported by MOH capacity, civil society capacity, and community capacity. In addition, they included culture and communication in the political and ecological environment. The components and elements in the sustainability framework guided the planning reflected in the roadmaps.

Comparative analysis of roadmap priorities

We compared roadmap priorities (**Table 2**) and identified a few patterns among the prioritized elements in different project areas. Overall, every project area identified priorities related to policy and coordination of external stakeholders including funders; supply chain management; service delivery and referral system; and communication and social mobilization, indicating that these factors have persisted despite program maturity, and are also of concern to new programs. Four program areas identified internal planning and coordination; supervision; and, quality assurance for services as priorities. Countries with either a mature iCCM program (Malawi) or mature CHW program (Mozambique) did not identify general human resource issues, including training, capacity building and recruitment, as a priority, which emerged as a priority for the other program locations. However, stakeholders in Malawi identified specific human resource issues pertaining to CHW deployment, and internal planning and coordination remains a challenge in Mozambique. Data management, including data use, was identified as a priority for the newer iCCM programs, including the programs in Niger, and Abia and Niger States in Nigeria.

Synthesis of progress and recommendations

Table 3 reports the vision statements and summarizes progress in RAcE project sites and recommendations for sustaining iCCM programs. Each vision statement articulates a "big picture" goal for child health. The team in Malawi, which works with the most mature iCCM program among RAcE project sites, outlined the most specific vision, calling out critical elements of iCCM programs including personnel, supplies, and system supports.

Community engagement, supply management, data processes, government leadership, and CHW remuneration or retention were recurrent themes in most project areas during the transition period and some examples are presented here. Social mobilization activities were conducted with RAcE support in Niger State, but some Village Development Committees had yet to be established in

Table 2. *Prioritized roadmap elements and locations*

	DRC	MALAWI	MOZAM-BIQUE	NIGER	ABIA STATE, NIGERIA	NIGER STATE, NIGERIA
Financing	X		X	X	X	X
Government ownership		X		X		
Policy, programme development, and coordination (external)	X	X	X	X	X	X
Advocacy for partnerships					X	
Human resources (including training, capacity building and recruitment)	X			X	X	X
Internal planning, coordination and policy	X		X	X	X	X
Supply chain management	X	X	X	X	X	X
Supervision	X	X	X	X	X	
Monitoring and evaluation, and health information systems	X		X	X		X
Service delivery and referral system	X	X	X	X	X	X
Quality assurance for services	X	X	X	X	X	
Communication and social mobilisation	X	X	X	X	X	X
Monitoring and evaluation, and health information systems (pertaining to civil society capacity)	X		X			
Data quality		X		X		X
CHW* residency, training or transportation challenges		X				
Low utilization of iCCM* by communities		X				
Data management (including data use)				X	X	X
Health advocacy and resource mobilization				X		
Advocacy for high-quality health services and data					X	
Incentives for CHWs					X	
Monitoring policy development (through TWG* or Task Force)					X	
Policy, advocacy and strategy at community levels						X
Human resources – engagement with community leaders						X

DRC – Democratic Republic of the Congo, CHW – community health workers, iCCM – integrated community case management, TWG – technical working group

Table 3. *Vision statements, summary of progress, and recommendations*

	Democratic Republic of Congo	Malawi	Mozambique	Niger	Abia State, Nigeria	Niger State, Nigeria
Vision statements						
	*D'ici fin 2030, zéro décès lié au Paludisme, à la Diarrhée et à la Pneumonie des enfants de moins de cinq (5) ans grâce à la mise en place d'un système durable de PEC-C à tous les niveaux avec le concours de tous les partenaires impliqué**	By 2021 all children under five years of age in hard-to-reach areas with pneumonia, diarrhoea, and malaria receive prompt treatment around the clock from personnel who are trained, equipped, resourced, supervised, mentored, and practicing iCCM; residing in the catchment area with a good house, adequate drug supply, clinic structure, and functional referral system; using data for planning and decision making; within a knowledgeable and enabling political community and enabling political environment to attain zero avoidable under-five deaths.	*Reduzida a mortalidade em crianças menores de cinco anos de idade, expandindo a cobertura de serviços de qualidade através de um sistema de saúde primário reforçado.†*	*D'ici 2026, un paquet complet de services curatifs, préventifs et promotionnels de qualité est rendu accessible à tous les enfants de moins de cinq (5) ans, d'une manière durable et équitable par des relais communautaires motivés dans toutes les communautés du Niger avec leur pleine participation.‡*	State government and stakeholders (community institutions, volunteers, local and international partners) will provide the resources (funds, environment, policy and capacity) to end preventable deaths of children 0-59 mo due to malaria, pneumonia and diarrhoeal diseases by 2030.	To implement iCCM in Niger State through institutionalizing sustainable support systems to reduce by 95% preventable deaths due to malaria, pneumonia, and diarrhoea in children between 0-59 mo, especially in hard to reach communities, by 2025.
Progress as of May, 2017:						
		HSA mapping activity conducted.	Not monitored due to project ending.	MSP continues to need transportation to supervise RCom in some districts.	The State Ministry of Health (SMOH) took over training on data management and use, and all refresher trainings for CORPs, community health extension workers (CHEWs), and local government area (LGA) focal persons.	LGA team members, the iCCM coordinator, and Malaria Consortium jointly conducted mentoring and coaching sessions for all CORPs and CHEWs.
	Each health zone integrated community health site coverage plans in operating plans.					
	All health zones had computers and tools to compile data.	Some facilities are using commodities intended for village clinics.		The national strategic plan for iCCM has not yet been adopted, delaying inclusion of iCCM costs in the state budget. [The plan was adopted in 2018.]	A formal data flow was established between the Abia State Primary Health Care Development Agency and state officials, and between state officials and the federal MOH.	SMOH was trained in data management.

Table 3. *Continued*

	DEMOCRATIC REPUBLIC OF CONGO	MALAWI	MOZAMBIQUE	NIGER	ABIA STATE, NIGERIA	NIGER STATE, NIGERIA
	Provincial MOH office took over monitoring and evaluation activities.	Discussions occurring to ensure that MOH procures all drugs.		Community leaders have verbally committed to supporting RComs, but there is no documentation about budgeting or other efforts.	Development of incentives program and fundraising activities were planned.	All CORPs were supervised by CHEWs with standard supervision tools.
	IRC still retaining ReCos and working with government partners to order, store, and distribute commodities and supplies.	Communication materials about iCCM were printed and planned for distribution at facilities.		Medicines are not consistently available at facilities.	Some Village Development Committees have not yet been established.	Uneven provision of incentives for CORPs by communities.
		Transportation for supervision is an ongoing challenge.		Referral system is not always accessible; slips are not consistently available at facilities.		Social mobilization activities continued with support from MC.
		Refresher training for HSAs included how to complete referral and counter-referral forms.				RAcE project procured and distributed all commodities
		Lack of political will at district level.				
Recommendations:	Identify people who would be responsible for strategic guidance and oversight of the iCCM program, develop a harmonised plan and financing protocols for iCCM among donors, and identify and coordinate engagement with communities.	Engage communities through a consultative problem solving process.	Decentralize decision making to include contributions from civil society, community health committees, and other health system levels to improve demand for iCCM.	Find solutions to RCom remuneration and supervision. Explore cost sharing among key stakeholders.	Develop an incentives programme for CORPs.	Engage Ward Development Committees and Village Development Committees in commodity management to ensure that CORPs are fully stocked.

Table 3. *Continued*

Democratic Republic of Congo	Malawi	Mozambique	Niger	Abia State, Nigeria	Niger State, Nigeria
More thinking and planning is required regarding governance and financing issues for the health system overall, and for iCCM services within that system.	Avoid overburdening HSAs with other interventions that could fragment the iCCM program.	Incorporate APEs formally in the MISAU human resource structure.	Adopt a validated national strategic plan for integrated community case management and child health.	Advocate with state officials to ensure the establishment of Village Development Committees, budgeting for iCCM programme costs, and supervision of community-based health workers.	Secure funding and commitment for social mobilisation activities.
Central MOH should provide more leadership.	Critically review the performance of current stock management programs (c-stock).	Create a structure in MISAU to oversee iCCM activities, increase government ownership, and streamline technical support.	Identify and remedy bottlenecks in the supply chain.	Obtain lists of NGOs and other community-level actors to engage.	SMOH to take ownership of the HMIS.
Mobilizing funding for the recruitment of more ReCos.	Ensure IMCI Unit participates in development of community health strategy so that iCCM roadmap priorities are incorporated in it.	Improve collaboration in MISAU departments and across ministries to maximise efficiencies and leverage key resources for APEs and the iCCM programme.	Strengthen the referral system.	Define the roles and responsibilities of the members of the iCCM Task Force to aid in organising its efforts to work with the state government to sustain the iCCM programme.	Develop a human resource plan, including job descriptions for staff at all levels.
	Engage funding partners such as the Global Fund to assist with financing challenges.	Increase accountability to local communities to further enable MISAU and its partners to improve child health.	Formally situate the iCCM programme within the MSP so there is a clear line of support.	Establish an operations plan with a budget, a M&E plan, mentoring schedule for CORPs and CHEWs, state HMIS and procurement system for commodities.	Develop a data management plan.

Table 3. *Continued*

DEMOCRATIC REPUBLIC OF CONGO	MALAWI	MOZAMBIQUE	NIGER	ABIA STATE, NIGERIA	NIGER STATE, NIGERIA
	Implement supportive policies to address HSA residency issue.		Improve data collection and quality through standard protocols and tools and integrate data in HMIS.		Incorporate data use into M&E plan.
	Establish a leadership structure within MOH to support the iCCM program.				Develop a community engagement strategy with social mobilization and communication activities.
	Discuss HSA retention data at annual meetings and facilitate participant problem solving.				Develop a supply chain plan that addresses forecasting, procurement and distribution.
					Include iCCM as a core component in the State Primary Healthcare Strategy.
					Create terms of reference for iCCM Task Force.

CHW – community health worker, iCCM – integrated community case management, MOH – Ministry of Health, HSA – health surveillance assistant, CHEW – community health extension workers, MISAU - Ministerio da Saude, CORP - community-oriented resource person, SMOH – State Ministry of Health, APE – Agentes Polivalentes Elementares, NGO – non-governmental organization, HMIS – health management information system, RECO – *relais communautaires*

*Translation: By the end of 2030, zero deaths due to malaria, diarrhoea, and pneumonia of children under five (5) years through the establishment of a sustainable system of integrated community case management at all levels, with all involved partners.
†Translation: Reduced mortality among children under five years of age through expanded coverage of quality services in a strengthened primary health system.
‡Translation: By 2026, a comprehensive package of quality curative, preventative and promotional services is made available to all children under five (5) years of age, in a sustainable and equitable manner by community-based relays motivated in all communities of Niger with their full participation.

Abia State and social mobilization was carried out by a local NGO (Gracodev). In most areas, the RAcE project was still procuring and distributing supplies, although discussions with governments about taking over those tasks were under way. Some trainings in data collection and management had occurred, eg, in Niger State and in Malawi. In addition, health zones in DRC had tools to compile data. The Provincial MOH took over M&E activities in DRC and local government worked with the RAcE project to jointly mentor and coach CHWs in Niger State. However, a lack of district interest was noted in Malawi, and the national strategic plan for iCCM had not yet been adopted in Niger. Community support for CHWs was deemed important, but progress was uneven. In Niger State, some communities provided support through food and other incentives, while others did not. Community leadership did not move beyond verbal commitment in Niger. The RAcE project was still retaining ReCos in DRC. Although we could not monitor the transition in Mozambique due to the project ending, persistent threats to the APE programme in Mozambique have been noted, including donor-dependent funding for monthly incentives [13] and heavy workloads. In addition, stakeholders noted that MISAU has a limited capacity to manage, implement, and finance the iCCM programme.

Two recommendations for all project areas are to use the iCCM roadmap to guide future investments and efforts, and to update it regularly as the programs mature. **Table 3** lists other recommendations addressing the common themes of community engagement, supply management, data processes, government leadership, and CHW remuneration or retention. Specifically, identifying champions and creating structures within the government to support iCCM programs emerged as an important step in the immediate term to sustain the programs. For example, given that iCCM was recently introduced in Abia State, focused advocacy efforts will be needed to ensure state ownership of the program. Other strategies for engaging communities, improving data management, strengthening supply chains and supporting CHWs were also made.

DISCUSSION

In this paper we reported the process and outputs of a sustainability planning initiative for RAcE project sites. We also compared roadmap priorities, progress against roadmaps, and recommendations among the project sites. We found that every project area identified priorities related to policy and coordination of external stakeholders including funders; supply chain management; service delivery and referral system; and communication and social mobilization. Moreover, community engagement, supply management, data processes, government leadership, and CHW remuneration or retention were recurrent themes in most project areas during the transition period. Identifying champions and creating structures within the government to support iCCM programs emerged as an important step in the immediate term to sustain the programs.

Sustaining iCCM programmes can be crucial to sustaining improvements in child and community health outcomes in some settings, and is an emerging priority [8,11]. The framework we created incorporates the elements of a health system approach [41], while expanding service planning and delivery to include civil society partners and a broader consideration of the political and ecological environmental context. Identifying programme priorities and documenting them in a roadmap, along with deliberately planning for transition from an external implementer to a national system, may facilitate positive sustainability efforts and outcomes. These processes incorporate policy history and context, which have been deemed critical for national iCCM program support [7], through the engagement of stakeholders at multiple levels and through multiple sectors. Although this approach should be formally tested, we have shown that adapting and using it in different contexts creates an inclusive and expansive (ie, multi-level and multisectoral) dialogue about systemic factors that influence the sustainability of a health service or programme.

The process of designing roadmaps included working with practical tools and guidance that facilitated thinking about specific issues related to implementing iCCM. This process included identifying critical challenges, involving multiple stakeholders, thinking across multiple sectors beyond the health system, establishing timeframes for achieving benchmarks, and building on established country or state strengths. Technical Working Groups (TWGs) formed at the conclusion of each workshop continued to advise roadmap updates in program areas. Ideally, this group will be able to continually update the roadmap so that it is contextually current and responsive, a critical feature of working toward sustainability within a changing environment [38]. The feasibility of full transition from externally guided implementation to autonomous implementation in each project setting was variable, and in most countries it was evident that limited resources would not allow for the same level of iCCM services without donor funding. All RAcE projects were able to transition some roles, responsibilities, and activities for iCCM to the MOH and other local partners. Common aspects of programme implementation that were transitioned included monitoring and evaluation activities, supervision, training, and data management. It should be noted that, as LMIC economies grow, they may be able to assume a greater role in the administration of programs currently funded by donors, although poorer countries are more susceptible to political corruption and violent conflict which undermine progress [42]. In addition, the fluctuations of global markets create uncertainty about sustained capacity to implement health and other programs. Further, climate change has a disproportionate impact on LMIC [43].

Although the transition experienced some successes, a longer transition period would have been beneficial, meaning that planning for sustainability at the beginning of a project may have afforded a stronger "end game" for transition. Ideally, a sustainability framework should be used during programme planning to ensure that a programme is designed to be sustained [39]. This approach offers the advantage of providing an opportunity to build the capacity of national and local stakeholders in a measured and deliberate manner. In addition, convening key stakeholders to establish a TWG early in programme implementation would enable that group to exercise an important role in coordination and planning throughout program implementation.

Finally, this process seeks to address practical realities to sustaining iCCM programs through country-specific dialogue and solutions. While there is ongoing global dialogue about the best ways to finance iCCM programs [44] and retain CHWs [45], countries and donors continue to grapple with how to ensure smooth transitions from external to internal funding and management. These discussions within countries naturally require multi-level and multisectoral conversations, which this sustainability planning process supports. But donors, too, could participate in sustainability planning dialogues and serve countries better by aligning investments with roadmap priorities, to ultimately move programs closer to sustainment.

There are some limitations to this analysis. It was both comparative and summative; it was infeasible to analyze every roadmap element in detail. This approach necessarily tends toward superficiality; however, it is useful to look across programs to review the emerging priorities for iCCM sustainability. Although limited conclusions can be drawn from the comparative analysis, and priorities and challenges are specific to context, the process and tools we described could be adapted for other settings, and should be formally tested. As iCCM grows as a health care delivery strategy in many countries, engaging stakeholders in processes to create TWGs and produce roadmaps could assist program implementers with identifying and addressing the challenges that their programs face, and ultimately sustaining health gains. In addition, our definition of sustainability is limited here to program sustainability. The framework omits some relevant factors such as antimicrobial resistance and does not specify elements such as climate change, which is becoming increasingly important for health service planning. Further, future studies may consider power dynamics among stakeholders to elucidate relevant factors affecting sustainability [46,47], and macro-level factors that can counteract system strengthening efforts, such as competing priorities and the hierarchical structure of personnel roles in a system [48]. Global reviews of iCCM implementation will continue to inform sustainability planning by identifying emerging factors to incorporate in relevant frameworks [49].

CONCLUSIONS

In conclusion, the expectation for the sustainability of a health service is that the local system that produces health (inclusive of policy makers, programme implementers and service providers, and community members) is robust and resilient enough to maintain health coverage and outcome gains while adapting to changing conditions. Embarking on a process to plan for the sustainability of iCCM services optimizes investments in the programme by ensuring that life-saving curative services will continue to be available to children in hard-to-reach areas when funding and other conditions change. Areas where work remains to increase the likelihood of iCCM program sustainability included political leadership; supply chain management; human resource capacity, supervision and retention; data management; and, community engagement. Future investments in iCCM programs should assist country teams to address these issues.

Acknowledgements: *We thank the following individuals for their review of, and contributions to, previous drafts of this manuscript: Gunther Baugh, WHO, Geneva; Dr Francisco Mbofana, Ministério da Saúde, Mozambique; Grace Nganga, formerly of World Vision, Niamey, Niger; Dr Andrew L. Mbewe, WHO, Abuja, Nigeria; and, Dr Elvina Orji, Abia State Primary Health Care Development Agency, Abia State, Nigeria.*

Funding: *Funding from Global Affairs Canada.*

Authorship contributions: *JY, LMD, and RH drafted the manuscript. All other authors provided inputs relevant to their areas of expertise.*

Competing interests: *To the best of our knowledge, no authors have competing interests in relation to this article. We have tried to reach all authors, but some live and work in remote areas and were unable to respond by the time of the publication of this article. All other authors completed the ICMJE COI form (available upon request from the corresponding author), and declare no conflict of interest.*

Additional material
Online Supplementary Document

References

1 Rabin BA, Brownson RC, Haire-Joshu D, Kreuter MW, Weaver NL. A glossary for dissemination and implementation research in health. J Public Health Manag Pract. 2008;14:117-23. Medline:18287916 doi:10.1097/01.PHH.0000311888.06252.bb

2 United States Agency for International Development and Maternal and Child Health Integrated Program. Integrated community case management of childhood illnesses: documentation of best practices and bottlenecks to program implementation in the Democratic Republic of Congo (DRC). Available: https://www.mchip.net/sites/default/files/mchipfiles/DRCLongEnglish.pdf. Accessed: 20 May 2018.

3 Sarriot EG, Swedberg E, Ricca J. Pro-sustainability choices and child deaths averted: from project experience to investment strategy. Health Policy Plan. 2011;26:187-98. Medline:20823216 doi:10.1093/heapol/czq042

4 Goldberg J. Country ownership and capacity building: the next buzzwords in health systems strengthening or a truly new approach to development? BMC Public Health. 2012;12:531. Medline:22818046 doi:10.1186/1471-2458-12-531

5 Bao J, Rodriguez DC, Paina L, Ozawa S, Bennett S. Monitoring and evaluating the transition of large-scale programs in global health. Glob Health Sci Pract. 2015;3:591-605. Medline:26681706 doi:10.9745/GHSP-D-15-00221

6 World Health Organization, United Nations Children's Fund. Joint statement on integrated community case management: An equity-focused strategy to improve access to treatment services for children. Available: https://www.unicef.org/health/files/iCCM_Joint_Statement_2012.pdf. Accessed: 20 May 2018.

7 George A, Young M, Nefdt R, Basu R, Sylla M, Clarysse G, et al. Community health workers providing government community case management for child survival in sub-Saharan Africa: who are they and what are they expected to do? Am J Trop Med Hyg. 2012;87:85-91. Medline:23136282 doi:10.4269/ajtmh.2012.11-0757

8 Rasanathan K, Muniz M, Bakshi S, Kumar M, Solano A, Kariuki W, et al. Community case management of childhood illness in Sub-Saharan Africa: findings from a cross-sectional survey on policy and implementation. J Glob Health. 2014;4:020401. Medline:25520791

9 Young M, Wolfheim C, Marsh DR, Hammamy D. World Health Organization/United Nations Children's Fund joint statement on integrated community case management: An equity-focused strategy to improve access to essential treatment services for children. Am J Trop Med Hyg. 2012;87:6-10. Medline:23136272 doi:10.4269/ajtmh.2012.12-0221

10 Boschi-Pinto C, Labadie G, Dilip TR, Oliphant N, Dalglish SL, Aboubaker S, et al. Global implementation survey of Integrated Management of Childhood Illness (IMCI): 20 years on. BMJ Open. 2018;8:e019079. Medline:30061428 doi:10.1136/bmjopen-2017-019079

11 Daelmans B, Seck A, Nsona H, Wilson S, Young M. Integrated community case management of childhood illness: What have we learned? Am J Trop Med Hyg. 2016;94:571-3. Medline:26936992 doi:10.4269/ajtmh.94-3intro2

12 Bennett S, George A, Rodriguez D, Shearer J, Diallo B, Konate M, et al. Policy challenges facing integrated community case management in Sub-Saharan Africa. Trop Med Int Health. 2014;19:872-82. Medline:24750516 doi:10.1111/tmi.12319

13 Chilundo BG, Cliff J, Mariano A, Rodriguez D, George A. Relaunch of the official community health work program in Mozambique: is there a sustainable basis for iCCM

policy? Health Policy Plan. 2015;30:ii54-64. Medline:26516151 doi:10.1093/heapol/czv014

14 Daviaud E, Besada D, Leon N, Rohde S, Sanders D, Oliphant N, et al. Costs of implementing integrated community case management (iCCM) in six African countries: Implications for sustainability. J Glob Health. 2017;7:010403. Medline:28702174 doi:10.7189/jogh.07.010403

15 George A, Rodriquez DC, Rasanathan K, Brandes N, Bennett S. iCCM policy analysis: Strategic contributions to understanding its character, design and scale up in sub-Saharan Africa. Health Policy Plan. 2015;30:ii3-11. Medline:26516148 doi:10.1093/heapol/czv096

16 Hamer DH, Marsh DR, Peterson S, Pagnoni F. Integrated community case management: next steps in addressing the implementation research agenda. Am J Trop Med Hyg. 2012;87:151-3. Medline:23136291 doi:10.4269/ajtmh.2012.12-0505

17 Vogus A, Graff K. PEPFAR transitions to country ownership: review of past donor transitions and applications of lessons learned to the eastern Caribbean. Glob Health Sci Pract. 2015;3:274-86. Medline:26085023 doi:10.9745/GHSP-D-14-00227

18 Oberth G, Whiteside A. What does sustainability mean in the HIV and AIDS response? Afr J AIDS Res. 2016;15:35-43. Medline:26785676 doi:10.2989/16085906.2016.1138976

19 Dalglish SL, George A, Shearer JC, Bennett S. Epistemic communities in global health and the development of child survival policy: a case study of iCCM. Health Policy Plan. 2015;30:ii12-25. Medline:26516146 doi:10.1093/heapol/czv043

20 Rodríguez DC, Shearer J, Mariano ARE, Juma PA, Dalglish SL, Bennett S. Evidence-informed policymaking in practice: country-level examples of use of evidence for iCCM policy. Health Policy Plan. 2015;30:ii36-45. Medline:26516149 doi:10.1093/heapol/czv033

21 Dalglish SL, Rodríguez DC, Harouna A, Surkan PJ. Knowledge and power in policymaking for child survival in Niger. Soc Sci Med. 2017;177:150-7. Medline:28167340 doi:10.1016/j.socscimed.2017.01.056

22 Sarriot E, Morrow M, Langston A, Weiss J, Landegger J, Tsuma L, et al. A causal loop analysis of the sustainability of integrated community case management in Rwanda. Soc Sci Med. 2015;131:147-55. Medline:25779620 doi:10.1016/j.socscimed.2015.03.014

23 Strachan C, Wharton-Smith A, Sinyangwe C, Mubiru D, Ssekitooleko J, Meier J, et al. Integrated community case management of malaria, pneumonia and diarrhoea across three African countries: a qualitative study exploring lessons learnt and implications for further scale up. J Glob Health. 2014;4:020404. Medline:25520794 doi:10.7189/jogh.04.020404

24 Martin NA, Hulland KRS, Dreibelbis R, Sultana F, Winch PJ. Sustained adoption of water, sanitation and hygiene interventions: systematic review. Trop Med Int Health. 2018;23:122-35. Medline:29160921 doi:10.1111/tmi.13011

25 Ministère du Plan et Suivi de la Mise en oeuvre de la Révolution de la Modernité (MPSMRM), Ministère de la Santé Publique (MSP), ICF International. Chapter 10: child health. Democratic Republic of Congo demographic and health survey 2013-14: key findings. Rockville, MD, USA: MPSMRM, MSP, and ICF International; 2014:144–156.

26 United States Agency for International Development and Maternal and Child Health Integrated Program. Integrated community case management of childhood illnesses: documentation of best practices and bottlenecks to program implementation in the Democratic Republic of Congo (DRC). Available: https://www.mchip.net/sites/default/files/mchipfiles/DRCLongEnglish.pdf. Accessed: 20 May 2018.

27 World Health Organization. Democratic Republic of Congo: WHO statistical profile. Available: http://www.who.int/gho/countries/cod.pdf?ua=1. Accessed: 20 May 2018.

28 National Statistical Office/Malawi and ICF. Malawi demographic and health survey 2015-16. Zomba, Malawi: National Statistical Office and ICF; 2017.

29 World Health Organization Regional Office for Africa, Global Health Observatory. Malawi: WHO statistical profile. Available: http://www.who.int/gho/countries/mwi.pdf?ua=1. Accessed: 20 May 2018.

30 Nsona H, Mtimuni A, Daelmans B, Callaghan-Koru JA, Gilroy K, Mgalula L, et al. Scaling up integrated community case management of childhood illness: update from Malawi. Am J Trop Med Hyg. 2012;87:54-60. Medline:23136278 doi:10.4269/ajtmh.2012.11-0759

31 Countdown to 2015: Maternal, Newborn, and Child Survival, 2015.

32 Ministerio da Saude. Relatorio Anual das Actividades do Programa de Agentes Polivalentes Elementares (APEs) do Ano 2013. Maputo, Mocambique: Ministry of Health; 2014. [Translation: 2013 Annual Report of the APE Programme].

33 da Saude M. (MISAU)/Moçambique, Instituto Nacional de Estatística (INE)/Moçambique, ICF International. Moçambique Inquérito Demográfico e de Saúde 2011. Calverton, MD, USA: MISAU/Moçambique, INE/Moçambique, and ICF International; 2013.

34 United Nations Development Programme. Data on under-five mortality rate (per 1,000 births). Available: http://hdr.undp.org/en/indicators/57506. Accessed: 20 May 2018.

35 United Nations Children's Fund Data and Analytics Section, Division of Data, Research and Policy. Child mortality estimates: global and regional child deaths by cause. Available: https://data.unicef.org/topic/child-survival/under-five-mortality. Accessed: 20 May 2018.

36 Institut National de la Statistique (INS)/Niger, ICF International. Niger Enquête Démographique et de Santé et à Indicateurs Multiples (EDSN-MICS IV) 2012. Calverton, Maryland, USA: INS/Niger and ICF International; 2013.

37 National Population Commission (NPC) [Nigeria], ICF International. Nigeria demographic and health survey 2013. Abuja, Nigeria, and Rockville, MD, USA: NPC and ICF International; 2014.

38 Chambers DA, Glasgow RE, Stange KC. The dynamic sustainability framework: addressing the paradox of sustainment amid ongoing change. Implement Sci. 2013;8:117. Medline:24088228 doi:10.1186/1748-5908-8-117

39 Sarriot E, Ricca J, Yourkavitch J, Ryan L, et al. Taking the long view: A practical guide to sustainability planning and measurement in community-oriented health programming et al. Taking the long view: A practical guide to sustainability planning and measurement in community-oriented health programming. Calverton, MD: Macro International Inc.; 2008.

40 Sarriot E, Kouletio M. Community health systems as complex adaptive systems: ontology and praxis lessons from an urban health experience with demonstrated sustainability. Syst Pract Action Res. 2015;28:255-72. doi:10.1007/s11213-014-9329-9

41 McGorman L, Marsh DR, Guenther T, Gilroy K, Barat LM, Hammamy D, et al. A health systems approach to integrated community case management of childhood illness: methods and tools. Am J Trop Med Hyg. 2012;87:69-76. Medline:23136280 doi:10.4269/ajtmh.2012.11-0758

42 Radelet S. The great surge: the ascent of the developing world. New York, NY: Simon and Schuster; 2015.

43 World Health Organization. Climate change and health fact sheet. Available: http://www.who.int/en/news-room/fact-sheets/detail/climate-change-and-health. Accessed: 30 September 2018.

44 Management Sciences for Health. iCCM costing and financing tool: implementation manual and user guide. 2010. Available: https://www.msh.org/sites/msh.org/files/iccm_costing_and_financing_tool_userguide_version1.0.pdf. Accessed: 29 July 2018.

45 World Health Organization. Increasing access to health workers in remote and rural areas through improved retention: global policy recommendations. Available: https://ccmcentral.com/wp-content/uploads/2014/04/Improving-CHW-Retention-Policy-recommendations_WHO_2010.pdf. Accessed: 29 July 2018.

46 Dalglish SL, Surkan PJ, Diarra A, Harouna A, Bennett S. Power and pro-poor policies: the case of iCCM in Niger. Health Policy Plan. 2015;30 Suppl 2:ii84-94. Medline:26516154 doi:10.1093/heapol/czv064

47 Dalglish SL. Methods for the strategic review of programmes for integrated management of childhood illness and community cases. BMJ. 2018;362:k2989. Medline:30061099 doi:10.1136/bmj.k2989

48 Thomas JC. Contextual factors affecting health information system strengthening. Glob Public Health. 2017;12:1568-78. Medline:27841079 doi:10.1080/17441692.2016.1256419

49 Dalglish SL, Sriram V, Scott K, Rodríguez DC. A framework for medical power in two case studies of health policymaking in India and Niger. Glob Public Health. 2019;14:542-54. Medline:29616876 doi:10.1080/17441692.2018.1457705

Effect of community-based intervention on improving access to treatment for sick under-five children in hard-to-reach communities in Niger State, Nigeria

Olusola Oresanya[1], Helen Counihan[2], Ibrahim Nndaliman[3], Ayodele Alegbeleye[3], Jonathan Jiya[4], Olatunde Adesoro[1], John Dada[1], Patrick Gimba[5], Lynda Ozor[6], Debra Prosnitz[7], Kolawole Maxwell[1]

[1] Malaria Consortium, Abuja, Nigeria
[2] Malaria Consortium, London, UK
[3] Malaria Consortium, Niger, Nigeria
[4] Malaria Consortium (retired), Niger, Nigeria
[5] Niger State Ministry of Health, Niger, Nigeria
[6] World Health Organization, Abuja, Nigeria
[7] ICF, Fairfax, Virginia, USA

Background Access to prompt and appropriate treatment is key to survival for children with malaria, pneumonia and diarrhoea. Community-based services are vital to extending care to remote populations. Malaria Consortium supported Niger state Ministry of Health, Nigeria, to introduce and implement an integrated community case management (iCCM) programme for four years in six local government areas (LGAs). The objective was to increase coverage of effective treatment for malaria, pneumonia and diarrhoea among children aged 2-59 months.

Methods The programme involved training, equipping, ongoing support and supervision of 1320 community volunteers (CORPs) to provide iCCM services to their communities in all six LGAs. Demand creation activities were also conducted; these included community dialogues, household mobilization, sensitization and mass media campaigns targeted at programme communities. To assess the level of changes in care seeking and treatment, baseline and endline household surveys were conducted in 2014 and 2017 respectively. For both surveys, a 30×30 multi-stage cluster sampling method was used, the sampling frame being RAcE programme communities.

Results Care-seeking from an appropriate provider increased overall and for each iCCM illness from 78% to 94% for children presenting with fever ($P < 0.01$), from 72% to 91% for diarrhoea cases ($P < 0.01$), and from 76% to 89% for cases of cough with difficult or fast breathing ($P < 0.05$). For diagnosis and treatment, the coverage of fevers tested for malaria increased from 34% to 77% ($P < 0.001$) and

ACT treatments from 57% to 73% (<0.005); 56% of cases of cough or fast breathing who sought care from a CORP, had their respiratory rate counted and 61% with cough or fast breathing received amoxicillin. At endline caregivers sought care from CORPs in their communities for most cases of childhood illnesses (84%) compared to other providers at hospitals (1%) or health centres (9%).This aligns with caregivers' belief that CORPs are trusted providers (94%) who provide quality services (96%).

Conclusion Implementation of iCCM with focused demand creation activities can improve access to quality lifesaving interventions from frontline community providers in Nigeria. This can contribute towards achieving SDGs if iCCM is scaled up to hard-to-reach areas of all states in the country.

Pneumonia, diarrhoea and malaria are major causes of mortality in children under five years (U5) in sub-Saharan Africa. While pneumonia and diarrhoea account for 16% and 8% of deaths in U5 children respectively, this age group accounts for an estimated 66% of all malaria deaths, [1] potentiated by underlying malnutrition. These deaths can be prevented with proven cost-effective interventions, [2] which are often not available for children living in rural and remote communities located far from health facilities. This increases the risk of rapid progression to fatality due to delayed treatment [3]. In Nigeria, low coverage of life-saving high-impact preventive and curative childhood interventions is a key factor in high U5 mortality. In 2008, only 37% of children with diarrhoea received any oral rehydration therapy or increased fluids to drink, with just 0.7% receiving zinc supplements, while the proportion of children with acute respiratory infections who were given antibiotics was 22.5% and of children with fever, only 6% received artemisinin-based combination therapy (ACT) [4]. Access to prompt and appropriate treatment are key to survival of children affected by these killer diseases [5,6].

Achieving universal health coverage is at the heart of the SDGs, [7,8] however, by definition this cannot be achieved without universal access [9]. Universal health coverage is said to be attained when people obtain the health services they need and are also protected from financial hardship due to out-of-pocket expenses and access to these services, meaning the opportunity or ability to do both [9,10]. The dimensions of access have been described as physical accessibility, financial affordability and acceptability in terms of willingness to seek services and not merely adequacy of supply [10,11]. Although many countries are far from universal coverage, they can take steps towards it by improving equitable access [12].

The United Nations Children's Fund (UNICEF) and World Health Organization (WHO) released a joint statement on integrated community case management (iCCM) of childhood illnesses in 2012 [13]. Following this, Nigeria, adopted iCCM as part of its Child Health policy and developed national guidelines for its implementation in 2013.

iCCM is a proven equity-focused intervention for extending affordable care to hard to reach communities to reduce deaths among U5s [14]. Prompt and effective community management of pneumonia, malaria, and diarrhoea, has been found to reduce mortality by 70%, 60% and 70%-90% respectively [14,15]. It can address the three dimensions of universal access by bringing treatment services for children U5 closer to the home thereby eliminating the geographical or physical barrier to access; mitigating financial barriers to demand for services when provided free of charge [16] and promoting acceptability when delivered by trusted members of the community nominated by the communities themselves [17].

The flagship Rapid Access Expansion (RAcE) iCCM programme for Nigeria launched in 2013 in Abia and Niger states was supported by WHO with funding from the Global Affairs Canada. Malaria Consortium supported Niger State Ministry of Health to introduce and implement iCCM for four years in six local government areas (LGAs). The objective was to increase the number of children 2-59 months receiving effective treatment for common illnesses through provision of iCCM services combined with demand creation activities for caregivers of young children. Children under five living in communities five kilometres or more from the nearest functional health facility were targeted.

Although a number of studies have documented the effect of iCCM on access to care in rural communities in African countries, [18,19] the acceptability and utilization of iCCM services provided by community volunteers in the Nigerian setting is yet to be documented. This study presents the findings from the endline assessment of the RAcE iCCM in Niger state, Nigeria.

METHODS

Programme implementation design

Niger State is located in North Central Nigeria and has a projected (2017) population of about 5 586 003. The state has the largest land mass in the country (76 263 km^2) and majority of the population are spread across rural areas, with 30 percent of the population living in urban areas. Their occupation is largely agrarian and they are Muslim and Christian with a small minority practising traditional beliefs. Literacy rate is less than 50 percent and under-five mortality rate is 100 per 1000 live births. According to NDHS 2013, health seeking for children with fever, diarrhoea and acute respiratory infections is 38 percent, 42 percent and 29 percent respectively. Prevalence of global acute malnutrition is 6.1 percent, severe acute malnutrition is 0.5 percent while moderate acute malnutrition prevalence is 5.6 percent.

The Niger State RAcE programme was designed to increase the coverage of diagnostic, treatment and referral services through capacity building and operational support to health workers, communities and ministries of health at state and national levels. Over 161 973 children U5 in hard-to-reach areas of selected six LGAs were targeted to be reached through trained and equipped volunteer community caregivers known as community-oriented resource persons (CORPs). 1320 CORPs were trained and equipped to diagnose and treat children free of charge. The trained CORPs were provided respiratory timers, malaria rapid diagnostic test kits, amoxicillin dispersible tablets, ACT, ORS and zinc, as well as reporting tools including Sick Child Recording Forms and CORP Registers. Each CORP had on an average 118 children in his/her catchment population. The CORPs were supervised and mentored by community health extension workers (CHEWs) based at the primary health care centres, who were also trained on integrated management of childhood illnesses (IMCI). This system supported CORPs' case management skills, as well as data collection and reporting needs. The supervision system followed the national recommendation of monthly visits to the CORPs by the CHEWs to check on competencies, supplies and record-keeping using standard checklists.

Eligible communities for iCCM were identified through a health facility assessment to ascertain functionality, and mapping of communities that were more than 5 km away from the nearest functional health facility. Selection of the CORPs was community-led and based on criteria recommended in the national guidelines, including residence in the community and ability to read and write. Under the RAcE Programme, CORPs and CHEWs participated in 6 days of iCCM training; the CHEWs had an additional three days training on supervision, which enhanced their capacity to supervise the CORPs. CORPs received an incentive of approximately 20 US dollars monthly to support transport costs for home visits and facility visits for replenishment of medicines and mentoring.

The behaviour change communication strategy designed and implemented for the programme, guided the development of appropriate messages and materials as well as innovative multi-channels to reach the caregivers and other key audiences. Community mobilization activities including community dialogues, household sensitization by specially trained social mobilisers, and mass media campaigns targeted at communities, were embarked on with the support of women's, religious and community leader groups, to increase care-seeking and uptake of services as well as to augment CORPs' credibility.

ICF International (ICF) provided technical support to strengthen routine data quality and programme evaluation surveys.

Study design and objective

There were two cross-sectional household surveys conducted, one at programme baseline in 2014 prior to iCCM implementation, and the other at endline in February, 2017.

The objectives of the surveys were to assess care-seeking behaviour for sick children; coverage of iCCM assessment and treatment; and caregiver knowledge, attitudes, and practices related to pneumonia, diarrhoea, and malaria. Baseline and endline results were compared to assess changes in sick child care-seeking, assessment, and treatment coverage as well as caregivers' knowledge of childhood illnesses and perceptions of CORPs' services.

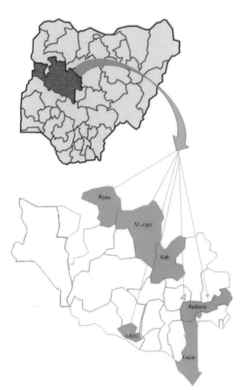

Study setting

Baseline and endline surveys were conducted across the six programme LGAs, Lapai, Paikoro, Rijau, Edati, Mariga and Rafi, before and after the intervention in 2014 and 2017 respectively (see **Figure 1**). There were no other community health interventions taking place in these LGAs during the programme implementation.

Sampling and study size

Primary caregivers of children aged 2–59 months living in the programme communities who reported that their children had diarrhoea, fever, or cough

Figure 1. *Study sites in Niger State, Nigeria.*

with rapid breathing in the two weeks prior to the survey, were considered eligible for inclusion in the survey. A 30x30 multi-stage cluster sampling method [20] was used to select 30 clusters using probability proportional to size, the sampling frame being RAcE programme communities. In order to detect a 20 percent difference in the sick child indicators that include all sick children for a specific illness (fever, diarrhoea, or cough with difficult or fast breathing) between baseline and endline at 90 percent power with a two-tailed test and 95 percent confidence using cluster sampling, 263 cases were needed for each illness, this was however rounded up to 300 cases per illness.

Data collection

Data was collected on key indicators related to caregiver knowledge of CORPs, caregiver perceptions of CORPs and care-seeking, assessment, treatment, referral adherence, and follow-up of sick children. To train the survey team, comprising of data collectors, supervisors and monitors, a training of trainers was held in Abuja from January 24 to 27, 2017 of supervisors and monitors while a cascade followed in Niger for the data collectors subsequently. Data collection was done using a standard household questionnaire comprising seven modules: caregiver and household background information; caregivers' knowledge of iCCM activities in their community; caregivers' knowledge of childhood illness danger signs; household decision-making; and a module for each major childhood illness: fever, diarrhoea, and fast breathing. The same questionnaires, which were developed by ICF and drawn from the Knowledge, Practice, Coverage (KPC) Survey tool, [21] were used for both baseline and endline except for the addition of two new questions at endline on whether caregivers sought care for their sick child and whether they sought care from a CORP. Participation in the study was voluntary, each provided written informed consent prior to interview. At the household level, the enumerator first determined whether an eligible child lived there. If there was an eligible child in the household, the interviewer administered the questionnaire, including all applicable illness modules, to the caregiver of the eligible child. If more than one child was eligible, and they were sick with different illnesses, their caregiver was asked about each instance of illness. If there was more than one eligible child in the household for an illness, the interviewer randomly selected one of the eligible children and interviewed his or her caregiver. If multiple children in the same household were reported to have symptoms in the preceding two weeks but had different caregivers, interviewers could interview multiple caregivers, as long as not more than one child from each household was included for each iCCM condition.

Quality control procedures during field work included daily spot checks by supervisors, during which they observed at least one interview per enumerator per day and also reviewed all completed questionnaires they received. In addition, one monitor was assigned to each LGA to ensure team compliance with the survey protocol and to provide further logistical, material, and technical support to the supervisors.

Data analysis

The baseline and endline CSPro data files were imported into Stata v14 (Stata Corp, College Station, TX, USA) and merged into one file for the analysis. Point estimates and 95 percent confidence intervals were calculated for the survey indicators accounting for cluster effects. Pearson χ^2 test was used to determine statistical significance for binary and categorical variables and regression for continuous variables. Changes between baseline and endline with p-values less than 0.05 were taken as statistically significant.

RESULTS

Participants background characteristics

A total of 899 primary caregivers of sick children were included in the survey at baseline and 630 at endline. **Table 1** shows the distribution of the disease condition among the eligible children surveyed. There was no significant difference in the sex and age distribution of the children, response rates for fever, diarrhoea, and cough with difficult or fast breathing cases targeted was 100 percent. Relatively more cases of fever, diarrhoea, and cough with difficult or fast breathing were captured at baseline (1,130) than endline (902) (**Table 1**).

Caregiver knowledge of illnesses and perception of CORPs

Over the course of program implementation, caregiver knowledge of two or more signs of childhood illness (eg, danger signs for sick children as well as symptoms and treatment of malaria and diarrhoea) increased significantly, from 56 percent at baseline to 68 percent at endline ($P < 0.05$) (see **Table 2**). Knowledge of the cause of malaria increased significantly, from 61 percent at baseline to 78 percent at endline, but knowledge of fever as a sign of malaria did not change significantly. Caregiver knowledge of correct malaria treatment (artemisinin-based combination therapy [ACT]) increased significantly between baseline and endline, from 26 percent at baseline to 73 percent at endline ($P < 0.0001$). Caregiver knowledge of correct diarrhoea treatment (oral rehydration solution [ORS] and zinc) also increased significantly, from 5 percent at baseline to 54 percent at endline ($P < 0.0001$).

Table 1. *Characteristics of sick children included in the survey*

CHILD CHARACTERISTIC	BASELINE % (95% CI)	ENDLINE % (95% CI)
Sex of sick children included in survey:		
Male, %	50.5 (47.0-54.0)	49.9 (45.0-54.7)
Female, %	49.5 (46.0-53.0)	50.2 (45.3-55.0)
Age (months) of sick children included in survey:		
2–11, %	20.2 (17.5-23.3)	15.0 (12.2-18.4)
12–23, %	21.1 (18.7-23.9)	22.1 (19.7-24.6)
24–35, %	17.1 (14.3-20.4)	22.1 (19.7- 4.6)
36–47, %	17.1 (14.3-20.4)	20.0 (17.1-23.3)
48–59, %	19.7 (16.8-22.9)	19.4 (16.5-22.7)
Two-week history of illness of sick children included in survey:		
Had fever, %	58.3 (52.9-63.5)	57.9 (53.9-61.9)
Had diarrhoea, %	47.9 (47.0-57.1)	46.9 (43.1-50.8)
Had cough with fast breathing, %	43.2 (38.1-48.4)	51.2 (47.7-54.7)
Average number of illnesses, N	1.5	1.6
Total number of sick children included in survey:	899	680
Cases of illness included in survey:		
Fever, N	413	301
Diarrhoea, N	374	300
Cough with fast breathing, N	343	301
Total number of illness cases among sick children included in survey	1130	902

CI – confidence interval

Table 2. *Caregiver knowledge of childhood illnesses*

CAREGIVER ILLNESS KNOWLEDGE	BASELINE % (95% CI)	ENDLINE % (95% CI)	P-VALUE
Knows 2+ child illness signs	55.9 (45.9-65.4)	68.2 (58.9-76.3)	0.0463
Knows cause of malaria	61.2 (52.5-69.2)	77.8 (68.8-84.8)	0.0154
Knows fever is a sign of malaria	57.7 (49.8-65.2)	63.9 (54.9-72.1)	0.3194
Knows malaria treatment	25.5 (20.3-31.5)	72.9 (63.7-80.6)	<0.0001
Knows diarrhoea treatment (ORS + zinc)	4.9 (2.8-8.4)	53.5 (42.2-64.5)	<0.0001
Total number of caregivers	**721**	**510**	

CI – confidence interval

At endline, caregivers generally had positive perceptions of CORPs. Ninety four percent of caregivers viewed CORPs as trusted health care providers, and 96 percent believed that CORPs provided quality services, and were a convenient source of treatment, and the same percentage found the CORP at the first care-seeking visit (**Table 3**).

Table 3. *Caregiver perceptions of iCCM-trained CORP*

CAREGIVER PERCEPTION OF CORP	ENDLINE % (95% CI)	ENDLINE N
Views the CORP as a trusted health care provider	94.1 (88.1-97.2)	474
Believes the CORP provides quality services	95.6 (89.7-98.2)	474
Cites the CORP as a convenient source of treatment	96.0 (90.7-98.3)	474
Found the CORP at first visit (for all instances of care-seeking included in survey)*	96.1 (93.7-97.6)	410

CI – confidence interval

*Includes only caregivers who report seeking care from a CORP for at least one sick child.

Care seeking

Table 4 presents results for all appropriate providers while **Figure 2** shows results for choice of CORPs as first source of care among those who sought any care for their children by illness. Overall, care-seeking for a sick child from

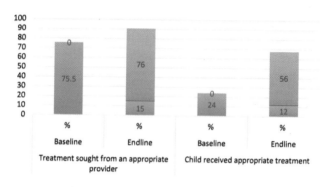

Figure 2. *Contribution of CORPs to appropriate treatment.*

Table 4. *Care seeking from appropriate provider*

ILLNESS	SOUGHT CARE FROM APPROPRIATE PROVIDER*		P-VALUE	CORP WAS FIRST SOURCE OF CARE	BASE-LINE N	END-LINE N
	Baseline % (95% CI)	Endline % (95% CI)		Endline % (95% CI)		
Overall	75.5 (68.3-81.5)	91.4 (87.2-94.3)	0.0000	76.6 (65.9-84.8)	1130	902
Fever	78.0 (70.6-83.9)	94.0 (88.8-96.9)	0.0001	78.4 (66.3-87.0)	413	301
Diarrhea	71.9 (64.3-78.5)	91.3 (86.7-94.4)	0.0000	75.7 (64.8-84.0)	374	300
Cough with fast or difficult breathing	76.4 (68.1-83.1)	88.7 (82.3-93.0)	0.0110	75.8 (64.4-84.4)	343	301

CI – confidence interval

*Appropriate providers include hospital, health centre, health post, clinic, CORP, or pharmacy.

an appropriate provider increased significantly, from 76% at baseline to 91% at endline (*P* <.001) as shown in **Table 4**. Care-seeking from an appropriate provider also increased for each iCCM illness from 78% to 94% for fever cases (*P* < 0.01), from 72% to 91% for diarrhoea cases (*P* < 0.01), and from 76% to 89% for cases of cough with difficult or fast breathing (*P* < 0.05).

The results also showed that CORPs contributed largely to the increase seen at endline in the percentage of children who received treatment from an appropriate provider. **Figure 2** shows a significant increase in the proportion of children who received care from an appropriate provider from 75 percent at baseline to 91 percent at endline, with CORPs contributing 76 percent and other providers 15 percent. Of those who sought care from appropriate providers at baseline, only 24 percent received appropriate treatment compared to 68 percent at endline, out of which CORPs constituted 56 percent.

In addition, source of care-seeking practices shifted substantially, with caregivers at endline selecting to seek care from CORPs in their communities for the majority of cases of all illnesses experienced by their children. Among those who sought any care, more than 82 percent of fever, diarrhoea and cough with fast or difficult breathing cases sought care form CORPs as the first source of care at endline. See **Figure 3**.

When analysed by type of facilities visited, a shift was noticed from hospitals and other health facilities as first source of care to CORPs. The baseline and endline pie charts in **Figures 4** and **Figure 5** show that among all cases of illness for which care was sought at baseline, when there were no CORPs, the majority of caregivers sought care at a hospital (39 percent) or a health centre

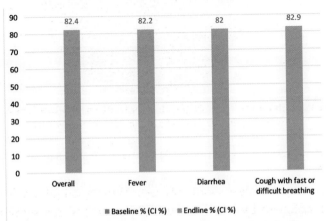

Figure 3. *Care seeking from CORPs as first source of care by illness.*

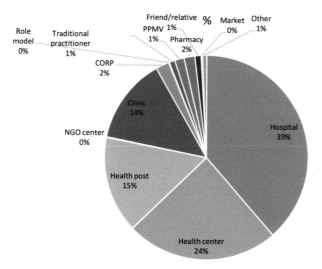

Figure 4. *Percentage of caregivers who sought advice or treatment for his or her sick child from a given location as the first source, among those who sought any care at baseline.*

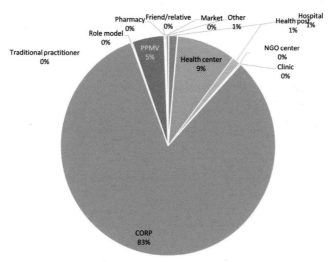

Figure 5. *Percentage of caregivers who sought advice or treatment for his or her sick child from a given location as the first source, among those who sought any care at endline.*

(24 percent); by endline, the majority of cases of illness sought care from CORPs (83 percent), followed by health centres (9 percent) with a significant drop in the cases that sought care at hospital as first source of care to one percent.

Sick child assessment and treatment

Overall, appropriate diagnosis and treatment of fever, diarrhoea and cough with fast or difficult breathing increased at endline. Among cases of fever who sought care from a CORP at endline, 77 percent received a malaria test, 90 percent of the caregivers reported receiving the result of the test, and 89 percent reported receiving ACT after a positive test (**Table 5**). Among children with fever who sought care from a provider other than a CORP at endline, 57 percent received a malaria test from the provider, 41 percent of their caregivers reported receiving the result of the test from the provider, and 48 percent received ACT from the provider after being confirmed for malaria. These results

Table 5. *Malaria and fast breathing assessment among children with fever or cough**

MALARIA AND FAST BREATHING ASSESSMENT	BASELINE % (95% CI)	ENDLINE % (95% CI)	P-VALUE	BASE-LINE N	END-LINE N
Fever cases in which care was sought from CORP:					
Child had blood drawn by CORP	0	77.1 (67.6-84.4)	0.0003	17	240
Caregiver received result of malaria test	0*	90.3 (0.8-1.0)	na	0	185
Blood test positive for malaria	0*	92.8 (0.9-1.0)	na	0	167
Received ACT after positive malaria test, among those who had a positive malaria test	0*	89.0 (0.8-1.0)	na	0	155
Fever cases in which care was sought from providers other than CORP:					
Child had blood drawn by other provider	99.4 (95.3-99.9)	57.1 (40.9-72.0)	0.0000	318	112
Caregiver received result of malaria test	27.9 (21.1-35.8)	40.6 (28.8-53.6)	0.0797	316	64
Blood test positive for malaria	79.6 (65.0-89.1)	96.2 (73.8-99.6)	0.0708	88	26
Received ACT after positive malaria test, among those who had a positive malaria test	68.6 (53.1-80.8)	48.0 (28.0-68.7)	0.0546	70	25
All cough with fast or difficult breathing cases:					
Respiratory rate assessed	47.8 (40.8-54.9)	62.1 (51.9-71.4)	0.0153	343	301
Cough with fast or difficult breathing cases in which care was sought from CORP					
Respiratory rate assessed	0†	55.8 (44.1-67.0)	na	17	231
Cough with fast or difficult breathing cases in which care was sought from provider other than CORP:					
Respiratory rate assessed	57.4 (50.0 – 64.5)	42.3 (30.9 – 54.3)	0.0161	256	102

n/a – not applicable, ACT – artemisinin-based combination therapy, CORP – community-oriented resource person
*Some cases sought care from multiple providers, which is why the sum of the endline N for those assessed by CORP and those assessed by other providers (333) is larger than endline N that had respiratory rate assessed (301) for fast breathing.
†There were no cases or the number of cases was too small to calculate a percentage.

indicate overall more appropriate assessment and treatment of fever cases by CORPs, compared to cases seen by other providers. The findings were similar for assessment of children with cough with fast or difficult breathing; overall, the proportion of children who had cough with fast or difficult breathing that had their respiratory rates assessed increased significantly from 48 percent at baseline to 62 percent at endline.

Among confirmed malaria cases, the percentage of children who received ACT within the same or next day following the onset of fever increased significantly, from 57 percent at baseline to 74 percent at endline ($P < 0.05$) (see **Table 6**). For cases of diarrhoea, treatment with ORS and zinc by any provider

Table 6. *Appropriate treatment coverage*

ILLNESS (TREATMENT)	BASELINE % (CI %)	ENDLINE % (CI %)	P-VALUE	BASE-LINE N	END-LINE N
Received treatment:					
Confirmed malaria (ACT same or next day following the onset of fever)*	56.9 (46.5-66.8)	73.9 (64.7-81.4)	0.0123	72	188
Diarrhoea (ORS)	68.2 (59.5-75.7)	88.3 (81.9-92.7)	<0.0001	374	300
Diarrhoea (zinc)	15.0 (10.5-20.9)	77.0 (66.8-84.8)	<0.0001	374	300
Diarrhoea (ORS and zinc)	12.8 (8.9-18.2)	74.0 (63.6-82.3)	<0.0001	374	300
Cough with difficult or fast breathing (amoxicillin)	28.6 (21.6-36.7)	60.5 (50.2-69.9)	<0.0001	343	301
Received treatment from CORP:					
Fever (ACT same or next day following the onset of fever)	0	55.5 (46.6-64.0)	na	413	301
Confirmed malaria (ACT same or next day following the on-set of fever)*	0	60.6 (50.0-70.4)	na	72	188
Diarrhoea (ORS)	0	75.3 (63.9-84.0)	na	374	300
Diarrhoea (zinc)	0	68.3 (57.5-77.5)	na	374	300
Diarrhoea (ORS and zinc)	0	66.3 (55.5-75.7)	na	374	300
Cough with difficult or fast breathing (amoxicillin)	0	47.2 (36.3-58.3)	na	343	301
Received treatment from provider other than CORP:					
Fever (ACT same or next day following the onset of fever)	25.2 (20.0-31.2)	9.0 (4.5-17.1)	0.0015	413	301
Confirmed malaria (ACT same or next day following the on-set of fever)*	56.9 (46.5-66.8)	13.3 (7.1-23.4)	<0.0001	72	188
Diarrhoea (ORS)	65.0 (55.5-73.4)	13.0 (7.6-21.4)	<0.0001	374	300
Diarrhoea (zinc)	12.8 (9.0-18.0)	9.7 (6.4-14.3)	0.3157	374	300
Diarrhoea (ORS and zinc)	11.8 (8.1-16.8)	7.7 (4.5-12.7)	0.1541	374	300
Cough with difficult or fast breathing (amoxicillin)	24.8 (18.0-33.1)	13.3 (8.1-21.0)	0.0212	343	301

CI – confidence interval, ACT – artemisinin-based combination therapy, na – not applicable, CORP – community-orientated resource person

*Denominator for confirmed malaria is restricted to those with a positive malaria diagnostic test result.

increased significantly, from 13 percent at baseline to 74 percent at endline ($P < 0.001$), and for cases of cough with difficult or fast breathing, treatment with amoxicillin by any provider increased significantly from 29 percent at baseline to 61 percent at endline ($P < 0.001$). At endline, treatments received from CORPs contributed significantly to the overall increase in prompt and appropriate treatments received by children 2-59 months compared to other providers. 61 percent out of 74 percent treated with ACTs following confirmation of malaria, were treated by CORPs. CORPs also contributed 75 percent to ORS treatment, 68 percent to zinc and 66 percent to ORS and zinc and 47 percent to amoxicillin treatment for fast breathing at endline.

DISCUSSION

Over the course of the intervention, there was significant increase in caregiver knowledge of two or more danger signs of childhood illness, cause of malaria, correct malaria treatment and correct diarrhoea treatment. Most caregivers of sick children, especially those who live in rural and remote communities, do not seek care from trained health personnel, [22] partly due to the knowledge level of caregivers. Studies have documented the relationship between knowledge of caregivers and care seeking [23-25]. Bruce et al in a study of the determinants of care seeking for children with pneumonia and diarrhoea in Guatemala documented mother's perception of illness severity and recognition of WHO-defined danger signs as predictors of care seeking for childhood illnesses [26]. Another study in Pakistan concluded that community mobilization and behaviour change activities should be included in community case management programmes rather than isolated strengthening of skills of community health workers (CHWs) [27]. The increase found in Niger state was likely boosted by the demand creation activities and behavioural change communication strategy implemented as part of the iCCM programme. Caregivers were targeted as the primary audience with the aim of improving their knowledge on childhood illnesses and promoting uptake of services provided by CORPs.

Caregivers in Niger State had positive perceptions about CORPs as trusted health care providers who were a convenient source of treatment and provided quality services. It is generally agreed that CORPs as community volunteers are critical in improving access to life saving interventions, however it is important that they are accepted and trusted by the communities they serve. Poor confidentiality and trust have been identified as key barriers to CHW acceptability in delivering maternal and child health services in the home [28,29].

Overall, this study found care-seeking for a sick child from an appropriate provider increased significantly for all three diseases of focus with a shift towards the CORPs in the communities as the first source compared to other sources of care. This fits with similar findings from previous studies which suggests that iCCM influences local care-seeking practices and reduces workload at already over-burdened health facilities [28,30,31]. We are not aware of any other programme being implemented during the project period which may have also contributed to the outcomes on health seeking behaviour presented here.

The study demonstrated a significant increase in diagnosis and treatment coverage for malaria, cough with fast or difficult breathing and diarrhoea in a timely manner with major contributions by CORPs as appropriate providers. Although interventions promoting care seeking improve mortality outcomes, timely care seeking from an appropriate care provider is also crucial [32]. Timely treatment is especially vital for children with symptoms of malaria and pneumonia, as improved outcomes have been associated with provision of treatment within 24 hours of onset of symptom [33]. The increased coverage could be attributable to the fact that 96 percent of the caregivers in the study perceived CORPs as a convenient source of care closer to the home and that they also provided quality services. Studies have documented a number of factors that influence care-seeking behaviour, which include perceptions of cause of illness, distance, cost, socio-cultural barriers, knowledge and information barriers and quality of available care among others [34,35]. The increased care seeking and treatment coverage found in this study further re-affirm the documented ability of iCCM to address geographical or physical barriers and improve access to care as evidenced by increased coverage of treatments [19,36-38].

Overall, there was better assessment and appropriate treatment of fever and suspected pneumonia cases and by CORPs, compared to cases managed by other providers, implying that community volunteers when trained, supported and well equipped can implement iCCM according to national guidelines. In all intervention areas, children with fever taken first to CORPs were significantly more likely to receive a test, to receive the test results, and to receive treatment with ACT than children taken to other providers, including primary health centres (PHCs). Children seen by CORPs were also more likely to have their respiratory rates assessed. This finding is comparable to a Mozambique study which found that only 41 percent of children with fever treated by first level health facility workers were tested with an RDT, and 19 percent of them received respiratory rates assessment compared to 60 percent and 68 percent of children seen by CHWs respectively [39]. It is however important to note that even though CORPs performed better than other providers in child assessment, the proportion of children who had their respiratory rates counted in this study remained low (56 percent). We also found that CORPs were less likely to treat children with fast breathing with amoxicillin than they were to treat cases of malaria and diarrhoea. Although reasons for these differences were not measured in this survey, it calls for closer supervision and mentoring of these community volunteers to ensure they are adhering to protocol.

A number of factors could have contributed to the sub-optimal performance of other providers, including PHCs, found in this study. Lack or outdated knowledge of treatment protocol or algorithm, non-availability of commodities for testing and treating the child, as well as lack of motivation and poor supervision, are possible factors as documented in other studies [40-42]. In order to maintain quality in the continuum of care, which should not be neglected for the sake of universal access, primary health care facilities, which should play supervisory roles for CORPs, must also be strengthened in terms of adherence to protocol, supportive supervision and uninterrupted supplies [43]. The overall benefit of iCCM in achieving universal access can only be harnessed when scaled up with good quality of care; and this will require not only community ownership of the intervention but also political commitment of governments to invest in it as required elements of sustainability.

Limitations

A major limitation that should be recognized while interpreting the results of this study is the that results of treatment of confirmed malaria are based on caregiver recall of receiving a finger or heel stick (rapid diagnostic test [RDT] or microscopy, depending on the provider), which can be poor [44].

CONCLUSION

Implementation of iCCM with focused demand creation activities contributed to improved timely and appropriate treatment for fever, diarrhoea and cough with fast or difficult breathing for children living in rural and remote areas in Nigeria. Scaling up of iCCM, using frontline community providers, to hard-to-reach areas across Nigeria can contribute towards achieving the SDGs.

Acknowledgements: *We acknowledge the contribution of ICF in the design of the sampling methodology and endline data analysis and WHO Country office staff who provided direct support for in country coordination and programme monitoring. We* acknowledge the immense contribution of Dr Salim Sadruddin and Gunther Baugh of WHO Geneva for their overall technical oversight of the programme. All staff of Malaria Consortium, RAcE programme team and Ministry of Health in Niger State who participated in the implementation of the intervention and monitoring of field work, are also acknowledged. We thank Mr. Olalekan Onitiju, who supported the field work and all the survey supervisors, data collectors, editors, clerks and drivers for their valuable work in ensuring that the data were properly collected and processed. We would also like to appreciate the community-oriented resource persons and community health extension workers who work hard to provide services to caregivers and children in communities, and the caregivers, who participated in the study.

Disclaimers: *The views expressed in this article are those of the authors and not of WHO or the Global Affairs Canada.*

Ethics approval: *The survey protocol received ethical approval from ICF's Institutional Review Board and from Nigeria's National Health Research Ethics Committee.*

Funding: *The RAcE programme and its baseline and endline surveys were funded by World Health Organization (WHO) through funding by Global Affairs Canada.*

Authorship contributions: *OO: Corresponding author/Technical support to Project implementation/first manuscript draft/consent to final version of manuscript. HC: Technical inputs/manuscript review & editing/consent to final version of manuscript. IN, AA, JJ, OA, JD and PG: Project implementation/management/manuscript review/ consent to final version of manuscript. LO: Technical support project implementation/manuscript review/ consent to final version of manuscript. DP: Contribution to data analysis/Technical inputs/ Manuscript review & editing/Consent to final version of manuscript. KM: Programme management/Manuscript review & editing/ Consent to final version of manuscript.*

Competing interests: *The authors completed the Unified Competing Interest form at www.icmje.org/coi_disclosure.pdf (available upon request from the corresponding author), and declare no conflicts of interest.*

References

1 World Health Organization. 2018. World Malaria Report 2018. Geneva: World Health Organization; 2018. Available: http://apps.who.int/iris/bitstream/hand le/10665/275867/9789241565653-eng.pdf?ua=1 Accessed: 28 November 2018.

2 World Health Organization and UNICEF. Ending preventable child deaths from pneumonia and diarrhoea by 2025—the integrated Global Action Plan for Pneumonia and Diarrhoea (GAPPD). Geneva/New York: WHO/UNICEF; 2013.

3 Berkley JA, Ross A, Mwangi I, Osier FH, Mohammed M, Shebbe MI, et al. Prognostic indicators of early and late death in children admitted to district hospital in Kenya: cohort study. BMJ. 2003;326:361. Medline:12586667 doi:10.1136/bmj.326.7385.361

4 National Population Commission (NPC), Marco O. Nigerian Demographic and Health Survey 2008.Calverton, MD: National Population Commission (NPC) and ORC Marco; 2009.

5   Christopher JB, Le May A, Lewin S, Ross D. Thirty years after Alma-Ata: a systematic review of the impact of community health workers delivering curative interventions against malaria, pneumonia and diarrhea on child mortality and morbidity in sub-Saharan Africa. Hum Resour Health. 2011;9:27-38. Medline:22024435 doi:10.1186/1478-4491-9-27

6   Anthony D, Mullerbeck E, editors. UNICEF. Committing to child survival: A promise renewed. New York: UNICEF; 2012.

7   Vega J. Universal health coverage: the post-2015 development agenda. Lancet. 2013;381:179-80. Medline:23332947 doi:10.1016/S0140-6736(13)60062-8

8   UNDP. 2018. Goal 3: Good health and well-being. Available: http://www.undp.org/content/undp/en/home/sustainable-development-goals/goal-3-good-health-and-well-being.html. Accessed: 2 June 2018.

9   Evans DB, Hsu J, Boerma T. Universal health coverage and universal access. Bull World Health Organ. 2013;91:546-546A. Medline:23940398 doi:10.2471/BLT.13.125450

10 Kutzin J. Health financing for universal coverage and health system performance: concepts and implications for policy. Bull World Health Organ. 2013;91:602-11. Medline:23940408 doi:10.2471/BLT.12.113985

11 Gulliford M, Figueroa-Munoz J, Morgan M, Hughes D, Gibson B, Beech R, et al. What does 'access to health care' mean? J Health Serv Res Policy. 2002;7:186-8. Medline:12171751 doi:10.1258/135581902760082517

12 The world health report 2010 – Health systems financing: the path to universal coverage. Geneva: World Health Organization; 2010. Available: http://www.who.int/whr/2010/whr10_en.pdf. Accessed: 12 June 2018.

13 Joint statement: management of pneumonia in community settings Geneva/New York: WHO/UNICEF; 2004 (WHO/FCH/CAH/04.06).

14 Young M, Wolfheim C, Marsh DR, Hammamy D. World Health Organization/United Nations Children's Fund joint statement on integrated community case management: an equity-focused strategy to improve access to essential treatment services for children. Am J Trop Med Hyg. 2012;87:6-10. Medline:23136272 doi:10.4269/ajtmh.2012.12-0221

15 Theodoratou E, Al-Jilaihawi S, Woodward F, Ferguson J, Jhass A, Ferguson J, et al. The effect of case management on childhood pneumonia mortality in developing countries. Int J Epidemiol. 2010;39:i155-71. Medline:20348118 doi:10.1093/ije/dyq032

16 World Health Organization. Technical consultation meeting report on universal access to core malaria interventions in high-burden countries 11–13 April 2018. Available: http://apps.who.int/iris/bitstream/handle/10665/272466/WHO-CDS-GMP-2018.08-eng.pdf?ua=1. Accessed: 12 June 2018.

17 Muhumuza G, Mutesi C, Mutamba F, Ampuriire P, Nangai C. Acceptability and utilization of Community Health Workers after the adoption of the Integrated Community Case Management Policy in Kabarole District in Uganda. Health Syst Policy Res. 2015;2:13. Medline:26998446

18 Buchner DL, Brenner JL, Kabakyenga J, Teddy K, Maling S, Barigye C, et al. Stakeholders' perceptions of integrated community case management by community health workers: a post-intervention qualitative study. PLoS One. 2014;9:e98610. Medline:24927074 doi:10.1371/journal.pone.0098610

19 Brenner JL, Barigye C, Maling S, Kabakyenga J, Nettel-Aguirre A, Buchner D, et al. Where there is no doctor: can volunteer community health workers in rural Uganda provide integrated community case management? Afr Health Sci. 2017;17:237-46. Medline:29026398 doi:10.4314/ahs.v17i1.29

20 Binkin N, Sullivan K, Staehling N, Nieburg P. Rapid nutrition surveys: How many clusters are enough? Disasters. 1992;16:97-103. Medline:20958740 doi:10.1111/j.1467-7717.1992. tb00383.x

21 CORE Group. 2001. Knowledge, practice, and coverage survey (KPC 2000+ Field Guide). Available: https://www.spring-nutrition.org/publications/tool-summaries/knowledge-practice-and-coverage-survey-kpc-2000-field-guide. Accessed: 22 June 2018.

22 Gupta GR. Tackling pneumonia and diarrhoea: the deadliest diseases for the world's poorest children. Lancet. 2012;379:2123-4. Medline:22682449 doi:10.1016/S0140-6736(12)60907-6

23 Ogunlesi TA, Abdul AR. Maternal knowledge and care-seeking behaviors for newborn jaundice in Sagamu, Southwest Nigeria. Niger J Clin Pract. 2015;18:33-40. Medline:25511341

24 Yansaneh AI, Moulton LH, George AS, Rao SR, Kennedy N, Bangura P, et al. Influence of community health volunteers on care seeking and treatment coverage for common childhood illnesses in the context of free health care in rural Sierra Leone. Trop Med Int Health. 2014;19:1466-76. Medline:25243929 doi:10.1111/tmi.12383

25 Burton DC, Flannery B, Onyango B, Larson C, Alaii J, Zhang X, et al. Healthcare-seeking behaviour for common infectious disease-related illnesses in rural Kenya: a community-based house-to-house survey. J Health Popul Nutr. 2011;29:61-70. Medline:21528791 doi:10.3329/jhpn.v29i1.7567

26 Bruce N, Pope D, Arana B, Shiels C, Romero C, Klein R, et al. Determinants of care seeking for children with pneumonia and diarrhea in Guatemala: implications for intervention strategies. Am J Public Health. 2014;104:647-57. Medline:24524510 doi:10.2105/AJPH.2013.301658

27 Sadruddin S, Khan IU, Bari A, Khan A, Ahmad I, Qazi SA. Effect of community mobilization on appropriate care seeking for pneumonia in Haripur, Pakistan. J Glob Health. 2015;5:010405. Medline:25798232 doi:10.7189/jogh.05.010405

28 Grant M, Wilford A, Haskins L, Phakathi S, Mntambo N, Horwood CM. Trust of community health workers influences the acceptance of community-based maternal and child health services. Afr J Prim Health Care Fam Med. 2017;9:e1-8. Medline:28582988 doi:10.4102/phcfm.v9i1.1281

29 Singh D, Cumming R, Negin J. Acceptability and trust of community health workers offering maternal and newborn health education in rural Uganda. Health Educ Res. 2015;30:947-58. Medline:26459326

30 Seidenberg PD, Hamer DH, Iyer H, Pilingana P, Siazeele K, Hamainza B, Brieger W, Yeboah-Antwi K. Impact of integrated community case management on health-seeking behavior in rural Zambia. Am J Trop Med Hyg. 2012;87(5 Suppl):105-10. Medline:23136285 doi:10.4269/ajtmh.2012.11-0799

31 WHO. Meeting report of workshop on the development of tools to promote improved care seeking 26–30 July 1999. Department of Child and Adolescent Health and Development, WHO/FCH/CAH/99.3. Geneva: WHO, 1999.

32 World Health Organization. Malaria Treatment Guidelines 2015. Available: http://www.who.int/malaria/publications/atoz/9789241549127/en/. Accessed: 22nd June 2018.

33 Hill Z, Kendall C, Arthur P, Kirkwood B, Adjei E. Recognizing childhood illnesses and their traditional explanations: exploring options for care-seeking interventions in the context of the IMCI strategy in rural Ghana. Trop Med Int Health. 2003;8:668-76. Medline:12828551 doi:10.1046/j.1365-3156.2003.01058.x

34 Dillip A, Hetzel MW, Gosoniu D, Kessy F, Lengeler C, Mayumana I, Mshana C, Mshinda H, Schulze A, Makemba A, Pfeiffer C, Weiss MG, Obrist B. Socio-cultural factors explaining timely and appropriate use of health facilities for degedege in south-eastern Tanzania. Malar J. 2009;8:144. Medline:19563640 doi:10.1186/1475-2875-8-144

35 Bedford JK, Sharkey AB. Local barriers and solutions to improve care-seeking for childhood pneumonia, diarrhoea and malaria in Kenya, Nigeria and Niger: A qualitative study. PLoS One. 2014;9:e100038. Medline:24971642 doi:10.1371/journal.pone.0100038

36 Mubiru D, Byabasheija R, Bwanika JB, Meier JE, Magumba G, Kaggwa FM, et al. Evaluation of integrated community case management in eight districts of Central Uganda. PLoS One. 2015;10:e0134767. Medline:26267141 doi:10.1371/journal.pone.0134767

37 Mugeni C, Levine AC, Munyaneza RM, Mulindahabi E, Cockrell HC, Glavis-Bloom J, et al. Nationwide implementation of integrated community case management of childhood illness in Rwanda. Glob Health Sci Pract. 2014;2:328-41. Medline:25276592 doi:10.9745/GHSP-D-14-00080

38 Kalyango JN, Alfven T, Peterson S, Mugenyi K, Karamagi C, Rutebemberwa E. Integrated community case management of malaria and pneumonia increases prompt and appropriate treatment for pneumonia symptoms in children under five years in Eastern Uganda. Malar J. 2013;12:340. Medline:24053172 doi:10.1186/1475-2875-12-340

39 Guenther T, Sadruddin S, Finnegan K, Wetzler E, Ibo F, Rapaz P, et al. Contribution of community health workers to improving access to timely and appropriate case management of childhood fever in Mozambique. J Glob Health. 2017;7:010402. Medline:28400951 doi:10.7189/jogh.07.010402

40 Hoque DM, Arifeen SE, Rahman M, Chowdhury EK, Haque TM, Begum K, et al. Improving and sustaining quality of child health care through IMCI training and supervision: experience from rural Bangladesh. Health Policy Plan. 2014;29:753-62. Medline:24038076 doi:10.1093/heapol/czt059

41 Alhassan RK, Spieker N, van Ostenberg P, Ogink A, Nketiah-Amponsah E, de Wit TF. Association between health worker motivation and healthcare quality efforts in Ghana. Hum Resour Health. 2013;11:37. Medline:23945073 doi:10.1186/1478-4491-11-37

42 Binyaruka P, Borghi J. Improving quality of care through payment for performance: examining effects on the availability and stock-out of essential medical commodities in Tanzania. Trop Med Int Health. 2017;22:92-102. Medline:27928874 doi:10.1111/tmi.12809

43 Chee G, Pielemeier N, Lion A, Connor C. Why differentiating between health system support and health system strengthening is needed. Int J Health Plann Manage. 2013;28:85-94. Medline:22777839 doi:10.1002/hpm.2122

44 Indicator guide: Monitoring and evaluating integrated community case management. Washington, DC: John Snow Inc., Karolinska Institute, Save the Children, Uppsala University, and the World Health Organization. Available: http://1rqxbs47ujl4rdy6q3nzf554.wpengine.netdna-cdn.com/wp-content/uploads/2016/07/iCCM-Indicator-Guide.pdf. Accessed: 22 June 2018.

Improving access to appropriate case management for common childhood illnesses in hard-to-reach areas of Abia State, Nigeria

Chinwoke Isiguzo[1,2], Samantha Herrera[3], Joy Ufere[4], Ugo Enebeli[1], Chukwuemeka Oluoha[5], Jennifer Anyanti[1], Debra Prosnitz[6]

[1] Society for Family Health Abuja, Nigeria
[2] Graduate School of Public Health, University of Pittsburgh, Pittsburgh, Pennsylvania, USA
[3] Save the Children, Washington, D.C., USA
[4] World Health Organization, Abuja, Nigeria
[5] Abia State Ministry of Health Umuahia, Abia State, Nigeria
[6] ICF, Rockville, Maryland, USA

Background Studies have demonstrated that trained community health workers can improve access to quality health services for under five children. Under the World Health Organization's Rapid Access Expansion Progamme, integrated community case management of childhood illnesses (iCCM) was introduced in Abia and Niger States, Nigeria in 2013. The objective of the program was to increase the number of children 2-59 months receiving quality life-saving treatment for malaria, pneumonia and diarrhoea by extending case management through community-oriented resource persons (CORPs). We present findings from household surveys comparing baseline and endline data to assess changes in sick child care-seeking, assessment, and treatment coverage provided over the project period in Abia State.

Methods A baseline household survey was conducted in May 2014 and an endline survey in February 2017. The surveys used multi-stage cluster sampling of primary caregivers of children aged 2-59 months who had been recently sick with diarrhoea, fever, or cough with difficult breathing.

Results Care-seeking from an appropriate provider improved significantly from 69% at baseline to 77% at endline (P<0.01). At baseline, patent and proprietary medicine vendors (PPMVs) (55%) and health centers (34%) were the main providers of care for iCCM services; by endline, CORPs became the main source of care (48%), followed by PPMVs (36%) and health centers (25%).

Conclusions Overall, the findings demonstrate improvements in care-seeking. Care-seeking practices shifted over the course of the project, with more caregivers seeking care from CORPs by the end of the project. The findings suggest that scaling up iCCM in Nigeria may improve access to appropriate treatment for under five children living in hard-to-reach areas.

The United Nations Inter-agency Group for Child Mortality Estimation (UN-IGME) reported that globally there were approximately 5.6 million deaths of children under five years in 2016. Over 25% of those deaths were attributed to diarrheoa (8%), malaria (5%) and pneumonia (13%) [1]; these are diseases that are preventable and relatively simple to treat. Sub-Saharan Africa has the greatest burden of child mortality, with the highest number of under-five deaths occurring in Nigeria [1]. According to the 2013 Nigeria Demographic Health Survey about one in every eight children in Nigeria died before their fifth birthday – around 21 times the average rate in developed countries [2].

The World Health Organization – United Nations Children's Fund (WHO – UNICEF) Joint statement on integrated community case management (iCCM), recommends iCCM as an equity-focused strategy to improve access to life saving interventions for children under the age of five [3]. The strategy targets treatable diseases that are the main causes of childhood deaths in low and middle-income countries – pneumonia, diarrhoea, malaria and malnutrition, using available efficacious treatment. This involves administration of oral antibiotics for pneumonia, zinc and low osmolarity oral rehydration salts (ORS) for diarrhoea and artemisinin-combination therapy for malaria by community health workers (CHWs) [4,5].

In November 2013, the WHO Rapid Access Expansion Programme (RAcE) was launched in Nigeria [6]. The program, which pioneered iCCM in the country, supported Abia and Niger States to train and deploy community health workers (CHWs) referred as community-oriented resource persons (CORPs), in underserved hard-to-reach communities of the states. The iCCM programme in Abia State targeted children under five years of age across hard-to-reach communities in 15 out of 17 local government areas (LGAs). We present the results of the changes in care-seeking, diagnostic and treatment coverage, after the introduction of iCCM in Abia state.

METHODS

Study setting

Abia State is in the South Eastern region of Nigeria. The state had an estimated population of 3.7 million in 2016. The population is predominantly rural (70%), with the agricultural sector employing a good proportion of the state's workforce [7].

The State Ministry of Health (SMOH) provides overall direction for the health services in the state and is responsible for health staff development and organization; and implementation of secondary health care. The SMOH, through the

Abia State Primary Health Care Development Agency (ASPHCDA), provides policies and guidelines for primary health care service delivery and supervises its implementation in the 17 LGAs in the state. The primary health care (PHC) system provides basic health services and is often the only source of health care available to persons living in the rural areas. However, over the years, issues of equity and disparity between disease burden and health expenditure have led to sub-optimal utilization of the PHC system. To this end, the ASPHCDA was established to improve access and quality of care provided at the PHC level. The ASPHCDA, whose mandate is to also provide community health services, led the iCCM programme with support from Society for Family Health (SFH), Nigeria. Using the national iCCM guideline, the iCCM programme was implemented in hard-to-reach areas, defined as areas outside the five-kilometer radius of a functioning primary healthcare center that has road accessibility, 24-hour health service provision, and adequate availability of human resources and medical supplies in 15 of 17 LGAs in Abia State.

After the baseline survey, CORPs were selected by community members and members of ward development committee based on the national criteria for CORPs selection [8]. The selected CORPs received a six-day training in iCCM at the Primary Health Centers (PHCs). The Federal Ministry of Health approved iCCM curriculum was used for training the CORPs. The Nigeria iCCM curriculum has been adopted from the WHO "Caring for sick child in the community" training. The CORPs training comprised of didactic and clinical sessions. The clinical sessions included assessment, classification and treatment of malaria, diarrhoea, and pneumonia, screening and referral of children with severe acute malnutrition, and severe illnesses. Following the training, CORPs were provided with medicines – artemisinin-based combination therapy (ACT) for malaria, oral amoxicillin for pneumonia, ORS and zinc for diarrhoea; diagnostics – Rapid Diagnostic Tests for malaria and respiratory rate timers for pneumonia, and recording and reporting tools. The CORPs after the iCCM training were deployed to their respective communities. The CORPs were supervised and mentored by community health extension workers (CHEWs) based at the PHCs. The CHEWs were supervised by LGA iCCM focal persons, who are trained nurses. At the time of the endline survey 1,251 iCCM-trained CORPs were active out of the 1,351 trained at the start of the programme.

Case definition

Care seeking

Defined as seeking care for malaria, diarrhoea and pneumonia from an appropriate provider, including community-oriented resource person. An appropriate provider was defined as seeking care from a public or private health facilities, a community-oriented resource person, or proprietary and patent medicine vendors.

Assessment/diagnosis

Children presenting with fever were tested and diagnosed using a Rapid Diagnostic Test for malaria by a CORP. To assess for fast breathing pneumonia, children with cough/difficult or rapid breathing had their respiratory rate counted by a CORP for one minute using a respiratory rate counting timer. Cases with respiratory rate above the WHO age-specific cut-off point were classified as pneumonia. (50 breaths or more per minute in a child age 2 months up to 11 months and 40 breaths or more per minute in a child age 12 months up to 5 years are considered fast breathing).

Treatment

Children between 6-59 months with a positive RDT for malaria received artemether-lumefantrine (AL). Children 2-59 months age with pneumonia were treated with amoxicillin dispersible tablets and those presenting with diarrhoea were treated with ORS and zinc.

Study design and sampling

Household surveys

Baseline and endline cross-sectional cluster-based household surveys were conducted in the iCCM programme areas at the start of the project in May–June 2014 and in February 2017. The aim of the household surveys was to assess changes in sick child care-seeking, assessment, and treatment coverage as well as caregivers' knowledge of childhood illnesses and perceptions of CORP services over the project period. The surveys interviewed primary caregivers of children age 2-59 months who had been sick with diarrhoea, fever, or cough / difficult or fast breathing in the two weeks prior to the survey. Information on background characteristics of the caregivers and children, and care-seeking, assessment, and treatment for the three illnesses was collected.

A 30×30 multi-stage cluster sampling methodology was used for both surveys. Thirty clusters were selected using probability proportional to size. Within each cluster, 10 interviews were conducted for each of the three illnesses (diarrhoea, fever, or cough with difficult or fast breathing) for a total of 30 interviews per cluster. Due to some changes in the project areas between the baseline and endline surveys, the clusters were redrawn at endline with an updated sampling frame that only included communities where the project was implemented.

Data management

Data collection for the baseline household survey was completed between May and June 2014 and for the endline household survey in February 2017. All survey team members were trained prior to the conduct of the surveys. The trainings included a pre-test of the survey instruments in one of the LGAs. For the household surveys, written informed consent was sought from each respondent prior to the administration of the questionnaire.

The household survey data were collected using paper questionnaires and entered into a CSPro database developed by the U.S. Census Bureau and ICF International with funding from U.S. Agency for International Development USA. Data were double-entered and checked for consistency. Any discrepancies were checked and resolved.

Data analysis

Survey data were analyzed using Stata version 14. Frequency estimates and 95% confidence intervals were calculated for all household survey indicators collected. Estimates were adjusted for cluster effects. Pearson's chi-square test was computed to assess significant changes between baseline and endline indicator estimates.

Ethical approval

The household survey protocol was reviewed and approved by the ICF Institutional Review Board and from the National Health Research Ethics Committee in Nigeria.

RESULTS

Characteristics of sick children and caregivers

At baseline and endline, there was an equal representation of sick children by sex and an even distribution across the age groups (**Table 1**). The most commonly reported illness at both baseline and endline was fever (66.0% and 74.3%, respectively). There was a higher report of all three illnesses at endline compared to baseline. Majority of caregivers were between the age 25-34 (just under 50% in both surveys), had a secondary or higher level of education (68.7% and 75.5% at baseline and endline, respectively), and were currently married or living with a partner as if married (just under 90% in both surveys) (**Table 2**). Overall, the characteristics of the sick children and caregivers were similar across the baseline and endline household surveys.

Table 1. *Characteristics of sick children from household surveys at baseline and endline*

CHARACTERISTIC	BASELINE	ENDLINE
Sex (%):		
Female	50.9	50.8
Age (months, %):		
2-11	21.5	18.9
12-23	17.6	17.4
24-35	22.2	18.8
36-47	17.9	20.3
48-59	20.8	24.6
Two-week history of illness (%):		
Had fever	66.0	74.3
Had diarrhoea	45.1	58.9
Had cough with difficult or fast breathing	49.9	62.8
Total number of sick children in survey	585	506
Cases of illness among sick children (number):		
Fever	386	376
Diarrhoea	264	298
Cough with difficult or fast breathing	292	318
Total number of sick child cases	942	992

Table 2. *Characteristics of caregivers of sick children from household surveys at baseline and endline*

CHARACTERISTIC	BASELINE (%)	ENDLINE (%)
Age (years):		
15-24	19.7	18.8
25-34	49.9	46.6
35-44	22.7	25.1
45+	7.7	9.5
Education level:		
None	6.7	4.4
Primary	24.6	20.2
Secondary or higher	68.7	75.5
Marital status:		
Currently married or living with partner as if married	88.7	86.8
Not in union	11.3	13.2
Total number of caregivers (n):	585	506

Caregiver knowledge of illnesses

Caregiver knowledge of two or more childhood illness danger signs increased significantly, from 65% at baseline to 78% at endline ($P<0.01$) (**Table 3**). Knowledge on the cause and signs and symptoms of malaria, however, remained relatively stable between baseline (70%) and endline (70%). Caregiver knowledge of correct malaria treatment (artemisinin-based combination therapy [ACT]) improved significantly, from 30% at baseline to 54% at endline ($P<0.0001$). Caregiver knowledge of correct diarrhoea treatment (oral rehydration solution [ORS] and zinc) also increased significantly, from 1% at baseline to 25% at endline ($P<0.0001$).

Caregiver perceptions of iCCM-trained CORP

Table 3. *Caregiver knowledge of childhood illnesses*

INDICATOR	BASELINE % (95% CI)	ENDLINE % (95% CI)	P-VALUE	BASELINE N	ENDLINE N
Knows 2+ child illness danger signs	65.3 (60.3-70.0)	77.5 (70.3-83.3)	0.0044	585	506
Knows cause of malaria	69.2 (64.8-73.4)	70.8 (65.3-75.7)	0.6795	585	506
Knows malaria signs and symptoms	62.7 (56.3-68.8)	68.6 (62.2-74.3)	0.1413	585	506
Knows malaria treatment	30.1 (24.7-36.1)	53.6 (46.5-60.5)	< 0.0001	585	506
Knows diarrhoea treatment	0.7 (0.2-2.2)	25.1 (20.3-30.6)	< 0.0001	585	506

CI – confidence interval

Overall, most caregivers had good perceptions of the CORPs working in their community by endline, with more than 80% of caregivers reporting that they viewed the CORP as a trusted health care provider, that CORPs provide quality services, and that CORPs are a convenient source of treatment. In addition, at endline, 88% of caregivers reported that they found the CORP at their first visit, demonstrating high accessibility (**Table 4**).

Care-seeking for fever, diarrhoea, and cough with difficult or fast breathing

Overall, care-seeking from an appropriate provider, defined as seeking care from a public or private health facilities, a community-oriented resource person, or proprietary and patent medicine vendors increased over the course of the RAcE project from 68.7% to 76.8% ($P<0.01$); primarily due to increases in care-seeking for children with diarrhoea ($P<0.05$) and children with cough with difficult or fast breathing (*P*<0.0001) (**Table 5**). Source of care-seeking shifted substantially over the project period; with more caregivers selecting to seek care from CORPs in their communities by endline (48.1%) and fewer seeking care from hospitals (10.8% at baseline to 6.6% at endline), health centers (34.0% to 24.8%) and propriety and patent medicine vendors (55.1% to 36.2%).

Table 4. *Caregiver perceptions of CORPs*

INDICATOR	BASELINE % (95% CI)	ENDLINE % (95% CI)	P-VALUE	BASELINE N	ENDLINE N
View CORPs as trusted health care providers	na	82.8 (77.7-86.9)	na	12	331
Believe CORPs provide quality services	na	84.0 (77.5-88.9)	na	12	331
Found the CORP at first visit	na	87.8 (82.3-91.8)	na	2	230
Cite the CORP as a convenient source of treatment	na	88.2 (82.4-92.3)	na	12	331
View CORPs as trusted health care providers	na	82.8 (77.7-86.9)	na	12	331

CORP – community-oriented resource person, CI – confidence interval, na – not applicable

Table 5. *Care-seeking from an appropriate provider* and by specific source of care sought*

	BASELINE % (95% CI)	ENDLINE % (95% CI)	P-VALUE	BASE-LINE N	ENDLINE N
Care-seeking from an appropriate provider:					
Overall	68.7 (4.5-72.6)	76.8 (71.8-81.2)	0.0032	942	992
Fever	86.0 (81.5-89.6)	84.0 (79.1-88.0)	0.4721	386	376
Diarrhoea	74.2 (68.3-79.4)	81.9 (76.6-86.2)	0.0172	264	298
Cough with difficult or fast breathing	40.8 (34.4-47.4)	63.5 (56.1-70.3)	<0.0001	292	318
Care-seeking by source of care (all illnesses):					
Hospital	10.8 (8.2-14.0)	6.6 (4.5-9.6)	0.0389	808	852
Health center	34.0 (26.9-42.0)	24.8 (19.8-30.5)	0.0753		
Health clinic or post	2.9 (1.6-4.9)	1.5 (0.8-3.0)	0.1476		
CORP	0.0	48.1 (38.5-57.9)	<0.0001		
Traditional practitioner	1.0 (0.4-2.6)	0.7 (0.3-1.7)	0.6307		
Propriety and patent medicine vendor (PPMV)	55.1 (47.9-62.0)	36.2 (29.9-42.9)	0.0001		
Pharmacy	2.4 (1.3-4.1)	4.5 (2.5-7.8)	0.1112		
Other	6.0 (4.1-8.6)	4.8 (3.2-7.3)	0.3617		

CI – confidence interval, CORP – community-oriented resource person
*Appropriate provider included seeking care from a public or private health facilities, a CORP, and PPMV.

Assessment of sick children

The percentage of children with fever in the two weeks preceding the survey who had blood drawn (proxy measure for receipt of an RDT) increased from 9.3% at baseline to 41.0% at endline ($P<0.0001$) (**Table 6**). For children with fever who had a blood test, the percentage of caregivers who received the result of the test also improved from 72.2% at baseline to 90.3% at endline ($P<0.01$). For children with fever who sought care from a CORP, 77.3% had their blood drawn at endline and 93.8% of their caregivers reported having received the result of the test. A similar increase was also observed in assessment of cough with difficult or fast breathing; improving from 21.2% to 42.8% over the project period (**Table 6**). Among the children with cough and difficult or fast breathing who sought care from a CORP, 70.1% had their respiratory rate assessed at endline.

Table 6. *Assessment coverage among children with fever and with cough and difficult or fast breathing for all providers and for care sought by CORP*

INDICATOR	BASELINE % (95% CI)	ENDLINE % (95% CI)	P-VALUE	BASELINE N	ENDLINE N
All fever cases					
Child had blood drawn	9.3 (6.3-13.6)	41.0 (32.2-50.4)	<0.0001	386	376
Caregiver received result of blood test	72.2 (51.9-86.3)	90.3 (84.5-94.1)	0.0031	36	154
Fever cases in which care was sought from CORP:					
Child had blood drawn	0.0	77.3 (68.7-84.0)	na	0	167
Caregiver received result of blood test	0.0	93.8 (86.1-97.4)	na	0	129
All cough with difficult or fast breathing cases:					
Respiratory rate assessed	21.2 (15.6-28.2)	42.8 (34.9-51.0)	0.0001	292	318
All cough with difficult or fast breathing cases in which care was sought from a CORP					
Respiratory rate assessed	0.0	70.1 (59.5-78.9)	na	0	127

na – not applicable, CI – confidence interval, CORP – community-oriented resource person

Treatment coverage

Receipt of treatment among all cases of confirmed malaria (fever cases that had a positive RDT), diarrhoea, and cough with difficult or fast breathing increased significantly between baseline and endline (**Table 7**). Among confirmed malaria cases, receipt of ACT within 2 days increased from 25.0% to 66.9% ($P<0.01$) over the project period. Among confirmed malaria, diarrhoea,

Table 7. *Treatment coverage among children with confirmed malaria, diarrhoea, and cough with difficult or fast breathing for all providers and for care sought by CORP*

	Baseline % (95% CI)	Endline % (95% CI)	P-value	Baseline N	Endline N
Received treatment from any provider:					
Confirmed malaria received ACT	41.7 (15.9-72.9)	90.2 (82.7-94.7)	0.0003	24	133
Confirmed malaria received ACT within 2 days	25.0 (9.6-51.0)	66.9 (60.1-73.1)	0.0016	24	133
Diarrhoea case received ORS and zinc	6.4 (3.7-11.0)	35.2 (27.9-43.4)	<0.0001	264	298
Cough with difficult or fast breathing received amoxicillin	8.6 (5.3-13.6)	35.5 (28.3-43.5)	<0.0001	292	318
Overall (received treatment across all three illnesses) *	8.3 (6.1-11.1)	41.0 (35.2-47.0)	<0.0001	580	749
Received treatment among those that sought care from a CORP:					
Confirmed malaria received ACT	0.0	93.1 (85.5-96.9)	na	0	116
Confirmed malaria received ACT within 2 days	0.0	69.8 (61.3-77.2)	na	0	116
Diarrhoea case received ORS and zinc	0.0	64.7 (53.0-74.8)	na	0	116
Cough with difficult or fast breathing received amoxicillin	0.0	66.1 (56.0-75.0)	na	0	127
Overall (received treatment across all three illnesses) *	0.0	66.1 (60.8-71.1)	na	0	365

ACT – artemisinin-based combination therapy, na – not applicable, ORS – oral rehydration salts, CORP – community-oriented resource person
*The overall indicator was calculated to include the percentage of children with confirmed malaria that received an ACT within two days, children with diarrhoea that received ORS and zinc, and children with cough with difficult or fast breathing that received amoxicillin.

and cough with difficult or fast breathing cases for which care was sought from a CORP, 69.8%, 64.7%, and 66.1%, respectively received the appropriate treatment (ACT within 2 days, ORS and zinc, and amoxicillin, respectively) from a CORP at endline.

Among the children who sought care from a CORP for the three illnesses at endline, 62.3% received the first dose of treatment in the presence of a CORP, 98.4% of their caregivers received counselling on how to administer the treatment, and 69.8% of children received a follow-up visit from the CORP

(**Table 8**). Provision of the first dose of treatment, counselling, or follow-up visits by a CORP was similar across all illnesses.

Table 8. *Characteristics of the provision of treatment by CORP at endline, across all illnesses*

Illness (treatment received)	First dose of treatment received in presence of CORP	Caregiver counseled on treatment administration	CORP conducted follow-up visit with sick child	Endline N
Fever (ACT)	59.2 (49.5-68.1)	99.3 (94.9-99.9)	71.9 (62.2-79.9)	97
Diarrhoea (ORS and zinc)	64.6 (54.1-73.8)	98.7 (90.6-99.8)	69.0 (57.7-78.4)	79
Cough with difficult or fast breathing (amoxicillin)	65.5 (50.4-78.0)	96.4 (89.3-98.9)	67.7 (60.0-74.5)	84
Overall for all three illnesses	62.3 (53.6-70.3)	98.4 (96.1-99.3)	69.8 (61.7-76.8)	305

ORS – oral rehydration salts, ACT – artemisinin-based combination therapy, CORP – community-oriented resource person

DISCUSSION

This study examined changes in coverage of care-seeking, diagnostic and treatment services for diarrhoea, malaria, and pneumonia over the course of iCCM implementation in Abia state. The results demonstrate substantial improvements in access to appropriate case management of childhood illness between 2013 and 2017. Our results showed that in areas with access to iCCM, CORPs were the main source of care. Overall, care-seeking practices shifted over the course of the project, with more caregivers choosing to access care from a CORP by endline and less seeking care from PPMVs. The observed shift is likely due to proximity of caregivers to the CORPs, perceived quality and cost-savings, as PPMVs charge money for treatment, whereas treatment is provided free of charge by the CORPs. Several studies also have shown lower or sub-standard quality care provided by PPMVs; thus, perceived lower quality of care may also have influenced the shift away from PPMVs to CORPs [9-13].

Overall, caregivers also had good perceptions of the CORP working in their communities, with more than 80% reporting that they view the CORPs as trusted health care providers, that CORPs provide quality services, and that CORPs are a convenient source of treatment. Caregiver knowledge of child illness danger signs and knowledge of the correct treatment for malaria and diarrhoea all improved significantly between baseline and endline in the project areas.

Improvements in the appropriate assessment of children with fever and cough with difficult breathing were also observed over the RAcE project period, with higher coverage observed of administration of RDTs to assess for malaria and respiratory rate counting to assess for pneumonia among CORPs compared to coverage among all providers. Significant improvements in treatment coverage across all iCCM illnesses were also observed; with similarly higher coverage of appropriate treatment provided by CORPs compared to coverage among all providers. Of all iCCM illnesses, coverage of ACT treatment for confirmed malaria experienced the greatest improvement over the project period; though coverage of timely ACT treatment (within 24 hours) was lower among both CORPs and all providers. This signifies that greater efforts to enhance community awareness of the importance of early care seeking for febrile illness in children and the availability of trained and adequately supplied CORPs are needed to improve timely care-seeking. Our results provide evidence that well-supported CORPs can provide iCCM services consistent with country iCCM protocols. Other studies have demonstrated similar results to ours, indicating that when CHWs are trained and equipped, they can positively influence care-seeking behavior and improve access to appropriate treatment of common childhood illnesses, especially in hard-to-reach areas across sub-Saharan Africa [14-21].

While substantial increases were observed in care-seeking and appropriate case management of childhood illnesses over the life of the RAcE project; the results indicate that there are still areas for further improvement. Providing refresher trainings to CHWs and regular supervision and mentorship, ensuring CHWs have commodities, and providing recognition and other incentives to CHWs are strategies that have been shown to help improve the appropriate care provided by CHWs and their overall satisfaction and motivation for the work they do [22-25]. When CHWs are well-trained, supplied, and supervised, they can increase access to prompt and appropriate treatment of preventable childhood illnesses [22, 26-28]. These findings also highlight the importance of supporting CHWs as results were achieved within a well-supported iCCM program.

There are a few survey limitations to note. First, the survey findings are representative of the project areas as a whole; the survey was not powered to provide lower subnational-level estimates (eg, at the LGA level), and therefore we are not able to report on any differences in coverage across the project areas. Second, some programme areas changed from the initially selected areas at the start of the programme in Abia. These changes caused us to have to redraw the sample for the endline household survey, rather than using the same selected clusters for the baseline survey. Despite these changes, we do not believe this effected the results or the comparability of the baseline and endline surveys, as CORPs had not yet been operating in the programme areas at baseline and the initially selected areas were very similar in sociodemographic characteristics as the final selected areas for the programme. Last, there are known potential biases and limitations with the indicators that assess caregiver recall of malaria diagnostic testing and coverage of appropriate treatment for children with fever and cough with difficult or fast breathing.

CONCLUSIONS

The study results demonstrate that CHWs improve access to treatment of diarrhoea, malaria and pneumonia among children under five living in communities located far from health facilities. The health system in Nigeria is plagued with acute shortages in healthcare personnel and long distances to health facilities. The availability of CORPs can help address health access issues, especially in the rural areas, and support the Nigeria's policy goal to meet the universal health coverage and the health needs of the Nigerian population.

Acknowledgments *The authors wish to acknowledge the World Health Organization and the Global Affairs Canada. Our appreciation goes to the Community Resources Persons, Community Health Extension Workers in Communities where the RAcE Project was implemented, as well as caregivers of children under five who answered the survey questions. We also wish to thank the State Ministry of Health and Abia State Primary Health Care Development Agency for providing an enabling environment for the implementation of RAcE project in Abia State. We wish to thank all the project's Monitoring and Evaluation Officers for their assistance in field work management and survey training as well as Caroline Achi and Dr Elvina Orji for facilitating and supporting project management.*

Disclaimer: *The content of this publication is solely the responsibility of the authors and does not necessarily reflect the views or policies of World Health Organization or Global Affairs Canada.*

Ethics approval: *For each household survey, ethical approval was obtained from ICF's Institutional Review Board and the Nigerian National Health Research Ethics Committee.*

Funding: *The household surveys were funded under a contract with the World Health Organization (WHO) through funding by Global Affairs Canada.*

Authorship declaration: *CI, JA and CO conceptualized the study. CI, JU, UE, CO, JA and SH were involved in the data collection. CI and SH analysed and d⌐⌐⌐ manuscript. JU, UE, CO, JA, and DP provided critical reviews and content e manuscript drafts.*

Competing interests: *The authors have completed the Unified Competing Interest form at www.icmje.org/coi_disclosure.pdf (available on request from the corresponding author) and declare no conflicts of interest.*

References

1 You D, Hug L, Ejdemyr S, Beise J. Levels & trends in child mortality: Report 2015. New York, NY: United Nations Children's Fund, World Health Organization, The World Bank, United Nations Population Division; 2015.

2 National Population Commission (NPC) [Nigeria], ICF International. Nigeria demographic and health survey 2013. Abuja, Nigeria and Rockville, Maryland, USA: NPC and ICF International; 2014.

3 World Health Organization, United Nations Children's Fund (UNICEF). Integrated community case management (iCCM): An equity-focused strategy to improve access to essential treatment services for children. Geneva, Switzerland and New York, NY, USA: World Health Organization and United Nations Children's Fund; 2012.

4 George A, Rodriguez DC, Rasanathan K, Brandes N, Bennett S. iCCM policy analysis: Strategic contributions to understanding its character, design and scale up in sub-Saharan Africa. Health Policy Plan. 2015;30 Suppl 2:ii3-11. PubMed https://doi.org/10.1093/heapol/czv096

5 Collins D, Jarrah Z, Gilmartin C, Saya U. The costs of integrated community case management (iCCM) programs: A multi-country analysis. J Glob Health. 2014;4:020407. PubMed https://doi.org/10.7189/jogh.04.020407

6 World Health Organization. Rapid Access Expansion Programme in Nigeria. Geneva, Switzerland: World Health Organization; 2018. Available: https://www.who.int/malaria/areas/rapid_access_expansion_2015/nigeria/en/. Accessed: 4 February 2019.

7 Federal Republic of Nigeria. Abia State: South East Abuja, Nigeria: Federal Republic of Nigeria. Available: http://www.nigeria.gov.ng/index.php/2016-04-06-08-39-54/southeast/abia-state. Accessed:4 February 2019.

8 The Federal Ministry of Health Nigeria. National guideline for the implementation of integrated community case management of childhood illness in Nigeria. Abuja, Nigeria: The Federal Ministry of Health Nigeria; 2013.

9 Prach LM, Treleaven E, Isiguzo C, Liu J. Care-seeking at patent and proprietary medicine vendors in Nigeria. BMC Health Serv Res. 2015;15:231. PubMed https://doi.org/10.1186/s12913-015-0895-z

10 Beyeler N, Liu J, Sieverding M. A systematic review of the role of proprietary and patent medicine vendors in healthcare provision in Nigeria. PLoS One. 2015;10:e0117165. PubMed https://doi.org/10.1371/journal.pone.0117165

11 Awor P, Wamani H, Tylleskar T, Jagoe G, Peterson S. Increased access to care and appropriateness of treatment at private sector drug shops with integrated management of malaria, pneumonia and diarrhoea: A quasi-experimental study in Uganda. PLoS One. 2014;9:e115440. PubMed https://doi.org/10.1371/journal.pone.0115440

12 Rutebemberwa E, Kadobera D, Katureebe S, Kalyango JN, Mworozi E, Pariyo G. Use of community health workers for management of malaria and pneumonia in urban and rural areas in eastern Uganda. Am J Trop Med Hyg. 2012;87(5) Suppl:30-5. PubMed https://doi.org/10.4269/ajtmh.2012.11-0732

13 Liu J, Prach LM, Treleaven E, Hansen M, Anyanti J, Jagha T, et al. The role of drug vendors in improving basic health-care services in Nigeria. Bull World Health Organ. 2016;94:267-75. PubMed https://doi.org/10.2471/BLT.15.154666

14 Onwujekwe O, Uzochukwu B, Ojukwu J, Dike N, Shu E. Feasibility of a community health worker strategy for providing near and appropriate treatment of malaria in southeast Nigeria: An analysis of activities, costs and outcomes. Acta Trop. 2007;101:95-105. PubMed https://doi.org/10.1016/j.actatropica.2006.07.013

15 Perez F, Ba H, Dastagire SG, Altmann M. The role of community health workers in improving child health programmes in Mali. BMC Int Health Hum Rights. 2009;9:28. PubMed https://doi.org/10.1186/ 1472-698X-9-28

16 Yeboah-Antwi K, Pilingana P, Macleod WB, Semrau K, Siazeele K, Kalesha P, et al. Community case management of fever due to malaria and pneumonia in children under five in Zambia: A cluster randomized controlled trial. PLoS Med. 2010;7:e1000340. PubMed https://doi.org/10.1371/journal.pmed. 1000340

17 Brenner JL, Kabakyenga J, Kyomuhangi T, Wotton KA, Pim C, Ntaro M, et al. Can volunteer community health workers decrease child morbidity and mortality in southwestern Uganda? An impact evaluation. PLoS One. 2011;6:e27997. PubMed https://doi.org/10.1371/journal.pone.0027997

18 Kisia J, Nelima F, Otieno DO, Kiilu K, Emmanuel W, Sohani S, et al. Factors associated with utilization of community health workers in improving access to malaria treatment among children in Kenya. Malar J. 2012;11:248. PubMed https://doi.org/10.1186/1475-2875-11-248

19 Perry H, Zulliger R. How effective are community health workers? An overview of current evidence with recommendations for strengthening community health worker programs to accelerate progress in achieving the health-related Millenium Development Goals. Baltimore, MD: Johns Hopkins Bloomberg School of Public Health; 2012.

20 Seidenberg PD, Hamer DH, Iyer H, Pilingana P, Siazeele K, Hamainza B, et al. Impact of integrated community case management on health-seeking behavior in rural Zambia. Am J Trop Med Hyg. 2012; 87(5) Suppl:105-10. PubMed https://doi.org/10.4269/ajtmh.2012.11-0799

21 Yansaneh AI, Moulton LH, George AS, Rao SR, Kennedy N, Bangura P, et al. Influence of community health volunteers on care seeking and treatment coverage for common childhood illnesses in the context of free health care in rural Sierra Leone. Trop Med Int Health. 2014;19:1466-76. PubMed https://doi.org/10.1111/tmi.12383

22 Diaz T, Aboubaker S, Young M. Current scientific evidence for integrated community case management (iCCM) in Africa: Findings from the iCCM evidence symposium. J Glob Health. 2014;4:020101. PubMed

23 Hill Z, Dumbaugh M, Benton L, Kallander K, Strachan D, ten Asbroek A, et al. Supervising community health workers in low-income countries – A review of impact and implementation issues. Glob Health Action. 2014;7:24085. PubMed https://doi.org/10.3402/gha.v7.24085

24 Oliver K, Young M, Oliphant N, Diaz T, Kim J. Review of systematic challenges to the scale-up of the integrated community case management: Emerging lessons & recommendations from the Catalytic Initiative (CI/IHSS). New York, NY: UNICEF Health Section, Program Division; 2012.

25 Young M, Sharkey A, Aboubaker S, Kasungami D, Swedberg E, Ross K. The way forward for integrated community case management programmes: A summary of lessons learned to date and future priorities. J Glob Health. 2014;4:020303. PubMed https://doi.org/10.7189/jogh.04.020303

26 de Sousa A, Tiedje KE, Recht J, Bjelic I, Hamer DH. Community case management of childhood illnesses: Policy and implementation in Countdown to 2015 countries. Bull World Health Organ. 2012; 90:183-90. PubMed https://doi.org/10.2471/BLT.11.093989
27 Kalyango JN, Rutebemberwa E, Alfven T, Ssali S, Peterson S, Karamagi C. Performance of community health workers under integrated community case management of childhood illnesses in eastern Uganda. Malar J. 2012;11:282. PubMed https://doi.org/10.1186/1475-2875-11-282
28 Bagonza J, Kibira SP, Rutebemberwa E. Performance of community health workers managing malaria, pneumonia and diarrhoea under the community case management programme in central Uganda: A cross sectional study. Malar J. 2014;13:367. PubMed https://doi.org/10.1186/1475-2875-13-367

Community engagement and mobilisation of local resources to support integrated Community Case Management of childhood illnesses in Niger State, Nigeria

Ayodele Alegbeleye[1], John Dada[2], Olusola Oresanya[2], Jonathan Jiya[1], Helen Counihan[3], Patrick Gimba[4], Lynda Ozor[5], Kolawole Maxwell[2]

[1] Malaria Consortium, Minna, Niger state, Nigeria
[2] Malaria Consortium, Abuja, Nigeria
[3] Malaria Consortium, London, UK
[4] Niger State Ministry of Health, Minna, Nigeria
[5] World Health Organization, Abuja, Nigeria

Background Despite strong evidence of integrated community case management (iCCM) of childhood illnesses being a proven intervention for reducing childhood morbidity and mortality, sustainability remains a challenge in most settings. Community ownership and contribution are important factors in sustainability. The purpose of this study was to document the process and scale achieved for community engagement and mobilisation to foster ownership, service uptake and sustainability of iCCM services.

Methods A review of data collected by the RAcE project was conducted to describe the scale and achievement of leveraging community resources to support the community-oriented resource persons (CORPs). The Rapid Access Expansion (RAcE)-supported iCCM programme in Niger state (2014-2017), aimed at improving coverage of case management services for malaria, pneumonia, and diarrhoea, among children aged 2–59 months. Resources contributed by the community were documented and costed based on the market value of goods and services at the time. These monetary valuations were validated at community dialogue meetings. Descriptive statistics were used to summarise quantitative variables. The mean of the number of CORPs in active service and the percentages of the mobilised resources received by CORPs were calculated.

Results The community engagement activities included 143 engagement and advocacy visits, and meetings, 300 community dialogues, reactivation of 60 ward development committees, and 3000 radio messages in support of iCCM. 79.5% of 1659 trained CORPs were still in active iCCM service at the end of the project. We estimated the costs of all support provided by the community to CORPs in cash and kind as US$ 123 062. Types of support included cash; building materials; farming support; fuel for motorcycles, and transport fares.

Conclusions The achievements of community engagement, mobilisation, and the resources leveraged, demonstrated acceptability of the project to the beneficiaries and their willingness to contribute to uninterrupted service provision by CORPs.

In 2016, mortality among children under-five years (Cu5) in Nigeria was estimated at 104 deaths per 1000 live births [1]. Pneumonia, diarrhoea and malaria account for 32 percent, 16 percent and 19 percent of deaths in Cu5 in Nigeria [2]. Cu5 are more vulnerable to these diseases than other segments of the population, and can die without access to treatment, especially in rural areas, where access to the nearest health centre can be difficult. Mortality rates in rural areas are consistently higher than in urban areas linked to a relative dearth of human resources for health in those hard-to-reach areas [3]. In response to high morbidity and mortality among Cu5, WHO and UNICEF recommend integrated community case management [iCCM] as a strategy to provide timely and effective treatment of the three focal diseases: malaria, pneumonia and diarrhoea among children Cu5 [4]. iCCM is proven to be effective in increasing treatment coverage and delivering quality care for sick children, especially in areas with limited access to facility-based health care providers [4-7].

The service delivery for iCCM typically depends on lay, often volunteer, community health workers (CHWs) selected and trained to render the service in their communities [4]. Successful and sustainable iCCM services depend on appropriate selection, training, supervision and support to these CHWs [8-10]. However, there are challenges related to engagement and sustaining of volunteer health workers. The challenges include inadequate number of volunteers who have a suitable profile to perform as a CHW; inappropriate incentives and compensation for the volunteers; and lack of support from the formal health system and community leadership [11,12]. These challenges have resulted in varied rates of performance and retention among these workers with an attrition range of 3% to 77% documented in a variety of community health delivery programmes [12-14]. Attrition of CHWs negatively affects access to, and utilisation of, iCCM services [11,12]; and improvement in utilisation of services has been shown to be dependent on effective demand creation and social mobilisation [8,15].

Approaches used for demand creation and resource mobilisation for iCCM projects implemented previously have been documented. These often involve a three-pronged approach to include social and behaviour change communication, social mobilisation and advocacy [15]. Evidence has shown that social mobilisation is one of the key features of successful public health programmes [16,17]. However, the need to continue to assess and address the demand barriers for iCCM through behaviour change, community engagement and social mobilisation activities was identified at an international symposium in 2014 on lessons and priorities for iCCM [8].

Community Engagement and Mobilisation for RAcE Project

The Rapid Access Expansion 2015 (RAcE) project was the first iCCM programme at scale in Nigeria. It was implemented in collaboration with state government and partners, led by Malaria Consortium in Niger State, and funded by Global Affairs Canada through WHO. The partnership for the project included state government, the six focal local government areas (LGAs), and Federation of Muslim Women Association of Nigeria (FOMWAN), a faith-based non-governmental organisation (NGO). The goal of the project was to contribute to the reduction in mortality and morbidity among children aged 2 to 59 months. The emphasis was to increase access to correct diagnosis, treatment and referral for malaria, pneumonia and diarrhoea among Cu5 at the community level. The components of the RAcE project were service delivery, capacity building, demand creation, and monitoring and evaluation.

A key feature of the RAcE project was the selection and training of volunteers at the community level. The nomination of community members as volunteer CHWs was done by the community leaders, based on the selection criteria provided by the National iCCM Task Team. The main selection criteria were the volunteer's ability to read and write; and being resident in the communities where they will offer iCCM services. The nominees were trained by state trainers of CHWs, who were themselves trained at training of trainers organised by the state government, with the support of Malaria Consortium. Trainees whose performance at the training passed a required standard were selected as CHWs for iCCM. The trained volunteer CHWs are designated in Nigeria as community resource persons (CORPs), and they provide free iCCM services for the three focus diseases. To support this programme, another set of volunteers called social mobilisers (SMs) were selected in a process similar to that of the CORPs. They were trained to conduct mobilisation of community members to demand for, and to use, iCCM services as well as sensitising them on appropriate health seeking behaviour. The training and deployment of SMs was integral to community mobilisation.

The engagement and mobilisation component of the RAcE project was developed to strengthen links between iCCM services and the communities, and to engender ownership and sustainability of the project. The three broad communication approaches adopted were engagement and advocacy, communication, and social mobilisation (**Figure 1**), reflecting social and behaviour change communication frameworks from other public health programmes [17-19]. At the onset of the project, policy-level advocacy and engagement meetings were conducted. These included an inception meeting where government and other stakeholders at state and LGA levels were briefed on the objectives of the iCCM programme and the processes involved. Other platforms and opportunities were used to continually solicit support and commitment to sustain the gains of the project. An iCCM sustainability roadmap development workshop was organised by the state government and partners, where community leaders were invited to share their perspectives and make suggestions for community buy-in.

Advocacy and engagement activities at the community level were implemented in partnership with Federation of Muslim Women's Associations in Nigeria (FOMWAN) and other relevant community-based organisations (CBOs) as appropriate, and targeted at the community leaders as gatekeepers of the communities. The other CBOs included representatives of the women's wing of various Christian churches. FOMWAN and the women's organisations participated in identification of key advocacy issues, the advocacy visits, and presentations and follow-up actions to address the issues. A total of 143 advocacy visits and meetings were held at the community level with leadership of the

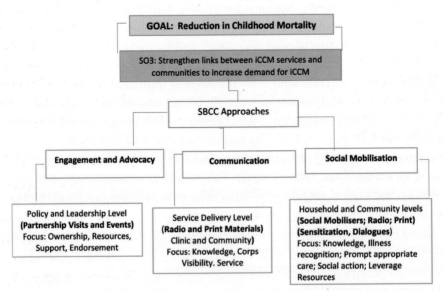

Figure 1. *Approaches and Components of Community Engagement and Mobilisation in RAcE project, Niger state. Adapted from Sharkey et al [15].*

communities. These included religious leaders, paramount traditional rulers, district heads and the leadership of faith-based organisations (FBOs) in the six focal LGAs. The iCCM-related advocacy needs and problems amenable to leadership support were presented to the leaders, who worked to promote iCCM. The key advocacy issues and the 'asks' included soliciting continuous leadership goodwill and support for iCCM, including their involvement in the selection of the CORPs, and provision of incentives and non-monetary support to the CORPs.

Key communication messages and materials were produced to support mobilisation activities and targeted at the community members. These messages in radio formats (mainly radio spots totalling 3000 slots), public service announcements and discussion programmes were aired to promote the CORPs, and the utilisation of iCCM services. The print formats involved production of flipcharts and motivational leaflets on iCCM, with images and basic information on the three focal diseases. The messages and materials were developed in English, and translated into three local languages.

The social mobilisation activities were conducted at the community level to introduce iCCM, explain its purpose, and benefits, and to and seek involvement and participation of the key audiences at the community level. The primary target were the caregivers and heads of households as community members. One hundred and twenty-six SMs were selected and trained for two days on community engagement and mobilisation approaches including sensitisation meetings, community dialogues, community level advocacy, resource mobilisation and other social mobilisation activities. The primary role of SMs was sensitising community members on appropriate health seeking behaviour, mobilising them to demand for iCCM services, supporting the reactivation and strengthening of community health structures such as village and ward development committees (WDCs) as well as mobilising community level support for CORPs.

The SMs were given data capturing tools to report and document their activities which were monitored and supervised by either the LGA Health Educators or FOMWAN officials trained to provide supervisory support to the SMs. A series of community dialogues (CDs) were conducted in small groups to achieve two purposes: initially to explore issues related to iCCM, and also to identify priority issues and develop follow-up actions to be jointly implemented by community members. Participants at the CDs were the community members, SMs, the CORPs and representatives of FOMWAN, CBOs and FBOs. The facilitators at the CDs were the SMs, and the LGA health educators and staff of Malaria Consortium. The needs of the CORPs and challenges related to their work were discussed during these CD sessions and community meetings, decisions taken on how to address them and follow up actions jointly implemented by community members, SMs and state iCCM team. One of the critical needs identified across all LGAs was the need to support the CORPs with monetary and non-monetary resources to enhance their commitment as volunteer health service providers.

As part of the engagement and mobilisation activities, 60 ward development committees (WDCs) were reactivated in the six focal LGAs. The WDCs were formed as part of the community engagement structure for primary health care programme. Committee members are made of representative of the different sector of development including health, education and agriculture. Their purpose is to work with government and partners to identify and collectively address key development issues at the community level. A summary of community engagement and mobilisation activities is presented in **Table 1**.

Table 1. *Engagement, audiences, and the outputs*

AUDIENCES FOR ENGAGEMENT	KEY OUTPUTS
Community members	Participation in the state roadmap workshop on iCCM
Traditional Rulers	CORPs (n=1659) selected and trained for ICCM
Religious leaders	143 advocacy visits conducted
Leadership of faith-based Organisation (FBOs)-WOWICAN, CAN	60 Ward Development Committees reactivated
Leadership of Ward Development Committees	Active participation in mobilisation activities (Regular attendance, motivating self and others, acceptance of roles, and follow-up on action points)
	Utilisation of ICCM services as indicated in the results quantified for the project

iCCM – integrated community case management, CORP – community-orientated resource person

As partners and stakeholders continue to address the challenges around sustainability of iCCM, this study was conducted to document the engagement, and the resources mobilised at the community level to support the CORPs in the RAcE project in Niger state; and as a key aspect of sustainability of iCCM in the state.

METHODS

This was a descriptive study focused on the scale and achievements of mobilisation of community resources as part of the engagement and community mobilisation component of the RAcE project, primarily by retrospectively reviewing data routinely collected by the project.

Project setting

The RAcE project (2014-2017) was implemented in six LGAs in Niger State, North Central Nigeria (**Figure 2**). The six LGAs: Edati, Lapai, Mariga, Paikoro, Rafi, and Rijau, had a combined population of 1 424 226 as at 2013, based on projections from the 2006 census [20]. Niger state comprises three main ethnic groups (Nupe, Hausa, and Gbagyi) with different religious and cultural backgrounds, and socio-economic status. Most project communities are without potable water and electricity and are located far away from health facilities. Niger State is largely rural and agrarian, with farming and fishing as main occupation; and with strong cultural structures and institutions, where there is high respect for traditional and religious leaders.

A total of 1659 volunteers trained as CORPs made up the study population, with 1320 confirmed to be still in active iCCM service through a validation exercise at the end of the third year of the project. The 1659 CORPs were considered the actual and potential beneficiaries of the engagement and mobilisation activities including resources mobilised from the community.

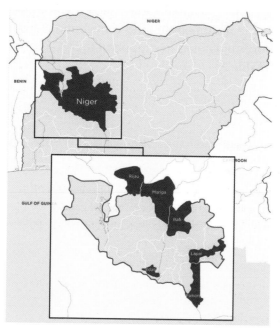

Figure 2. *RAcE project local government authority (LGAs) in Niger state.*

Data sources and collection

Mobilised resources as variables were assessed based on the estimation of the cost of these resources donated to support the CORPs and iCCM activities. Details of these resources, both monetary and non-monetary, and their value were described by community members and entered in a project resource mobilisation form by the SMs, under the guidance of the government staff, and officers of the RAcE project team. Entries on the resource mobilisation form were validated at community dialogue meetings, based on the market value of items at the time of the donation. Donated items and labour were costed based on the prevailing cost of goods and services at the time they were donated. The financial support, and estimated cost of the items donated to the CORPs in each LGA were aggregated for the period of three years, as the value under each of the categories of mobilised resources; and used as the quantitative data for this independent variable.

Community members attending community dialogues, and SMs, contacted representatives of trade and markets associations to determine the current market price of the items, labour, and gifts donated to the CORPs. The entries on the resource mobilisation form were only validated after the cost of the items have been confirmed by representatives of the trade and market associations, following due diligence with the associations. The approach adopted for costing of the items mobilised for the project conforms with the recommendation of how to document in-kind contributions to a project [21]. The category of resources mobilised in support of the CORPs and ICCM services are presented in **Table 2**.

Table 2. *Categories of monetary and non-monetary contributions by the community to support the CORPs for iCCM activities*

1. Cash.
2. Farming support & chemicals (labour as farming support).
3. Farm produce and animals (goats, ram, sheep, bags of grains).
4. Houses built (Building materials: mud blocks, roofing sheets, cement, sand provided to CORP for building house).
5. Logistics support/aids (Female CORP had firewood and water fetched for them; assisted with labour for laundry).
6. Motorcycle fuel or transport fare to collect drugs from supervising facilities.
7. Support to male CORPs to host marriage ceremonies.
8. Motorcycle and bicycle purchased for CORPs.

CORP – community-orientated resource person, RAcE – Rapid Access Expansion

Statistical methods

Frequency tables were generated for the resource mobilisation variables assessed. Descriptive statistics such as means were used to summarize quantitative variables while categorical variables were summarised with proportions. The mean of the number of CORPs in active service was calculated. The percentage of the mobilised resources received by CORPs in each LGA was calculated.

RESULTS

Monetary and non-monetary community support provided to the CORPs

The mobilised resources in support of the services of the CORPs were grouped into eight categories including monetary, and non-monetary incentives, as shown in **Table 1**. Many were in the form of support for farming and iCCM activities, including purchase of vehicles and support for construction of houses.

Over the period of 3 years (2015-2017), the total resources mobilised in support of the retained CORPs was estimated as the sum of US$ 123 062 of which 14.8% was monetary (cash) while the remaining 85.2% was in form of non-monetary incentives, including farm labour, building materials and others (**Table 3**). The mobilised resources included farming support and chemicals (55.21%); farm produces and animals (17.5%), financial assistance (4.8%), and support to CORPs for marriage (0.4%). The mobilised resources varied by LGA: Edati (37.7%), Lapai (33.42%) and Paikoro (1.64%).

Retention of CORPs in iCCM

A total of 1659 CORPs were trained, of which 1320 (79.5%) were in active iCCM service at the end of year 3 of the project (**Table 4**). The proportion of the active CORPs was highest in Rijau LGA (90.70%), followed by 88.21% and 77.10% in Lapai and Mariga LGAs respectively; with the lowest in Edati LGA (62.42%).

Other observed effects of resource mobilisation to support iCCM

Based on meeting records and anecdotal feedback from the community meetings and from the SMs and project staff, a number of further observations were made about the nature and consequences of this community engagement and mobilisation including resource mobilisation as follows:

Table 3. *Estimated community resources mobilised by recipient CORPs in the six local government areas (LGAs), RAcE Project*

Type of resources mobilised by number of CORPS (CORP No.) and estimated monetary value (EMV) in US$*		LOCAL GOVERNMENT AREAS						Total CORPs	Amount of resources mobilized, US$ (%)
		Paikoro	Rafi	Mariga	Edati	Lapai	Rijau		
Cash	CORP No	45	54	84	65	104	81	433	18 129 (14.8)
	Direct Cash (US$)	804	3908	1073	5229	6128	988		
Farming Support & Chemicals	CORP No.	15	58	43	69	68	49	302	67 787 (55.2)
	EMV	401	6654	1575	23 987	30 456	4715		
Houses Built/ mud blocks	CORP No.	–	6	2	2	–	2	12	12 657 (10.1)
	EMV	–	4670	843	5348	–	1797		
Logistics Support/Aid	CORP No.	12	8	8	2	3	14	47	1436 (1.2)
	EMV	253	235	281	17	96	554		
Support for Marriage for CORPs	CORP No.	1	4	–	–	1	–	6	530 (0.4)
	EMV	63	354	0	0	112	0		
Motorcycle/ Bicycle purchased for CORPs	CORP No.	1	4	1	–	–	1	7	1014 (0.8)
	EMV	352	349	240	0	0	73		
Farm Produce/ Animals	CORP No.	4	16	69	66	41	105	301	21 508 (17.5)
	EMV	134	740	222	11 778	4243	4391		
Total	EMV	2008 (1.6)	16 911 (13.7)	4234 (3.4)	46 359 (37.7)	41 036 (33.3)	12 479 (10.2)		123 062 (100.0)

CORP – community-orientated resource person, RAcE – Rapid Access Expansion

*Resources estimated in Naira and converted to US$ at exchange rate of U$ 1 = N 312.99; the parallel market rate in the country between 2016 and 2017.

Table 4. *Active CORPS, RAcE Project, Niger state*

LGAs	Number CORPS trained; Years 1-3	Number and % of CORPs in active iCCM service by end of Year 3	% of CORPs in active iCCM service by end of Year 3 in 6 LGAs
Paikoro	213	159 (74.65)	79.57
Rafi	265	202 (76.23)	
Mariga	393	303(77.10)	
Edati	189	118(62.42)	
Lapai	212	187(88.21)	
Rijau	387	351(90.70)	
TOTAL	1659	1320	

LGA – local government authority, iCCM – integrated community case management, CORP – community-orientated resource person, RAcE – Rapid Access Expansion

- All the CORPs, irrespective of their gender, enjoyed recognition in their communities

- The community members showed their appreciation and commonly referred to the CORPs as "local doctors", in recognition of their services.

- In Rafi LGA, two communities dedicated common farmland to iCCM programme from which the harvest will be sold and the money used to fund iCCM activities. A bi-weekly contribution of US$ 0.80 per head was levied to fund iCCM activities at the community level. Some communities have also indicated willingness to sustain procurement of iCCM drugs and commodities after the close-out of the RAcE project.

- Election of two CORPs as Ward Councillors, a position at the lowest level of political administration in the country but one of important standing in the community

- A female CORP in one of the six LGAs was engaged by the LGA Primary Health Care department as staff following her commitment and high-quality support for Cu5 care while her other colleagues enjoyed monthly support of the LGA leadership to collect drugs and other commodities from the supporting health facilities

- The paramount traditional leader of Lapai, in his public support for CORPs, noted that "there is no greater work than providing good health, and there is no greater worker that should be appreciated than the person who is trying to improve your health".

- A popular religious leader in Lapai LGA, whose child has been a direct beneficiary of the ICCM intervention noted "I advise parents to take their sick children to the CORPs; urged government and communities to support the CORPs".

DISCUSSION

Monetary and non-monetary community support provided to the CORPs

While many studies have indicated that community appreciation and support are important motivators for CHWs [22], the type and scale of community level resources mobilised in support for the RAcE iCCM project have rarely, if ever, been previously documented from other similar CHW programmes in the same level of detail. The generated resources in the form of monetary and non-monetary community level support for the trained CORPs were substantial, considering the bulk were contributed from meagre resources of subsistence farmers, technicians and artisans. Although the community resources mobilised for the CORPs varied by LGA, it was particularly high in two LGAs, Edati and Lapai, where nearly three quarters of the entire resources were mobilised.

It was not a surprise that about four-fifths of the resources mobilised to support the CORPs were non-monetary, just as the finding that over half of the estimated support was in the form of family support and agrochemicals for farming. Only resources considered crucial and most needed by CORPs were agreed at community dialogue sessions. Farming remains the main occupation in the project communities, and the entire state, which made chemicals for farming highly valuable. A study on non-financial incentives for CHW in Ethiopia indicated that young age and being married were significant factors associated with motivation of the volunteers [23]. The majority of the CORPs were young or middle-aged, married men, many of whom were engaged with farming. In addition, the few women CORPs, needed and appreciated support for domestic chores, which they may not have had the time to do adequately while they volunteered as CORPs.

While it appeared reasonable and important for the community leaders and members in project communities to mobilise resources to support iCCM and the CORPs, some communities found the need more compelling than others. In LGAs where the resources mobilised were much lower, the communities and leaders were less responsive to advocacy and mobilisation activities.

Retention of CORPs in iCCM

Nearly four-fifths of CORPs were active at the end of three years on the RAcE iCCM project, which was impressive, and higher than many other volunteer CHW programmes [24]. The self-esteem of CORPs was shown to be boosted, as community members showed their appreciation and commonly referred to them as "local doctors", in recognition of their services. Although there are few quantitative studies on attrition or retention of volunteer CHWs, other authors have reported the proportion of volunteers remaining in active service as between 43.0% and 74.42% over a period of one to four years, in different community-based programmes [24]. In a recent study, a high attrition rate of 46.8/1000 person years was reported among CHWs in a maternal and child health project in Kenya [25]. Given this study was conducted retrospectively, it was beyond the study scope to learn more from CORPs about their reasons for leaving as none of the one-fifth of the trained CORPs that dropped out of the project was available to be interviewed. However, reports from community members showed that attritions were mainly due to relocations because of marriage, education, search for better livelihood and also because of death. Other authors have documented reasons why volunteer CHW were inactive or dropped out of service, including inadequate and irregular pay, lack of family support, receiving no feedback from supervisors, age, poor selection, absence of refresher training, and economic opportunities [25-27]. In this study we did not correlate levels of CORP retention directly with levels of community resources mobilised for their support. This is because there are many other factors, which were beyond the scope of this study to measure, which could have affected the levels of retention and thereby confounded any attempt to demonstrate causality of resource mobilisation on CORP retention. For example, the resources mobilised in Edati LGA were the highest in monetary value, yet the LGA had the lowest retention of CORPs. Other possible reasons for this high attrition rate may include more education or employment opportunities in other locations for example. It is important to note that this study also did not explore other possible contributing motivating factors for CORP retention including an individual's work-related goals, his/her sense of altruism or self-efficacy, job satisfaction, community valuation of CHW work, and fulfilment of pre-hire expectations among others [13].

Resource mobilisation and sustainability

Two LGAs, Lapai and Rijau had proportionally more CORPs still active at the end of the project implementation than the others, and it was observed by the project team that the community and religious leaders in both were highly supportive of CORPs and actively promoted iCCM. In Lapai LGA, where about one-third of the total community resources were mobilised, there was a very high level of support to iCCM by the traditional and religious leaders.

The open demonstration and declaration of support for the CORPs by the community leaders in some of the LGAs was observed as an impetus for the communities to provide resources for their CORPs, mainly farm produce and animal husbandry. Further, Rijau LGA has many very hard-to-reach areas in terms of terrain, and many communities in the LGA were completely cut-off from health facility for nearly 6 months' during the rainy season every year. This could imply that it was an important priority for the communities facing a daily challenge of lack of health facilities and inadequate professional health workers, to provide the necessary support to the service of the CORPs. This fits with another study on hard-to-reach communities in a district in Kenya, where community and health system support were identified as crucial factors in sustaining and prolonging the service of CHWs [28].

In order to catalyse the duplication of success stories across project communities, best practices were shared at monthly LGA review meetings which encouraged other communities to replicate achievements. This was reported to have stimulated healthy competition among several communities who will not want to be seen as left behind.

In Niger state and in many parts of Nigeria, traditional and religious leaders are highly regarded as the "gatekeepers" of community norms. The public acknowledgment and appreciation of the importance of the work of the CORPs provided by the paramount traditional leader and popular religious leader of Lapai were a source of motivation for community members to mobilise resources for the CORPs.

The social bond between the memberships of the several benefitting communities has improved as a result of the iCCM services. Some community members would not attend meetings called by their leaders previously, however with the advent of iCCM community bonds have been strengthened. With the establishment and re-activation of the Village Health Committees (VHCs) and the Ward Health Development Committees (WHDCs) community responses to health issues have been strengthened. In addition to the WHDCs taking up projects such as the renovation of dilapidated Health Care centres and building new ones, the community members are now transformed advocates of iCCM, placing demand on the government to sustain iCCM.

The sustainability of iCCM is hinged on the resources dedicated to it. The effects of engagement and resource mobilisation which were observed by the project team have actual or potential positive effects on the sustainability of iCCM. The boosted self-esteem of CORPs may have made some difference in the motivation and aspirations of the CORPs. Self-esteem is one of the crucial factors that determines the job satisfaction or otherwise of a worker, which is related to remaining in-post and motivated to doing good work [10,29,30]. The election of CORPs as Ward Councillors can be motivating for existing CORPs or other CHWs, to be more dedicated to iCCM service, with the hope of a reward of traditional or political position in future. The healthy competition among communities, which resulted in a dedicated farm for iCCM, and the levy of amount considered affordable, are signs of community ownership of iCCM, which, if encouraged, will enhance sustainability of the project. The possibility of stoppage of donation and compensation is also a reason for the monthly levies, or dedicated farmland to plant crops and make sales, as communal effort to support iCCM.

Beyond the levy and dedicated farmland, the state government is also developing plans to harmonise and further institutionalise community health delivery services by adopting the Community Health Influencers, Promoters and Services (CHIPS) programme. The CHIPS programme was recently initiated by the National Primary Health Care Development Agency (NPHCDA) and recommended to state governments, as an approach to help institutionalize all CHWs, as integral to strengthening community health services. As part of CHIPS, all CHWs, irrespective of the content and type of their project, will have same designation; their selection, training, supervision, and compensation standardised and harmonized; as it is for other primary health care workers. Hopefully, when the CHIPS programme is operational, and the CORPs are absorbed into it, many of the issues related to drop-out of CHWs will be addressed.

Study limitations and implications for future research

This study was a descriptive one and was not designed to present statistically significant data. Other limitations include the estimation of the in-kind, labour and gifts provided in support of the CORPs as a potential source of bias. The local resources mobilised for RAcE project were estimated based on the current market value of the in-kind contribution of community resources, as confirmed by the trade and market associations. For this study, the validation of the CORPs in active iCCM service was done in the third year of the project. Some trained CORPs have been active but were not available at the period of the validation, while others who were not usually available, just happened to be available by chance at the time the validation was done. Future research needs to consider assessment of the community resources mobilised and attrition of CHWs on more regular interval of one to two years to enable trend analyses to inform programme review. It is important to also conduct correlation of CORPs retention with levels of community resources mobilised for in-depth analysis of the factors that have implications for policy and service delivery. This is in view of the vital contribution of the CHWs to the initiatives towards universal health coverage.

CONCLUSION

Mobilising local resources to support the RAcE project was informed by the need to motivate and support the CORPs, as identified in series of community dialogues. The level of community support in both monetary and non-monetary forms was high and appeared linked to the engagement and support of community leaders and mobilisers. Overall, the findings show the acceptability of iCCM in benefiting communities, and their willingness to contribute to uninterrupted service by CORPs to enhance sustainability of the project.

The achievements of community engagement, mobilisation, and the resources leveraged demonstrates the acceptability of the project by benefiting communities and their willingness to contribute to uninterrupted service provision by CORPs.

Acknowledgements: *We acknowledge first and foremost the communities of Niger state in which the RAcE project was implemented. We also wish to acknowledge the efforts of all staff of Malaria Consortium, RAcE project team and Ministry of Health in Niger State who participated in the implementation of the intervention and monitoring of field work. Also the WHO Country office staff including Dr Joy Ufere, who provided direct support for the project. We appreciate the community-oriented resource persons and community health extension workers, social mobilisers and the local government staff and members of FOMWAN who contributed immense efforts to the project.*

Funding: *This work was made possible through the RAcE project, funded by the World Health Organization through funding from Global Affairs Canada.*

Authorship contributions: *AA and JD conceived and designed the community engagement component of the project; AA and JD led on the research design and analysis, with support from OO; AA, JD, JJ and PG supported the data collection and analysis; HC, OO and KM provided technical inputs into the analysis and presentation of the findings; AA and JD co-drafted the manuscript with support from HC and OO; all authors reviewed and approved the final version of the paper.*

Completing interests: *The authors completed the Unified Competing Interest form at www.icmje.org/coi_disclosure.pdf (available upon request from the corresponding author), and declare no conflicts of interest.*

References

1   United Nations Children's Fund Levels and Trends in Childhood Mortality Report, 2017. Available: http://www.childmortality.org/files_v21/download/IGME%20report%202017%20child%20mortality%20final.pdf. Accessed: 26 June 2018.

2   World Health Organisation. Global Health Observatory data repository. Available: http://apps.who.int/gho/data/view.main.ghe3002015-CH9?lang=en. Accessed: 30 August 2018.

3   National Population Commission (NPC) [Nigeria] and ICF International. Nigeria Demographic and Health Survey, 2013. Abuja, Nigeria, and Rockville, Maryland, USA: *NPC and ICF International*, 2014. Available: https://dhsprogram.com/publications/publication-fr293-dhs-final-reports.cfm. Accessed: 30 August 2018.

4   World Health Organisation and United Nations Children's Fund Joint Statement Integrated Community Case Management. (iCCM), 2012. Available: http://www.who.int/maternal_child_adolescent/documents/statement_child_services_access_whounicef.pdf. Accessed: 26 May 2018.

5   Escribano Ferrer B, Schultz Hansen K, Gyapong M, Bruce J, Narh Bana SA, Narh CT, et al. Cost-effectiveness analysis of the national implementation of integrated community case management and community-based health planning and services in Ghana for the treatment of malaria, diarrhoea and pneumonia. Malar J. 2017;16:277. Medline:28679378 doi:10.1186/s12936-017-1906-9

6   Marsh DR, Hamer DH, Pagnoni F, Peterson S. Introduction to a special supplement: evidence for the implementation, effects, and impact of the integrated community case management strategy to treat childhood infection. Am J Trop Med Hyg. 2012;87(5 Suppl):2-5. Medline:23136271 doi:10.4269/ajtmh.2012.12-0504

7   Rasanathan K, Muñiz M, Bakshi S, Kumar M, Solano A, Kariuki W, et al. Community case management of childhood illness in Sub–Saharan Africa: findings from a cross–sectional survey on policy and implementation. J Glob Health. 2014;4:020401. Medline:25520791

8   Young M, Sharkey A, Aboubaker S, Kasungami D, Swedberg E, Ross K. The way forward for integrated community case management programmes: a summary of lessons learned to date and future priorities. J Glob Health. 2014;4:020303. Medline:25520789 doi:10.7189/jogh.04.020303

9   Yansaneh AI, Moulton LH, George AS, Rao SR, Kennedy N, Bangura P, et al. Influence of community health volunteers on care seeking and treatment coverage for common childhood illnesses in the context of free health care in rural Sierra Leone. Trop Med Int Health. 2014;19:1466-76. Medline:25243929 doi:10.1111/tmi.12383

10 Strachan DL, Källander K, ten Asbroek AH, Kirkwood B, Meek SR, Benton L, et al. Interventions to improve motivation and retention of community health workers delivering integrated community case management (iCCM): Stakeholder perceptions and priorities. Am J Trop Med Hyg. 2012;87(5 Suppl):111-9. Medline:23136286 doi:10.4269/ajtmh.2012.12-0030

11 Sharma R, Webster P, Bhattacharyya S. Factors affecting the performance of community health workers in India: a multi-stakeholder perspective. Glob Health Action. 2014;7:25352. Medline:25319596 doi:10.3402/gha.v7.25352

12 Olang'o CO, Nyamongo IK, Aagaard-Hansen J. Staff attrition among community health workers in home-based care programmes for people living with HIV and AIDS in western Kenya. Health Policy. 2010;97:232-7. Medline:20807685 doi:10.1016/j.healthpol.2010.05.004

13 Rahman SM, Ali NA, Jennings L, Seraji MH, Mannan I, Shah R, et al. Factors affecting recruitment and retention of community health workers in a newborn care intervention in Bangladesh. Hum Resour Health. 2010;8:12. Medline:20438642 doi:10.1186/1478-4491-8-12

14 Glenton C, Scheel IB, Pradhan S, Lewin S, Hodgins S, Shrestha V. The female community health volunteer programme in Nepal: decision makers' perceptions of volunteerism, payment and other incentives. Soc Sci Med. 2010;70:1920-7. Medline:20382464 doi:10.1016/j.socscimed.2010.02.034

15 Sharkey AB, Martin S, Cerveau T, Wetzler E, Berzal R. Demand generation and social mobilisation for integrated community case management (iCCM) and child health: lessons learned from successful programmes in Niger and Mozambique. J Glob Health. 2014;4:020410. Medline:25520800 doi:10.7189/jogh.04.020410

16 World Health Organization. Regional Framework for Advocacy, Communication and Social Mobilization, 2011. Available: http://apps.searo.who.int/PDS_DOCS/B4739. pdf?ua=1. Accessed: 2 June 2018.

17 World Health Organization. UNDP. Health in SDGs Policy brief 3: Social mobilization. Retrieved from: http://www.who.int/healthpromotion/conferences/9gchp/policy-brief3-social-mobilization.pdf. Accessed: 1 November 2018.

18 Nigeria Federal Ministry of Health – National Malaria Elimination Programme. Malaria ACSM guidelines: Strategic Framework and implementation guide for advocacy, communication and social mobilisation programmes, 2014. Available: http://gbchealth. org/wp-content/uploads/2015/05/Nigeria-Malaria-ACSM.pdf. Accessed: 2 June 2018.

19 Farnsworth SK, Böse K, Fajobi O, Souza PP, Peniston A, Davidson LL, et al. Community engagement to enhance child survival and early development in low– and middle–income countries: an evidence review. J Health Commun. 2014;19 Suppl 1:67-88. Medline:25207448 doi:10.1080/10810730.2014.941519

20 National Population Commissions (NPC). Census 2006: Population distribution by sex state, LGA and senatorial districts, 2008. Available: http://www.population.gov.ng/ index.php/censuses. Accessed: 1 June 2018.

21 Corporation for National and Community Service – Valuing. documenting, and recording in-kind – a tutorial. Available: https://www.nationalservice.gov/sites/default/files/olc/moodle/fm_key_concepts_of_cash_and_in_kind_match/viewb83c.html?id=3213&chapterid=2269. Accessed: 2 June 2018.

22 Greenspan JA, McHanon SA, Chebet JJ, Mpunga M, Urassa DP, Winch P. Sources of Community Health worker motivation: A qualitative study in Morogoro Region, Tanzania. Hum Resour Health. 2013;11:52. Medline:24112292 doi:10.1186/1478-4491-11-52

23 Haile F, Yemane D, Gebreslassie A. Assessment of non-financial incentives for volunteer community health workers–the case of Wukro district, Tigray, Ethiopia. Hum Resour Health. 2014;12:54. Medline:25245633 doi:10.1186/1478-4491-12-54

24 Nkonki L, Cliff J, Sanders D. Lay health worker attrition: Important but often ignored. Bull World Health Organ. 2011;89:919-23. Medline:22271950 doi:10.2471/BLT.11.087825

25 Ngugi AK, Nyaga LW, Lakhani A, Agoi F, Hanselman M, Lugogo G, et al. Prevalence, incidence and predictors of volunteer community health worker attrition in Kwale County, Kenya. BMJ Glob Health. 2018;3:e000750. Medline:30105093 doi:10.1136/bmjgh-2018-000750

26 Bhattacharyya K, Winch P, LeBan K, Tien M. Community Health Worker Incentives and Disincentives: How They Affect Motivation, Retention, and Sustainability. Available: http://www.chwcentral.org/community-health-worker-incentives-and-disincentives-how-they-affect-motivation-retention-and. Accessed: 14 June 2018.

27 Sommanustweechai A, Putthasri W, Nwe ML, Aung ST, Theint MM, Tangcharoen-sathien V, et al. Community health worker in hard-to-reach rural areas of Myanmar: Filling primary health care service gaps. Hum Resour Health. 2016;14:64. Medline:27769312 doi:10.1186/s12960-016-0161-4

28 Owek C, Abong'o B, Oyugi H, Oteku J, Kaseje D, Muruka C, et al. Motivational factors that influence retention of community health workers in a Kenyan district. Public Health Research. 2013;3:109-15.

29 Alam K, Tasneem S, Oliveras E. Retention of female volunteer community health workers in Dhaka urban slums: a case-control study. Health Policy Plan. 2012;27:477-86. Medline:21900361 doi:10.1093/heapol/czr059

30 Kok M. Improving the performance of community health workers: What can be learned from the literature? Available: http://www.chwcentral.org/blog/improving-performance-community-health-workers-what-can-be-learned-literature. Accessed: 28 May 28, 2018.

iCCM data quality: an approach to assessing iCCM reporting systems and data quality in 5 African countries

Lwendo Moonzwe Davis[1], Kirsten Zalisk[1], Samantha Herrera[1,2], Debra Prosnitz[1], Helen Coelho[1], Jennifer Yourkavitch[1]

[1] ICF, Rockville, Maryland, USA
[2] Save the Children, Washington, D.C., USA

Background Ensuring the quality of health service data is critical for data-driven decision-making. Data quality assessments (DQAs) are used to determine if data are of sufficient quality to support their intended use. However, guidance on how to conduct DQAs specifically for community-based interventions, such as integrated community case management (iCCM) programs, is limited. As part of the World Health Organization's (WHO) Rapid Access Expansion (RAcE) Programme, ICF conducted DQAs in a unique effort to characterize the quality of community health worker-generated data and to use DQA findings to strengthen reporting systems and decision-making.

Methods We present our experience implementing assessments using standardized DQA tools in the six RAcE project sites in the Democratic Republic of Congo, Malawi, Mozambique, Niger, and Nigeria. We describe the process used to create the RAcE DQA tools, adapt the tools to country contexts, and develop the iCCM DQA Toolkit, which enables countries to carry out regular and rapid DQAs. We provide examples of how we used results to generate recommendations.

Results The DQA tools were customized for each RAcE site to assess the iCCM data reporting system, trace iCCM indicators through this system, and to ensure that DQAs were efficient and generated useful recommendations. This experience led to creation of an iCCM DQA Toolkit comprised of simplified versions of RAcE DQA tools and a guidance document. It includes system assessment questions that elicit actionable responses and a simplified data tracing tool focused on one treatment indicator for each iCCM focus illness: diarrhea, malaria, and pneumonia. The toolkit is intended for use at the national or sub-national level for periodic data quality checks.

Conclusions The iCCM DQA Toolkit was designed to be easily tailored to different data reporting system structures because iCCM data reporting tools and data flow vary substantially. The toolkit enables countries to identify points in the reporting system where data quality is compromised and areas of the reporting system that require strengthening, so that countries can make informed adjustments that improve data quality, strengthen reporting systems, and inform decision-making.

Quality of data refers to the degree to which the data collected measure what they were intended to measure. Data quality is a multi-dimensional concept, inclusive of several elements: accuracy, availability, completeness, confidentiality, integrity, precision, reliability, and timeliness [1,2]. Many factors can impact the quality of data collected, including inappropriate or inadequate data collection instruments and procedures, poor recording and reporting, and errors in data processing [3]. For routine health information data, data quality assessments (DQAs) play an important role in determining if data meet the quality required to support their intended use, identifying data quality challenges, and providing recommendations to improve the quality of data. DQAs should also assess data collection processes and data use [4]. DQAs are especially important as many monitoring systems fail to deliver data that are relevant, complete, timely, and accurate. Further, in the field of global health there has been a push for data-driven or evidence-based decision-making [5-11]. However, many program managers are ill-equipped and do not have the data needed for informed decision-making [5,12-15]. Even when data are available, their quality may be weak, limiting their usefulness for appropriate decision-making [13].

Community-based interventions are expanding in technical and geographic scope in an effort to improve health service coverage and equity. Evidence is needed to inform community-based programming, and to ensure its quality. As such, the quality of data generated at the community level is especially important. Integrated community case management (iCCM) is increasingly being used as a strategy to enable community health workers (CHWs) to diagnose and provide treatment for pneumonia, diarrhea, and malaria, the three major causes of childhood mortality [16,17] iCCM strategy is employed in communities defined as hard-to-reach due to their limited access to a health facility. For iCCM interventions, routine data are vital to assess program performance and identify areas for improvement [13,14,18,19]. However, iCCM data face several data quality problems, both due to challenges specific to CHWs and because adding another level to the reporting system creates more opportunities for errors. CHWs, who generate iCCM data, have varied, but often limited, literacy and numeracy levels, limited time or tight timeframes to record and report data, limited resources, minimal training on data recording and reporting, poor physical infrastructure for submitting reports in a timely manner, and few incentives [14,20,21]. Errors in data recording and aggregation introduce further challenges in ensuring data quality [22]. DQAs play an important role in identifying and making recommendations to address some of these problems. However, literature and published guidance on how to conduct DQAs specifically for community-based interventions, such as iCCM programs, is limited [21,23]. Several studies have also noted the importance of documenting and describing the process used to conduct DQAs, especially for data originating from the community level [24].

The World Health Organization (WHO) launched the Rapid Access Expansion Programme (RAcE) in the Democratic Republic of Congo, Malawi, Mozambique, Niger and Nigeria in 2013. Under RAcE international non-governmental organizations (NGOs) and WHO supported Ministries of Health (MOH) to implement iCCM programs. The RAcE programme had two primary objectives: to catalyze the scale-up of community case management of malaria (CCMm) and iCCM, and to stimulate policy review and regulatory updates in each country on disease case management. Throughout the implementation of RAcE, ICF provided independent technical support for monitoring and evaluation activities, which included designing and conducting DQAs.

In this article, we describe the process used to create and adapt RAcE DQA tools and develop the iCCM DQA Toolkit, which enables countries to carry out regular and rapid DQAs. Drawing on our DQA protocols and reports, we also provide examples of how we used results to generate recommendations for project implementing partners and national-level stakeholders.

METHODS

In 2013, ICF designed DQA tools to assess the quality of iCCM data and the iCCM data collection, reporting, and management system for RAcE. The DQA tools were adapted from the Global Fund's DQA tool developed by MEASURE Evaluation for facility-based HIV and AIDS treatment programs to focus on iCCM data generated at the community level and iCCM data reporting and management system. Papers by Nyangara et al. 2018 and Yourkavitch et al. 2016 provide further details on the methods utilized for the RAcE DQAs [16,25]. In each of the six RAcE project areas, two DQAs were conducted one to two years apart (**Table 1**). The time between the first and second DQAs allowed grantees and project stakeholders to make modifications to the reporting system based on DQA findings and recommendations to improve data quality.

Although there were slight variations in the DQA methodology across project sites and sometimes between rounds, all of the DQAs had three primary objectives:

Table 1. *Timing of RAcE DQAs*

PROJECT SITE	ROUND 1 DQA	ROUND 2 DQA
Democratic Republic of Congo	June 2014	September 2015
Malawi	January 2014	February 2016
Mozambique	June 2015	October 2016
Niger	April 2014	June 2015
Nigeria (Abia State)	October 2015	November 2016
Nigeria (Niger State)	October 2015	December 2016

RAcE – Rapid Access Expansion, DQA – data quality assessment

- To assess the effectiveness of the grantee data collection system, and identify any bottlenecks in the national health information system that affected grantee routine reporting

- To assess the integrity of project data, including CHW and supervisor registers, and data on services provided/case management, supervision and commodity stockouts

- To provide guidance and recommendations to grantees and national stakeholders in the generation of quality data to guide the implementation of the project and improve data quality

In each DQA, ICF evaluated data quality through several exercises including: mapping the data flow, tracing and verifying the data, and assessing the iCCM data reporting system in place. ICF also provided detailed recommendations based on the findings from each DQA. At the request for an external assessment by the WHO, ICF staff and in-country consultants conducted the DQAs, with logistic support and engagement of grantee staff. The DQAs utilized both quantitative and qualitative data collection methods to accomplish the aforementioned objectives. We briefed grantee, MOH, and other national stakeholder staff prior to DQA fieldwork and debriefed them with preliminary results immediately following fieldwork. Also at the request of WHO, ICF developed the iCCM DQA Toolkit, intended to be a resource for MOH staff. The toolkit includes data collection and analysis tools and accompanying guidance necessary to carry out routine DQAs.

RESULTS

Tool development process

ICF developed DQA tools to assess the iCCM data reporting system and to trace iCCM indicators through this system. We adapted the conceptualization and methodology for the RAcE DQAs from the Global Fund's DQA for HIV and AIDS treatment programs [25] (**Figure 1**).

The design of the DQA tools was based on MEASURE Evaluation's Excel-based tool to assess the quality of HIV/AIDS treatment data emanating from facility-based services [2]. However, to fit the purposes of the assessed iCCM programs, we modified the tool to focus on iCCM, extend data collection from the facility level to the community level, and incorporate qualitative data collection to complement findings from quantitative data. In modifying the MEASURE Evaluation tool, iCCM data flows were mapped using iCCM data collection and reporting tools and we reviewed grantees' RAcE performance monitoring frameworks (PMFs) to determine which indicators or data fields to trace. After conducting the first DQA in Malawi, we developed custom-ized paper "tracker forms" to record data extracted from iCCM registers and reporting forms, which we later entered into the Excel (Microsoft Inc, Seattle, WA, USA) tool.

Mapping the data flow

Reporting systems varied by country and a critical step of adapting the tools was to understand the data flow. In DRC, Malawi, Mozambique and Niger, data flowed from the CHW or community level to the facility level, to an

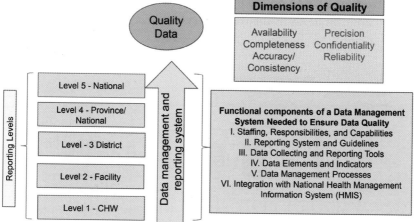

Figure 1. *Rapid Access Expansion (RAcE) data quality assessment (DQA) toolkit conceptual framework adapted from MEASURE Evaluation, Data Quality Audit Tool, 2008.*

intermediate aggregation level (eg, district, province), and then in parallel to the central/national and grantee levels. However, in Nigeria there were no systems in place to report community-level data to the central or national level. Data from the community level in Nigeria were submitted to the grantees and available to the State Ministries of Health (SMOH). Because the DQAs were conducted to assess the RAcE grantees' reporting systems, iCCM data were traced from the community level to the grantee level. Due to the variation of each data reporting system, it was critical to map out the systems to tailor the DQA tools. For instance, in the majority of RAcE sites, CHWs generated monthly iCCM reports using the data in their iCCM registers and submitted them to the health facility level, but in two project areas, CHW supervisors generated comparable reports. In two RAcE project areas, CHW-generated data were aggregated at the facility level, but in the other four project areas, data were passed from the facility level to the next reporting level by CHWs. At this next reporting level, staff entered data into an electronic data management system, into a database, or into another paper form, depending on the RAcE project area, and sometimes depending on the location within the RAcE project area. **Figure 2** is an example of a CHW register from Nigeria (samples of other registers are available on the CCM Central Website: https://ccmcentral.com/resources-and-tools/tools-for-chws/).

Indicators traced

As part of the DQA planning processes, we selected key iCCM indicators from the grantees' PMFs to trace. The DQA tools were then adapted for each RAcE project area based on the indicators which were traceable through the data flow and the fields in the data collection and reporting tools. Selecting

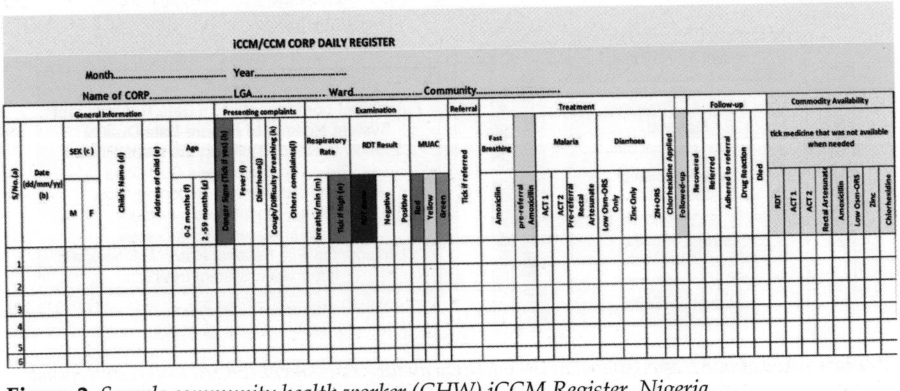
iCCM/CCM CORP DAILY REGISTER
Month.................... Year....................
Name of CORP.................... LGA.................... Ward.................... Community....................
General Information: S/No.(a); Date (dd/mm/yy) (b); SEX (c) M F; Child's Name (d); Address of child (e); Age: 0-2 months (f), 2-59 months (g)
Presenting complaints: Danger Signs (Tick if yes) (h); Fever (i); Diarrhoea(j); Cough/Difficulty Breathing (k); Others complaints(l)
Examination: Respiratory Rate: breaths/min (m), Tick if high (n); RDT Result: Negative, Positive; MUAC: Red, Yellow, Green
Referral: Tick if referred
Treatment: Fast Breathing: Amoxicilin, pre-referral Amoxicilin; Malaria: ACT 1, ACT 2, Pre-referral Rectal Artesunate; Diarrhoea: Low Osm-ORS Only, Zinc Only, ZN+ORS; Chlorhexidine Applied
Followed-up
Follow-up: Recovered; Referred; Adhered to referral; Drug Reaction; Died
Commodity Availability: tick medicine that was not available when needed: RDT, ACT 1, ACT 2, Rectal Artesunate, Amoxicilin, Low Osm-ORS, Zinc, Chlorhexidine
1
2
3
4
5
6

Figure 2. *Sample community health worker (CHW) iCCM Register, Nigeria.*

indicators, reviewing the data elements needed to calculate each indicator, and then ensuring that the iCCM data collection and reporting tools captured these data elements were critical steps in DQA planning. In some countries, this planning process revealed that reporting tools were not accurately capturing data elements needed to calculate iCCM indicators, and that consequently data grantees reported were inaccurate. Across all sites, we examined indicators related to treatment of diarrhea, malaria, and pneumonia over a three-month period that aligned with the grantees' last completed RAcE reporting quarter. We also examined stockout and supervision indicators if the information was available in the reporting forms.

Data collection methods

The DQA tools implemented a mixed-method approach consisting of qualitative and quantitative methods to assess data quality and the reporting system, summarized in **Table 2**.

Qualitative methods were used to capture involvement of and perceptions from stakeholders across all levels of the reporting system and to assess how systems functioned. Specific areas of inquiry covered in the interview guide included data use, understanding and adequacy of data collection and reporting tools, training and supervisory support provided and received to complete data

Table 2. *Summary of data collection tools, sources and outputs*

	QUALITATIVE METHODS	QUANTITATIVE METHODS
Tool	• Interview Guide* (Word Document)	• Data tracing and verification (Excel) • Systems assessment (Excel)
Data Sources	• Central level staff, intermediate aggregation level staff, CHW supervisor and CHW involved in iCCM data collection, management or reporting	• Data collection and reporting tools, including iCCM registers, paper reporting forms, and electonic data files • Central level staff, intermediate aggregation level staff and CHW supervisor involved in iCCM data collection, management or reporting
Outputs	• Interview notes	• Availability and completeness measures • Verification ratios* • Consistency ratios • Absolute counts and differences among data sources • Scorecard with average scores for each component across each level assessed

RAcE – Rapid Access Expansion, CHW – community health worker
*Included in RAcE DQAs but not included in the iCCM DQA Toolkit.

collection forms, and perceptions of workload. Qualitative data collection also enabled us to learn more about the data quality challenges associated with the collection, management, and reporting system(s) in place. We collected qualitative data through key informant interviews and document reviews. Although the specific types and numbers of individuals interviewed varied, the DQA team conducted interviews with individuals who were involved in iCCM data collection, reporting, or data management at each level of the reporting system. Across RAcE project areas, the DQA team interviewed one iCCM CHW supervisor and one randomly selected CHW at each sampled facility. Interviews were conducted using a semi-structured interview guide and were either audio recorded or documented with notes. Local consultants conducted interviews in the local languages or through a translator and ICF staff conducted other interviews in English, French, or Portuguese. The DQA team also conducted comprehensive reviews of all RAcE grantee and applicable iCCM data collection and reporting tools, and the data and information flow to assess their quality and to identify any potential bottlenecks or challenges.

Quantitative methods were used to assess the quality of the data collected at each reporting level with a focus on key project indicators. Data were collected and scored using the systems assessment tool, and CHW counts of treatments were verified and traced through the reporting system using the data tracing tool. The systems assessment included standardized questions across five dimensions as identified in **Figure 1**: (1) Monitoring and Evaluation (M&E) structures, functions, and capabilities, 2) indicator definitions and reporting guidelines, 3) data collection and reporting forms, 4) data management processes, and 5) links with the national reporting system. Although we standardized the questions across all RAcE project sites, depending on the systems, we excluded some questions that were not applicable. For instance, if RAcE project sites did not enter data into an electronic data management system or database at the sub-national reporting level, we excluded the questions about electronic data entry from the systems assessment for that level.

The DQAs used data tracing and verification to detect inconsistencies and unexpected values in the information reported. The DQAs also collected quantitative data to assess the availability and completeness of data collection and reporting forms. At each facility visited, the DQA team reviewed the iCCM registers for all CHWs who reported to that facility. The DQA team also reviewed any monthly reports that the CHWs submitted to the health facility. At the next level of the reporting system, the DQA team reviewed the reports from the facilities submitted to the sites visited at that level (eg, district, provincial or local government authority (LGA) health offices). At the grantee's office, the

DQA team reviewed the data that they received and the data in their project database, if they had one. Data for the traced indicators were extracted from the iCCM registers and reporting forms, then recorded on the paper tracker sheets and entered into the data tracing Excel tool.

Sampling methodology

Understanding the reporting system and data flow was critical to the site selection for each DQA to ensure that sites at each level of the reporting system were included. In all RAcE project areas, CHWs reported to a facility-based supervisor. In order to select the sample, we needed a complete list of the program health facilities, including the number of supervisors at each facility and the number of CHWs who reported to each supervisor. We developed the sampling strategy implemented in the DQAs to be logistically feasible and to provide a snapshot of what was happening in each project area; it was not intended to be statistically representative, but rather to highlight key themes around data quality that needed to be addressed. The iCCM DQA Toolkit (available at http://ccmcentral.com/) discusses further sampling considerations, such as funding, timeframe for the assessment, and other logistical considerations.

Across the RAcE project areas, there were several considerations made for site selection. In some cases, we used multi-stage sampling to make the DQA fieldwork more feasible within a two to three week period. For example, in Mozambique's second DQA, we randomly selected two of the four RAcE supported provinces; however, within those provinces we excluded districts that were unsafe and those that were not yet using the new reporting forms. Additionally in Mozambique, because of the geographic spread of RAcE project areas, we accounted for distance in the sampling to ensure feasibility of data collection. We then selected facilities based on having at least one active CHW for the entire reporting period. Back-up facilities were also selected in the event that one of the original facilities was inaccessible. In DRC, conflicts in one of the health zones forced suspension of implementation in that health zone and cut off access to other health zones that could only be reached by traveling through the conflict area. Therefore, we implemented a purposeful sampling approach. In all other RAcE project areas, we implemented a random selection approach.

A larger number of facilities was sampled in the first DQAs in Malawi and Niger. For logistic feasibility, we sampled eight facilities in subsequent DQAs, but the number of CHWs associated with each of the selected facilities varied

(**Table 3**). Additionally, the number of CHWs whose data were verified and traced may have been less than the total number of CHWs who reported to the sampled facilities, if for example, on the day of the DQA team's visit, a CHW did not report to or bring their iCCM registers to the facility. The DQA teams traced and verified for all CHWs present; however, they randomly selected one CHW at each facility for an interview. **Table 3** summarizes the number of facilities sampled for each DQA and the number and type of CHWs that reported to each sampled facility and were included in the DQA.

Table 3. *Samples for first and second RAcE DQAs*

RAcE Project and DQA	Number of nistricts, LGA, Health zones	Num- ber of Facili- ties	Number of CHWs included in assessment	CHW cadre
DRC (DQA 1)	4	8	60	*Relais Communautaire* (RCom)
DRC (DQA 2)	3	8	52	
Malawi (DQA 1)	4	10	52	Health Surveillance Assistant (HSA)
Malawi (DQA 2)	4	8	34	
Mozambique (DQA 1)	6	8	31	*Agente Polivalente Elementar* (APE)
Mozambique (DQA 2)	4	8	23	
Niger (DQA 1)	2	16	83*	*Relais Communautaire* (RCom)
Niger (DQA 2)	4	8	85	
Nigeria – Abia State (DQA 1)	4	8	67	Community- Oriented Resource Persons (CORPs)
Nigeria – Abia State (DQA 2)	4	8	48	
Nigeria – Niger State (DQA 1)	3	8	30	
Nigeria – Niger State (DQA 2)	6	8	61	

RAcE – Rapid Access Expansion, DQA – data quality assessment, LGA – local government authority, CHW – community health worker
*Only 83 of 146 RCom were included in the DQA. Others were ill, had dropped out of the CHW program, or were not available for other reasons.

Systems assessment

For each dimension of the reporting system, the systems assessment included a series of questions. Each question is scored on a scale that ranges from 1 to 3 (1 = no, not at all; 2 = yes, partly; 3 = yes, completely). Scores of 1 or 2 automatically generate a field for the assessor to note reasons for the score. The scores of individual questions are then averaged to produce a score for each dimension by each site included in the assessment, by reporting level, and across all reporting levels. The closer the scores are to 3, the stronger or more functional the reporting system is for that dimension. The systems assessment tool was programmed to automatically calculate the scores. Spider diagrams were used to visually display the overall results (an example is shown in **Figure 3**).

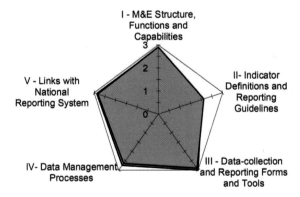

Figure 3. *Example of overall Rapid Access Expansion (RAcE) data quality assessment (DQA) systems assessment scores by dimension.*

Data verification

Data verification assessed reporting performance (the availability and completeness of reports) and the consistency of the data across the levels of the reporting system. In most cases, we were unable to assess timeliness because submission dates were not recorded. We programmed data tracing results to automatically populate, however this process required substantial customization to account for variations in data reporting systems before fieldwork and data cleaning to account for missing data after fieldwork. The reporting performance results presented the percentage of available and complete data collection and reporting forms by reporting level for the time-period assessed.

We calculated verification ratios for treatments recorded in the CHWs' iCCM registers to assess if CHWs were appropriately filling out their registers when they recorded that they provided treatment to a sick child. The verification ratios compared the counts recorded in the treatment fields of the registers to the number of treatments appropriately recorded, by illness. We considered recorded treatments as appropriately recorded if the register entries included the appropriate corresponding symptomatic and diagnostic information. See **Figure 4** for an example of verification ratio trends for the three treatment indicators comparing recorded treatments to appropriately recorded treatments in CHW registers. This figure indicates that diarrhea in particular, and to a lesser extent pneumonia, were often not recorded appropriately.

We also calculated consistency ratios for each indicator to describe data consistency between reporting levels for the indicators traced in the DQA. These measures assessed data accuracy throughout the system. For these ratios, a

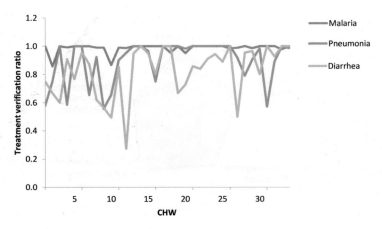

Figure 4. *Treatment verification ratios example.*

value of 1 indicated agreement between the two counts being compared. Consistency ratios greater than 1 indicated under-reporting and consistency ratios less than 1 indicated over-reporting. Reasons the data may not match across forms include errors in calculation or transcription, different interpretations of data to be reported, missing or illegible data, or corrections made to errors that occurred on one form but were not corrected on the other form. For example, we compared the values reported in the health facility monthly reports by the health facilities included in the DQA with the sum of the values that CHWs reported in their summary reports for three treatment indicators and an amoxicillin stockout indicator (**Figure 5**). **Figure 5** shows that amoxicillin stockout was often over-reported to the next level.

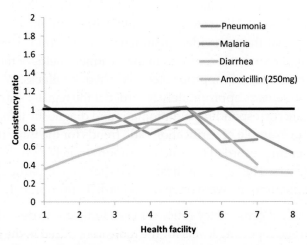

Figure 5. *Facility reporting consistency ratios example.*

Table 4. Data verification results of counts and differences for malaria treatment

District	Facility	SELECTED FACILITIES							
		Verified counts in CHW Registers	Counts in Summary Form of CHW Registers	Difference: Summary Form of CHW Registers minus CHW Registers	Counts in Facility Supervisor Summary Form	Difference: Facility Supervisor Summary Form minus Summary Form of CHW Registers	Counts in National HIS minus selected facilities	Difference: National HIS minus Facility Supervisor Summary Form	Difference: National HIS minus CHW Registers
1	1	69	64	-5	64	0	64	0	-5
2	2	275	299	24	327	28	327	0	52
	3	1035	1066	31	991	-75	1092	101	57
3	4	190	182	-8	183	1	245	62	55
	5	105	107	2	106	-1	106	0	1
4	6	121	125	4	120	-5	120	0	-1
	7	620	836	216	829	-7	829	0	209
	8	982	1153	171	1150	-3	1170	20	188

CHW – community health worker, HIS – health interview survey

In addition to the verification and consistency ratios, the DQA reports presented the counts verified in the CHWs' iCCM registers and the counts reported by reporting tool to show the differences in counts between the various reporting tools and levels. These differences provide information about the magnitude, as well as the direction, of discrepancies and complements the consistency ratios, see **Table 4** for an example of the verification result counts for malaria treatment.

Dissemination and recommendations

Dissemination of findings and provision of recommendations were important aspects of the DQAs. At the conclusion of each DQA, we conducted a debriefing with initial results in-country for key stakeholders. A comprehensive DQA report, which included recommendations based on the findings, was drafted and reviewed by WHO and grantees prior to the finalization. WHO then facilitated dissemination in-country to present and discuss recommendations with the MOH. ICF supported some grantees to develop specific action plans to address DQA recommendations. **Table 5** presents some examples of recommendations that resulted from the DQAs. See Yourkavitch et al. (2018) for discussion on the steps taken by MOHs and grantees to implement recommendations [26].

Table 5. *Examples of recommendations from DQAs*

RECOMMENDATIONS
Develop a systematic training plan for staff at all levels. A training plan should be developed to ensure that all staff at different levels of the iCCM reporting system receive the necessary training they need to be effective in their work. The training plan will ensure ongoing capacity building of CHWs, CHW supervisors, and M&E officers to improve the accuracy of the data they collect and report. The training plan should also include scheduled refresher trainings on data quality sessions during monthly or quarterly meetings. A good start would be a review of the existing training plans mentioned during the DQA interviews, then adapt and customize them for the national, district, facility and community levels.
Support the MOH iCCM unit with the development of written guidance and procedures. The systems assessment found data management practices to be the weakest point of the M&E system, primarily because written procedures do not exist to address issues with late, incomplete, inaccurate, and missing reports. Despite this, all of the licensed nurses interviewed could correctly describe what should be done in case of problems with the data. ICF recommends that the grantee support the MOH iCCM unit in the development, documentation, and implementation of standard procedures for each level of the CHW reporting system.
Create a standardized process to ensure that information is properly transferred on duplicate and triplicate copies of registers and summary forms. Often, the information recorded on the duplicate or triplicate copies is not an accurate reflection of what was recorded on the original copy. Reasons for such mistakes include the use of pencil, misalignment or improper placement of carbon copy paper, or failure to use a cardboard divider when recording information. This standard process should also be emphasized during supervisory visits.
Track CHW-level consumption information separately. Currently, CHW data related to medical supplies and commodities consumption are aggregated at the health facility level. These consolidated data do not flow to the district or provincial level. Hence, there is no mechanism for making data-driven estimates for CHW consumption and supply. The MOH should develop a system that enables consumption data specific to the CHW level to be reported through the CHW program and general supply chain.

iCCM data quality assessment toolkit and guidance

Throughout the DQA process, RAcE grantees and MOH staff increasingly recognized the importance of data quality and the need to routinely and rapidly measure the quality of iCCM data. At the request of WHO, ICF developed an iCCM DQA Toolkit to address this need. We designed the iCCM DQA Toolkit for MOH or implementing partner staff at the national and sub-national levels to conduct periodic data quality checks. Specifically, the toolkit is designed to assess the data recorded by CHWs as they are aggregated through the reporting system, from the community to the national level. The toolkit includes two Excel-based tools, the systems assessment tool and the data-tracing tool.

- The systems assessment tool includes a set of modules, one for each level of the data reporting system. The DQA team records and scores each item in the module, and the tool generates a scorecard to display the results.

- The data-tracing tool includes data collection and analysis worksheets for tracing selected indicators through the iCCM data reporting system. The DQA team uses the tool to review and collect information from the iCCM data collection and reporting tools at each level of the data reporting system at the sites selected for assessment. The tool then uses these data to calculate measures of data availability, completeness, and consistency as the data are aggregated through the iCCM data reporting system. A series of charts and tables included in the tool display these measures.

Development of the iCCM DQA Toolkit was a participatory process. After ICF developed the draft toolkit, we piloted both the systems assessment and data tracing tools in Abia State, Nigeria. We conducted the pilot over a period of four days. Site visits took place in three health facilities, an LGA office (intermediate aggregation level), and the State Ministry of Health. The first day included holding a toolkit orientation with MOH staff and conducting the systems assessment with the LGA focal point and the State and Federal officers. Facility visits took place on the second and third days of the pilot. At the facilities, we conducted the systems assessment with the CHW supervisor and used the data tracing tools to extract data from CHW, CHW supervisor, and LGA data collection and reporting tools. The fourth day of the pilot included entering the field data into the Excel tool, reviewing the data analysis process, and gathering feedback on the overall process and tools with MOH and LGA staff.

The toolkit has an accompanying guidance document, which provides detailed information on various aspects of the toolkit and guidance on DQA implementation. Specifically, the guidance document describes the purpose and structure of the iCCM DQA toolkit; considerations for determining personnel and logistics, selecting the sample, and preparing for fieldwork; instructions for adapting the tools; guidance on how to use the tools to implement a DQA; and guidance for analyzing, visualizing, and interpreting the data collected during the DQA. The complete toolkit and accompanying guidance document are available on http://ccmcentral.com/. It is important to note that some of the elements described above as part of the RAcE DQAs are not included in the iCCM DQA Toolkit or guidance; specifically there are not qualitative data collection tools nor is there provision for the calculation of verification ratios from iCCM registers. We excluded these two elements to facilitate a rapid and routine process.

DISCUSSION

Through RAcE, ICF conducted several comprehensive DQAs of routine iCCM data generated by CHWs. The DQAs evaluated the data reporting systems in place and provided recommendations on how to improve data quality. Details on some of the DQAs conducted under RAcE have been published elsewhere [21,23]. In general, however, there is limited literature on the process of conducting DQAs, specifically for data generated at the community level. Such accounts are especially important for iCCM programs that have additional challenges as they rely on community health systems that are overstretched and CHWs that often times are volunteers with limited formal education or training and low literacy levels. The communities that iCCM programs primarily target face other resources challenges such as poor infrastructure, transport, roads, electricity and mobile network/internet coverage challenges that place additional strains on the reporting system. However, the data collected by CHWs are critical to inform decisions about implementation and to demonstrate program successes and challenges.

ICF developed DQA tools to assess the iCCM data reporting system and to trace iCCM indicators through this system. Because data reporting tools and flows vary by country, a critical first step in conducting a DQA is to understand the data flow and reporting tools and customize DQA tools accordingly. The iCCM DQA Toolkit provides a starting point for designing a DQA for a specific iCCM reporting system. The DQA tools have proven to be effective, efficient, and generated recommendations to facilitate improving data quality. The DQAs conducted through RAcE took 2-3 weeks to complete, which could be burdensome for MOH staff. The iCCM DQA Toolkit is streamlined to be less burdensome and enable countries to more readily identify points in the reporting system where data quality is compromised and which dimensions of the reporting system require strengthening. We conducted the pilot exercise in Abia State, Nigeria in 3.5 days.

The toolkit includes systems assessment questions that elicit actionable responses, and the data tracing tool is simplified to focus on one indicator for each of the three iCCM-focus illnesses. The systems assessment examines the functional dimensions of the data reporting system that are needed to ensure data quality. Adapted from the MEASURE Evaluation conceptual framework, the RAcE DQA tools examined five dimensions: M&E structures, functions and capabilities; indicator definitions and reporting guidelines; data collection and reporting forms and tools; data management processes; and links with national reporting systems. The conceptual framework has since been updated to include a sixth component, use of data for decision making [2]. Elements to assess if data are being used for decision making include visualizing data through the development of charts, graphs, maps or other resources; ability to interpret and analyze data; access to guidance or technical assistance on data use; presentation and dissemination of data to key stakeholders; and evidence of decisions taken based on the analyzed data and results [2].

The toolkit also provides guidance on modifications national and sub-national MOH staff can make to tailor the tools to meet their iCCM program needs and yield DQA findings that improve data quality, strengthen reporting systems, and inform decision-making. Although there are several toolkits and guidance documents in existence [2,27-29], these tools to do not factor in the community level and thus, the feedback loop to the lowest (community) level and a thorough assessment of the data collection and reporting systems at the community level is often missing.

CONCLUSIONS

The process of implementing a DQA not only improves data quality, but is also beneficial to the DQA team. We recommend that staff at the national or sub-national level use the iCCM DQA Toolkit for periodic data quality checks or as part of routine supervision of iCCM programs. In this vein, the DQA would serve multiple purposes including capacity building, supervision, and identification of challenges or bottlenecks by those in a position to implement changes.

Acknowledgements: *The authors would like to thank the implementing NGOs – The International Rescue Committee, Malaria Consortium, Save the Children, Society for Family Health, and World Vision – the Ministries of Health, and the WHO representatives in each of the RAcE countries for sharing their data, time, thoughts, and experiences. We would like to thank the ICF staff and consultants that were involved in the DQA data collection and reporting efforts. We would also like to thank Salim Sadruddin and Gunther Baugh of the WHO for their inputs and support. Finally, we want to thank the community health workers who work hard to provide services to caregivers and children in communities. The content of this publication is solely the responsibility of the authors and does not necessarily reflect the views or policies of WHO or Global Affairs Canada. ICF obtained ethical approval from ICF's Institutional Review Board.*

Funding: *The Data Quality Assessments and Development of the iCCM Data Quality Assessment Toolkit was conducted by ICF under a contract with the WHO through funding by Global Affairs Canada.*

Disclaimer: *The views expressed in this manuscript are those of the authors.*

Authorship contributions: *SH conceptualized the paper and LMD drafted the manuscript. DP, HC, JY, KZ, and SH provided critical review and content edits on manuscript drafts.*

Competing interests: *WHO contracted ICF to conduct the DQAs in RAcE project areas. ICF developed the DQA tools, iCCM DQA Toolkit described in this paper. For each of the DQAs ICF conducted the assessments, interpreted the results, and provided recommendations, and this information was presented in the form of reports. WHO reviewed all DQA related tools and reports prior to providing approval. The affiliation of co-author Samantha Herrera, with Save the Children, occurred after the completion the project. The authors have completed the Unified Competing Interest form at www.icmje. org/coi_disclosure.pdf (available on request from the corresponding author) and declare no further competing interests.*

References

1 Brown W, Stouffer R, Hardee K. Data quality assurance tool for program level indicators. Chapel Hill, NC: MEASURE Evaluation; 2007.

2 MEASURE Evaluation. Routine data quality assessment tool: user manual. Chapel Hill, NC: MEASURE Evaluation; 2017.

3 Shrestha LB, Bodart C. Data transmission, data processing, and data quality. Design and implementation of health information systems. Gneva: WHO; 2000. pp 128-45.

4 Chen H, Hailey D, Wang N, Yu P. A review of data quality assessment methods for public health information systems. Int J Environ Res Public Health. 2014;11:5170-207. Medline:24830450 doi:10.3390/ijerph110505170

5 AbouZahr C, Boerma T. Health information systems: the foundations of public health. Bull World Health Organ. 2005;83:578-83. Medline:16184276

6 Clancy CM, Cronin K. Evidence-based decision making: global evidence, local decisions. Health Aff (Millwood). 2005;24:151-62. Medline:15647226 doi:10.1377/hlthaff.24.1.151

7 Sterman JD. Learning from evidence in a complex world. Am J Public Health. 2006;96:505-14. Medline:16449579 doi:10.2105/AJPH.2005.066043

8 Sauerborn R. Using information to make decisions. Design and implementation of health information system. Geneva: World Health Organisation; 2000:33-48.

9 Pappaioanou M, Malison M, Wilkins K, Otto B, Goodman RA, Churchill RE, et al. Strengthening capacity in developing countries for evidence-based public health: the data for decision-making project. Soc Sci Med. 2003;57:1925-37. Medline:14499516 doi:10.1016/S0277-9536(03)00058-3

10 Brownson RC, Gurney JG, Land GH. Evidence-based decision making in public health. J Public Health Manag Pract. 1999;5:86-97. Medline:10558389 doi:10.1097/00124784-199909000-00012

11 World Health Organization. Framework and standards for country health information systems. Geneva: World Health Organization; 2008.

12 Chilundo B, Sundby J, Aanestad M. Analysing the quality of routine malaria data in Mozambique. Malar J. 2004;3:3. Medline:14998435 doi:10.1186/1475-2875-3-3

13 Laínez YB, Wittcoff A, Mohamud AI, Amendola P, Perry HB, D'Harcourt E. Insights from community case management data in six sub-Saharan African countries. Am J Trop Med Hyg. 2012;87:144-50. Medline:23136290 doi:10.4269/ajtmh.2012.12-0106

14 Guenther T, Laínez YB, Oliphant NP, Dale M, Raharison S, Miller L, et al. Routine monitoring systems for integrated community case management programs: lessons from

18 countries in sub–Saharan Africa. J Glob Health. 2014;4:020301. Medline:25520787 doi:10.7189/jogh.04.020301

15 Glèlè Ahanhanzo Y, Ouedraogo LT, Kpozèhouen A, Coppieters Y, Makoutodé M, Wilmet-Dramaix M. Factors associated with data quality in the routine health information system of Benin. Arch Public Health. 2014;72:25. Medline:25114792 doi:10.1186/2049-3258-72-25

16 Marsh DR, Hamer DH, Pagnoni F, Peterson S. Introduction to a special supplement: evidence for the implementation, effects, and impact of the integrated community case management strategy to treat childhood infection. Am J Trop Med Hyg. 2012;87:2-5. Medline:23136271 doi:10.4269/ajtmh.2012.12-0504

17 World Health Organization. WHO/UNICEF joint statement integrated community case management (iCCM): an equity-focused strategy to improve access to essential treatment services for children. Geneva and New York; 2012.

18 Young M, Sharkey A, Aboubaker S, Kasungami D, Swedberg E, Ross K. The way forward for integrated community case management programmes: A summary of lessons learned to date and future priorities. J Glob Health. 2014;4:020303. Medline:25520789 doi:10.7189/jogh.04.020303

19 Young M, Wolfheim C, Marsh DR, Hammamy D. World Health Organization/United Nations Children's Fund joint statement on integrated community case management: an equity-focused strategy to improve access to essential treatment services for children. Am J Trop Med Hyg. 2012;87:6-10. Medline:23136272 doi:10.4269/ajtmh.2012.12-0221

20 Mahmood S, Ayub M. Accuracy of primary health care statistics reported by community based lady health workers in district Lahore. J Pak Med Assoc. 2010;60:649-53. Medline:20726196

21 Yourkavitch J, Zalisk K, Prosnitz D, Luhanga M, Nsona H. How do we know? an assessment of integrated community case management data quality in four districts of Malawi. Health Policy Plan. 2016;31:1162-71. Medline:27162235 doi:10.1093/heapol/czw047

22 Helleringer S, Frimpong J, Phillips J, Awooner J, Yeji F, editors. Operational study of the quality of health data aggregated by community health workers in the Upper East Region of Ghana. American Public Health Association Annual Meeting; 2010.

23 Nyangara FM, Hai T, Zalisk K, Ozor L, Ufere J, Isiguzo C, et al. Assessment of data quality and reporting systems for underserved populations: the case of integrated community case management programs in Nigeria. Health Policy Plan. 2018;33:465-73. Medline:29447403 doi:10.1093/heapol/czy003

24 Mitsunaga T, Hedt-Gauthier B, Ngizwenayo E, Farmer DB, Karamaga A, Drobac P, et al. Utilizing community health worker data for program management and evaluation: systems for data quality assessments and baseline results from Rwanda. Soc Sci Med. 2013;85:87-92. Medline:23540371 doi:10.1016/j.socscimed.2013.02.033

25 Hardee K. Data quality audit tool: Guidelines for Implementation. Chapel Hill, NC: MEASURE Evaluation; 2008.

26 Yourkavitch J, Prosnitz D, Herrera S. Data quality assessments stimulate improvements to health management information systems: evidence from five African countries. Presented at the 148th meeting of the American Public Health Association, San Diego, CA, November 2018.

27 World Health Organization. Data quality review: a toolkit for facility data quality assessment. Geneva: World Health Organization; 2017.

28 MEASURE Evaluation. Data Quality Assurance Tool for Program Level Indicators 2007.

29 The Global Fund. MEASURE Evaluation. Data Quality Audit (DQA) Tool. 2012.

Data quality assessments stimulate improvements to health management information systems: evidence from five African countries

Jennifer Yourkavitch[1], Debra Prosnitz[1], Samantha Herrera[2]

[1] ICF, Rockville, Maryland, USA
[2] Save the Children U.S., Washington, D.C., USA

Background Health service data are used to inform decisions about planning and implementation, as well as to evaluate performance and outcomes, and the quality of those data are important. Data quality assessments (DQA) afford the opportunity to collect information about health service data. Through its Rapid Access Expansion Programme (RAcE), the World Health Organization (WHO) funded non-governmental organizations (NGO) to support Ministries of Health (MOH) in implementing integrated community case management (iCCM) programs in the Democratic Republic of Congo, Malawi, Mozambique, Niger and Nigeria. WHO contracted ICF to support grantee monitoring and evaluation efforts, part of which was to conduct DQAs to enhance program monitoring and decision making. The contribution of DQAs to data-driven decision making has been documented and the purpose of this paper is to describe how DQAs contributed to health management information system (HMIS) strengthening and the findings of subsequent DQAs in those areas.

Methods ICF created a mixed-methods DQA for iCCM data, comprising a review of the data collection and management system, a data tracing component and key informant interviews. The DQA was applied twice in each RAcE site, which enables a general comparison of system-level attributes before and after the first DQA application. For this qualitative assessment, we reviewed DQA reports to collate information about DQA recommendations and how they were addressed before a subsequent DQA, along with the findings of the second DQA.

Results Findings from the first DQA in each RAcE site stimulated NGO and MOH efforts to strengthen different aspects of the HMIS in each country, including modifying data collection tools in the Democratic Republic of Congo; training community health workers (CHWs) and supervisors in Malawi; strengthening supervision in Mozambique; improving CHW registers and strengthening staff capacity at all levels to report data in Niger; establishing a data review system in Abia State, Nigeria; and, establishing processes to improve data use and quality in Niger State, Nigeria.

Conclusion Data quality assessments stimulated context-specific efforts by NGOs and MOHs to improve iCCM data quality. DQAs can serve as a collaborative and evidence-based activity to influence discussions of data quality and stimulate HMIS strengthening efforts.

Given that health service data are used to inform decisions about planning and implementation, as well as to evaluate performance and outcomes, the quality of those data are important. Data quality assessments (DQA) afford the opportunity to collect information about health service data and to develop a profile of data quality, evaluating characteristics including accuracy, consistency, and the timeliness of data reports. DQAs can also provide information about the health management information system (HMIS) that may support or hinder data quality. The World Health Organization (WHO) and partners recently released a three-part manual to aid assessments of data quality, underscoring growing global interest in this topic [1].

Through its Rapid Access Expansion Programme (hereafter referred to as RAcE), the WHO funded non-governmental organizations (NGO) to support Ministries of Health (MOH) in implementing integrated community case management (iCCM) programs in the Democratic Republic of Congo, Malawi, Mozambique, Niger, and Nigeria. WHO contracted ICF to support grantee monitoring and evaluation (M&E) efforts, part of which was to conduct DQAs to enhance program monitoring and decision making. Grantee data were sourced from the iCCM data reported by community health workers (CHWs) and MOH staff in communities and facilities, so the DQAs were able to assess the quality of iCCM data and relevant aspects of the HMIS in each country. Results from the assessments informed recommendations to improve data collection and management.

The potential contribution of DQAs to data-driven decision making has been implied elsewhere [2-5]. The purpose of this paper is to describe how DQAs contributed to HMIS strengthening, specifically, the recommendations yielded by DQAs in each RAcE-supported programme area, the HMIS improvement efforts undertaken following the DQA, and the findings of subsequent DQAs in those areas.

METHODS

ICF created a mixed-methods DQA for iCCM data, described in detail elsewhere [6]. The assessment comprised a review of the data collection and management system at all levels (community, facility, district, and central), a component that traced data reported between levels, and key informant interviews. The DQA was applied twice in each RAcE site, which enables a general comparison of system-level attributes before and after the first DQA application. ICF obtained ethical approval from ICF's Institutional Review Board as well as from institutions in each country before conducting each DQA. This thematic meta-analysis of those DQAs does not constitute human subjects research.

For this qualitative assessment, we reviewed DQA reports to collate information about DQA recommendations and how they were addressed before a subsequent DQA, along with the findings of the second DQA. **Figure 1** illustrates a simple post-hoc theory of change for this analysis and a continuous improvement cycle that could be engendered with multiple DQAs.

We listed and compared system-wide assessment results between the two DQAs in each country. The system-level assessment measured data quality factors in these five domains: Monitoring and Evaluation Structure, Functions, and Capabilities; Indicator Definitions and Reporting Guidelines; Data Collection and Reporting Forms and Tools; Data Management Processes; and Links with the National Reporting System. We scored a series of indicators in each domain on a scale (1 = Low; 2 = Moderate; 3 = Strong) and then calculated an average score per domain. Online Resource 1 lists the indicators in each domain of the systems assessment of the DQA. We reported a relative, qualitative value for each DQA's findings in these descriptions and efforts to strengthen the HMIS in response to recommendations from the first DQA. We focused this qualitative, thematic analysis on a general comparison of findings between the two DQAs.

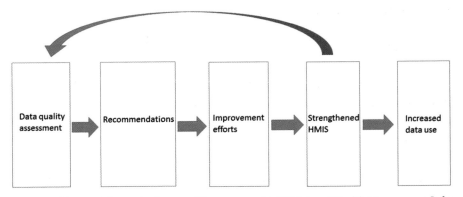

Figure 1. *Theory of change for Data quality assessments (DQAs) and Health Management Information System strengthening.*

RESULTS

The average interval between DQAs was 15 months. DQA timing depended on ICF, NGO, and MOH staff availability. While the short timeframe likely had an impact on the type of improvements that could be made (eg, "low-hanging fruit"), nonetheless, there is evidence that findings from the first DQA in each RAcE site stimulated grantee and MOH efforts to strengthen different aspects of the HMIS in each country (**Table 1**). A summary description of findings from this analysis is presented here.

The Democratic Republic of Congo

In the first DQA (2014), two domains scored lower than others: Indicator Definitions and Reporting Guidelines (moderately low) and Data Management Processes (very low). Regarding reporting, CHWs had seven forms to complete in a complex reporting process and their training seemed inadequate for the expectations of their service. There were no written guidelines for completing reporting forms or for aggregating and analyzing data at different levels of the health system. Written procedures for processing overdue or incomplete reports were not available at any level. Recommendations were to simplify the tools, translate the tools into the local language of CHWs, and bind reporting forms for easier maintenance and storage by CHWs. Recommendations also addressed weaknesses of the monitoring system including duplication of reporting at the health area level, and, specifically, holding refresher trainings for all staff involved in data collection.

In 2015, the system assessment showed stronger results in every area except the "indicator definitions and reporting guidelines" domain. Data collection tools had been modified and CHWs were comfortable using them although they reported that completing them was time consuming. There were still no written guidelines for completing forms. Recommendations included continuing to reinforce accurate reporting and extending the CHW pre-service training time devoted to data recording and reporting.

Malawi

In the first DQA (2014), two domains scored lower than others: Indicator Definitions and Reporting Guidelines (moderately low) and Data Management Processes (very low). Recommendations from that assessment focused on standardizing data reporting procedures, addressing late reports, missing

Table 1. *Summary of DQA recommendations, improvement efforts, and findings*

Country and first DQA year	Recommendations	Improvement efforts	Second DQA year and findings
Democratic Republic of Congo, 2014	-Address the weaknesses of the monitoring system, especially the duplication of reporting -Address the complexity of data collection tools -Translate tools into the local language of CHWs -Bind reporting forms for easier maintenance and storage *[Domains: Indicator Definitions and Reporting Guidelines, and Data Management Processes]*	Modified data collection tools	**2015 positive findings:** -Stronger results in all but one domain -CHWs were comfortable using reporting forms **Negative findings:** -No written guidelines for completing data reporting forms -Completing reporting forms is time consuming for CHWs
Malawi, 2014	-Standardize data reporting procedures -Address late reports, missing and implausible values, and incorrect aggregation -Conduct refresher trainings for CHWs and their supervisors *[Domains: Indicator Definitions and Reporting Guidelines, and Data Management Processes]*	-CHW and supervisor trainings on data collection and reporting -Job aid created to guide CHW reporting	**2016 positive findings:** -High scores in each domain -Trainings for CHWs and supervisors were conducted **Negative findings:** -Limited capacity in data management processes -No written reporting guidelines for district and central level -Supervisors did not spend much time on data quality -Lack of controls to prevent double counting and to identify people who do not follow referrals
Mozambique, 2015	Strengthen the reporting capacity of CHWs and supervisors Strengthen the supervision system Create standard protocols throughout the reporting system *[All domains were moderate or high.]*	M&E manual was updated to include information about managing data	**2016 positive findings:** iCCM data reporting system is well-established; all but one domain scored highly Regular CHW supervision visits occurred **Negative findings:** No process to track referrals No process to avoid double counting No systematic documentation of how data discrepancies were resolved

Table 1. Continued

Country and first DQA year	Recommendations	Improvement efforts	Second DQA year and findings
Niger, 2014	-Standardize and simplify CHW registers -Strengthen supervision by using a checklist -Provide written data management protocols for all levels of the reporting system *[Domains: Indicator Definitions and Reporting Guidance, Data Management Processes, and Links with the National Reporting System.]*	-Staff at all levels were trained on data reporting -Data collection process streamlined so that indicator points could be found on forms at each level -Registers revised to facilitate completion	**2015 positive findings:** -System assessment yielded moderate scores **Negative findings:** -Some supervisors did not have time for supervision -Reporting forms occasionally unavailable for CHWs -Could not integrate iCCM data with HMIS due to HMIS updating process
Nigeria (Abia State), 2015	-Create a data governance structure to clearly establish roles and responsibilities for iCCM data reporting at all levels of the system -Develop data reporting and management procedures at all levels and guidelines for how to complete reporting forms -Improve regular supervision Hold data review meetings and promote iCCM data use *[Domains: Indicator Definitions and Reporting Guidance, Data Management Processes, and Links with the National Reporting System.]*	-Refresher trainings for CHWs and supervisors -Development of an LGA summary reporting form to aggregate data from CHEWs and promote supervision of CHEWs at the LGA level -Held regular data review meetings	**2016 positive findings:** -High scores for all but one domain **Negative findings:** -Errors in aggregated data at supervisors' level -Written guidance for data reporting not available -iCCM data integration into HMIS under discussion
Nigeria (Niger State), 2015	-Organize additional trainings for CHWs -Hold data review meetings -Strengthen supervision -Create standard data management procedures *[Domain: Indicator Definitions and Reporting Guidelines]*	-Refresher training for supervisors -Processes to improve data use and quality established	**2016 positive findings:** Moderate scores Good understanding about iCCM data reporting at all levels well-established supervision system **Negative findings:** Data not used by CHWs or supervisors No written guidance for reporting data Data management responsibilities not well defined at upper levels of system

DQA – data quality assessment, CHW – community health worker, CHEW – community health extension worker, iCCM – integrated community case management, M&E – monitoring and evaluation, LGA – local government area and implausible values, and incorrect aggregation, and conducting refresher trainings for CHWs and their supervisors.

The second DQA (2016) yielded high scores in each domain; however, it also revealed several more areas for improvement. CHWs and their supervisors had been trained on data collection and reporting, and a new job aid in the register improved reporting guidance. However, CHWs had not been trained on data management. In addition, supervisors did not spend much time on checking data quality, as compared to checking performance of duties and supply stock. There were still no written guidelines on data reporting at central and district levels. Although supervision improved for CHWs that had poor data reporting, feedback to CHW supervisors about data reporting errors was not documented systematically and intervals between supervisory visits increased due to the number of CHWs to be visited. In addition, there remained a lack of controls for preventing double counting in the system and for identifying people who do not follow referrals. DHIS2 was introduced between the DQAs and that likely changed the reporting process in some ways.

Mozambique

The first DQA in Mozambique (2015) scored the system as "moderate" in all areas except for Links with National Reporting System, which scored highly. Recommendations included: strengthening the reporting capacity of CHWs and supervisors; strengthening the supervision system; and, creating standard protocols throughout the reporting system, including how to handle late submission of reports, missing values, incorrect aggregation, and implausible values.

The second DQA in 2016 found that the iCCM reporting system is well established and harmonized with the national reporting system, with designated staff at all levels to aggregate and review data. In addition, CHW reporting was found to be more consistent in this DQA. All domains scored highly except for data management processes. The M&E manual had been updated to include information about managing data after the first DQA. Supervision visits to CHWs occurred regularly. Additional supervision provided via phone or email was also implemented; however it was not documented. The main outstanding issues were the inability to track referrals and a lack of quality controls to avoid double-counting. In addition, there was no systematic documentation of how data discrepancies were resolved.

Niger

Part of the first DQA in Niger in 2014 could not be conducted due to incomplete CHW registers. Recommendations included standardizing and simplifying CHW registers, strengthening supervision by using a checklist, providing written data management protocols for all levels of the reporting system, and encouraging data use.

By the time of the second DQA in 2015, the quality of data in CHW registers had improved and the system assessment yielded moderate scores. Staff at all levels had been trained on data reporting and had a clear understanding of their roles in data reporting. The data collection process was streamlined after the first DQA, and the indicator data points reported in service delivery registers could be reported on forms to the next system level. Registers had been revised with pre-printed labels and more time was given to record keeping during CHW training. Nonetheless, challenges remained. Some supervisors did not have time for supervision duties, and reporting forms were occasionally unavailable for CHWs. There were challenges with integrating iCCM data into the HMIS because the HMIS was being updated. When CHWs felt overwhelmed with their work they could not prioritize data reporting.

Nigeria, Abia State

The first DQA in Abia State, Nigeria (2015) scored the system highly in "M&E Structure" and "Data Collection and Reporting Forms and Tools," but the other domains scored low, particularly "indicator definitions and reporting guidance." Recommendations included creating a data governance structure with clarified roles and responsibilities at all levels of the iCCM data reporting system, developing data reporting and management procedures at all levels, developing guidelines for completing the reporting forms, providing regular supervision, and promoting review and use of iCCM data through data review and feedback sessions.

The second DQA in 2016 showed high scores for all domains except "Indicator Definitions and Reporting Guidelines." Refresher trainings had been offered to CHWs and their supervisors. A summary form was developed and implemented at the local government area (LGA) level to improve data flow through the system and promote supervision at the LGA level. Regular data review meetings were implemented. However, some challenges remained. Errors were found after aggregation, suggesting that supervisors needed more training. Written guidelines for data reporting were not available at most system levels. At the time of the DQA, the state was in the process of determining which iCCM indicators would be included in the HMIS.

Nigeria, Niger State

The first DQA in Niger State, Nigeria in 2015 scored the system as "moderate" in all domains except "Indicator Definitions and Reporting Guidelines," which scored low. Recommendations included additional trainings for CHWs, holding data review meetings, strengthening supervision, and creating standard data management procedures.

The second DQA (2016) also yielded a moderate score for the "Reporting and Data Management System," but was weak in the "Link With National Reporting System" and "Indicator Definitions and Reporting Guidelines" domains. The DQA found a good understanding among staff at all levels of their roles in iCCM data collection and reporting; a well-established supervision system including joint supervision by local government areas, the State Ministry of Health, and grantee staff; and the use of national iCCM forms for data collection. There had been a refresher training for supervisors, and processes had been established to improve data use and quality including data display posters and supervision tools. However, iCCM data were not yet included in the HMIS at the State level, nor were there any written guidance for reporting data. In addition, responsibilities for data management were not defined well at upper levels of the system.

DISCUSSION

These examples indicate the utility of DQAs for stimulating HMIS improvements. Through support from RAcE, efforts were undertaken to improve data reporting systems and data quality between the DQAs in each area. While challenges remained, improvements in system capacity to support high quality data collection and reporting were evident at the time of the second DQAs.

Certainly, the ability of a health system to conduct DQAs, let alone act on the recommendations they produce, is dependent on the resources at hand. Programme resources are usually devoted to all that implementation requires, including training, supervision, and supplies, among other costs. Supervisors were tasked with both reviewing quality of care and quality of data, and with limited time often prioritized reviewing service delivery over data reporting. Rarely are resources devoted to system improvements to support data quality even though national and global policy makers and stakeholders rely on those data to direct further resource investment [6]. Areas supported by RAcE were uniquely positioned to benefit not only from iCCM programmes but also from strengthened data management systems. We presented evidence of health system strengthening efforts through (re)training staff and simplifying and streamlining data reporting. Future studies could attempt to link data quality to quality of care and system strengthening efforts supporting both.

RAcE-supported programmes had different histories with iCCM, eg, at the extremes, Malawi had been implementing an iCCM programme for eight years before RAcE started, while RAcE introduced iCCM for the first time in Nigeria. Thus, there were more challenges with establishing data management systems in Nigeria than there were in Malawi. But there was also an opportunity to instill an appreciation for data quality at all levels of the system there, even as the iCCM programme itself was being established. While in Malawi, challenges remained with ensuring adequate supervision for data quality. The service and associated reporting were not new but the need for some refinement to ensure data quality persisted.

Where the domain of data management processes had been found lacking in the first round of DQAs, this domain was generally found to be improved in the second round. However, the domain of "Indicator Definitions and Reporting Guidelines" remained challenging for most areas, in part because there were no written protocols or guidance for data reporting. Establishing these protocols would require leadership from the central level and a comprehensive dissemination strategy. Central level action on this topic may require additional advocacy and deserves internal and external investment. While some recommendations focused on central level leadership, the majority addressed practical issues at the CHW and facility levels. Increased use of data for decision making could lead naturally to greater attention to the quality of those data. Disseminating data reporting protocols throughout the health system could be accomplished through meetings at administrative levels and refresher trainings at service delivery levels. In addition, supervision protocols could incorporate attention to data quality directly.

There are some limitations to this analysis. In some cases, the assessments in each country were led by different staff and the scoring of consecutive assessments may differ, in part, for that reason. However, we focused here on qualitative evidence of HMIS strengthening activities, which should be free from interpretive bias. In addition, we likely did not report all system improvement efforts here. A lesson learned from the experiences of conducting two DQAs in each project area is the importance of documenting efforts to act on the first set of recommendations and linking that documentation to the second DQA report, so that there is a continuous record concerning data quality and related improvement efforts in a HMIS. Finally, the tool itself may be more suited to assessing the basics of a data management system rather than detailed refinements. We found that countries with systems needing basic supports scored lower than countries with established systems, but findings from the latter indicated significant room for improvement nonetheless. In addition, this DQA tool did not focus on data use, although that is clearly a concern (eg, see information presented about Abia State). Future efforts to assess data quality could specify a component related to data use, which is the ultimate purpose of a data system.

CONCLUSION

The DQAs conducted by ICF stimulated some efforts by NGOs and MOHs to improve iCCM data quality. Improvements were context-specific, but generally included the strengthening of staff skills, which is logically the place to begin data quality improvements. However, efforts to strengthen staff skills require system support to promote sustainable improvement. In addition to trainings, NGOs worked with MOHs to standardize or simplify reporting procedures. The importance of data quality for understanding health service performance and access to and equity in service delivery is clear, and additional resources are needed to improve data quality through system investments that support consistent data reporting. DQAs can serve as a collaborative and evidence-based activity to influence discussions of data quality and stimulate HMIS strengthening efforts.

Acknowledgements: *The authors would like to thank WHO, specifically Salim Sadruddin and Gunther Baugh, for their support to the RAcE Programme and to the data quality assessments. The authors also thank the ICF RAcE support team, including Helen Coelho, Kirsten Zalisk, and Yodit Fitigu. The authors are especially grateful for the hard work of Ministry of Health staff in the RAcE Programme countries and the RAcE grantee staff, including: Dr Jean Tony Bakukulu, Pascal Ngoy Leya, Gomezgani Jenda, Mr. Humphreys Nsona, Marla Smith, Dr Francisco Mbofana, Dr Aminata Tinni Konate, Grace Nganga, Dr Elvina Orji, Chinwoke Isiguzo, Dr Patrick B. Gimba, and Mr. Ibrahim Ndaliman. Disclaimer: The content of this publication is solely the responsibility of the authors and does not necessarily reflect the views or policies of World Health Organization or Global Affairs Canada. Ethics: ICF obtained ethical approval from ICF's Institutional Review Board as well as from institutions in each country before conducting each DQA. This thematic meta-analysis of those DQAs does not constitute human subjects research.*

Funding: *The evaluations were conducted by ICF under a contract with the World Health Organization (WHO) through funding by Global Affairs Canada.*

Authorship declaration: *Jennifer Yourkavitch conceptualized the study and drafted the manuscript. Debra Prosnitz and Samantha Herrera provided critical reviews and content edits on manuscript drafts.*

Competing interests: *The authors completed the Unified Competing Interest form at www.icmje.org/coi_disclosure.pdf (available upon request from the corresponding author), and declare no conflicts of interest.*

References

1 WHO. Data quality review: a toolkit for facility data quality assessment. Modules 1 - 3. Framework and metrics. Geneva: World Health Organization; 2017.

2 Lippeveld T, Sauerborn R, Bodart C. Design and implementation of health information systems. Geneva: World Health Organization; 2000.

3 AbouZahr C, Boerma T. Health information systems: the foundations of public health. Bull World Health Organ. 2005;83:578-83. Medline:16184276

4 Laínez YB, Wittcoff A, Mohamud AI, Amendola P, Perry HB, D'Harcourt E, et al. Insights from community case management data in six sub-Saharan African countries. Am J Trop Med Hyg. 2012;87:144-50. Medline:23136290 doi:10.4269/ajtmh.2012.12-0106

5 Guenther T, Laínez Y, Oliphant N, Dale M, Raharison S, Miller L, et al. Routine monitoring systems for integrated community case management programs: Lessons from 18 countries in sub-Saharan Africa. J Glob Health. 2014;4:020301. Medline:25520787 doi:10.7189/jogh.04.020301

6 Yourkavitch J, Zalisk K, Prosnitz D, Luhanga M, Nsona H. How do we know? An assessment of integrated community case management data quality in four districts of Malawi. Health Policy Plan. 2016;31:1162-71. Medline:27162235 doi:10.1093/heapol/czw047

Achievements and challenges of implementation in a mature iCCM programme: Malawi case study

Kirsten Zalisk[1], Tanya Guenther[2], Debra Prosnitz[1], Humphreys Nsona[3], Emmanuel Chimbalanga[4], Salim Sadruddin[5]

[1] ICF, Rockville, Maryland, USA
[2] Abt Associates Inc, Dili, Timor-Leste
[3] Republic of Malawi Ministry of Health, Lilongwe, Malawi
[4] Management Sciences for Health, Lilongwe, Malawi
[5] World Health Organization, Geneva, Switzerland

Background *Malawi has a mature integrated community case management (iCCM) programme that is led by the Ministry of Health (MOH) but that still relies on donor support. From 2013 until 2017, under the Rapid Access Expansion (RAcE) programme, the World Health Organization supported the MOH to expand and strengthen iCCM services in four districts. This paper examines Malawi's iCCM programme performance and implementation strength in RAcE districts to further strengthen the broader programme.*

Methods *Baseline and endline household surveys were conducted in iCCM-eligible areas of RAcE districts. Primary caregivers of recently-sick children under five were interviewed to assess changes in care-seeking and treatment over the project period. Health surveillance assistants (HSAs) were surveyed at endline to assess iCCM implementation strength.*

Results *Care-seeking from HSAs and treatment of fever improved over the project period. At endline, however, less than half of sick children were brought to an HSA, many caregivers reported a preference for providers other than HSAs, and perceptions of HSAs as trusted providers of high-quality, convenient care had decreased. HSA supervision and mentorship were below MOH targets. Stockouts of malaria medicines were associated with decreased care-seeking from HSAs. Thirty percent of clusters had limited or no access to iCCM (no HSA or an HSA providing iCCM services less than 2 days per week); 50% had moderate access (an HSA providing iCCM services 2 to 4 days per week; and 20% had high access (a resident HSA providing iCCM services 5 or more days per week). Moderate access to iCCM was associated with increased care-seeking from HSAs, increased treatment by HSAs, and more positive perceptions of HSAs compared to areas with limited or no access. Areas with high access to iCCM did not show further improvements above areas with moderate access.*

Conclusions *Availability of well-equipped and supported HSAs is critical to the provision of iCCM services. Additional qualitative research is needed to examine challenges and to inform potential solutions. Malawi's mature iCCM programme has a strong foundation but can be improved to strengthen the continuity of care from communities to facilities and to ultimately improve child health outcomes.*

Community health workers (CHWs), referred to as health surveillance assistants (HSAs), have been working in Malawi since the 1960s [1]. HSAs initially focused on health prevention and promotion activities, but in 2008, they began to take on curative activities when Malawi adopted integrated community case management (iCCM) and expanded the HSA workforce to help reach the country's goal of universal coverage of key child health interventions [1].

Integrated community case management (iCCM) is an equity-focused strategy that can improve access to and availability of essential treatment services for children by training, equipping, and supporting CHWs to manage – assess, classify, and treat – cases of malaria, pneumonia, and diarrhea among children under five years of age at the community level [2]. Communities farther than eight kilometers from a health facility or with difficult access because of geographical terrain or natural barriers were designated as being located in hard-to-reach areas (HTRAs) in Malawi and thus eligible for iCCM. District health management teams identified 3452 HTRAs [1], and iCCM rollout began in 2009 [3]. By September 2011, 2709 HTRAs had iCCM services [1]. Throughout its implementation, the iCCM programme in Malawi has benefited from the financial support received from global funding agencies and technical and logistical support from non-governmental organizations, primarily at the district or sub-district levels [4].

HSAs are centrally recruited and on the payroll of the MOH, but they are deployed to and stationed in the communities that they serve [5], providing iCCM services from their village clinics [6] in addition to providing other promotion and prevention activities at the community and health facility levels. HSAs are meant to serve approximately 1000 residents, but in practice they often have catchment areas of 2000 residents or more [5]. HSAs have at least 2 years of secondary school education and receive 10 weeks of pre-service training [1]. HSAs implementing iCCM complete six additional days of focused iCCM training [1] and are provided a drug box containing iCCM supplies. These supplies are replenished monthly at each HSA's supervisory health facility, where HSAs also submit their reporting forms and go for mentoring sessions with clinicians.

Responsibilities of HSAs providing iCCM services include assessing, classifying, and treating children ages 2-59 months who present with common childhood illnesses – fever, cough, fast or difficult breathing, diarrhea, and eye infections. HSAs also screen for malnutrition and identify signs of severe illnesses and refer those children, and other children with illness that they cannot treat, to a health facility. In addition to iCCM-related activities, HSAs are responsible for conducting health promotion, prevention, supervisory, surveillance, and assessment activities [1,7]. Because they are responsible for implementing numerous activities in their communities and at health facilities, they cannot provide iCCM services every day. At a minimum, HSAs are supposed to open their village clinics two days per week and provide iCCM services on demand outside of their village clinic hours [4].

The iCCM programme in Malawi is a mature one – having been rolled out almost a decade ago and scaled up to all districts. In 2013-2014, an independent national-level evaluation was conducted to assess the extent to which iCCM was associated with increases in care-seeking for childhood illness and accelerated declines in under-five mortality [8]. The evaluation showed that iCCM did not lead to an increase in care-seeking for childhood illness or impact under-five mortality, but it did show an increase in care-seeking from HSAs between 2010 and 2014 [8]. The evaluation further showed that iCCM implementation needed further strengthening. Among the 3717 surveyed HSAs trained in iCCM, 91% were providing iCCM services, but only 70% of those providing iCCM services lived in their catchment areas. Furthermore, during the three months prior to the assessment, 57% had key iCCM medicines in stock; 44% were supervised; and 58% received clinical mentorship, though results varied widely among the 27 districts included in the evaluation [4].

From 2013 until 2017, under the Rapid Access Expansion (RAcE) programme, the World Health Organization supported the MOH to expand and strengthen iCCM services in four districts: Dedza, Mzimba North, Ntchisi, and Ntcheu. When RAcE started, iCCM was well-established across Malawi, and more than 400 HSAs trained in iCCM were already working in the four project districts. The goal of RAcE Malawi programme, therefore, was to expand and strengthen iCCM by: (1) extending services to additional hard-to-reach areas, (2) supporting the shift in iCCM-eligible areas from areas more than 8 km to areas more than 5 km from a health facility, (3) introducing malaria rapid diagnostic tests (mRDTs) at the community level, and (4) updating the first-line antibiotic that HSAs use to treat children with pneumonia. RAcE also aimed to strengthen iCCM implementation by ensuring regular supply of iCCM medicines and other commodities, strengthening HSA supervision and mentorship, and increasing community awareness of and demand for iCCM services.

The purpose of this study is to examine iCCM implementation strength and programme performance in RAcE districts to further strengthen Malawi's mature iCCM programme.

METHODS

Study design

Two cross-sectional household surveys – the first at project baseline and the second at project endline – were conducted in HTRAs of the RAcE districts. The surveys used a 60×15 multi-stage cluster sampling methodology and targeted primary caregivers of children aged 2-59 months who had been sick with diarrhea, fever, or cough with difficult or fast breathing in the two weeks preceding the survey. The data were analyzed to assess changes in care-seeking and treatment over the project period. A survey of HSAs was conducted concurrently with the endline household survey to assess iCCM implementation strength. The objective of the HSA survey was to gain a better understanding of HSA background characteristics, activity levels, and support that they received to help interpret the household survey results. The baseline survey fieldwork was conducted in September 2013, and the endline survey fieldwork was conducted in August 2016.

Study area

The target population comprised the entire RAcE project area, iCCM-eligible areas more than 5 km from a health facility, of the four project districts. The primary sampling units were 2008 national census enumerations areas (EAs). All EAs located within 5 km of a health facility were excluded from the sampling frame before 60 EAs were randomly selected proportional to population size. The same EAs, or clusters, were included in both the baseline and endline surveys.

Within each cluster, all households were listed and those without children under five who had been sick with diarrhea, fever, or cough with difficult or fast breathing in the two weeks preceding the survey were removed from the list. The survey team then randomly selected 15 households from the list to visit and 15 back-up households. The survey team visited each selected household in the first group of 15 to obtain at least 5 interviews for each illness module – diarrhea, fever, and fast breathing – for a total of at least 15 interviews per cluster, or 300 interviews per illness across the project area. If the survey team did not obtain all necessary interviews, the survey team visited back-up households to fulfill the requirements for the cluster.

At each household, if there was an eligible child, the interviewer administered the questionnaire, including all applicable illness modules, to the caregiver of the eligible child. If multiple children were eligible, and they were sick with different illnesses, their caregiver was asked about each instance of illness. If multiple children in the household were eligible for the same illness, the interviewer randomly selected one of them and interviewed his or her caregiver. If there were multiple children selected for inclusion in the survey, and the children had different primary caregivers, each primary caregiver of the selected children was interviewed.

HSAs providing iCCM services in the 60 clusters selected for the household survey comprised the HSA survey target population. The clusters did not align perfectly with HSA catchment areas; therefore, if more than one HSA was providing iCCM services in a cluster, one eligible HSA was randomly selected for interview. If the survey team did not find an HSA eligible for interview in a cluster, they recorded the reason an iCCM-trained HSA was not available.

Survey questionnaire

The household survey questionnaire included seven modules: caregiver and household background information; caregivers' knowledge of iCCM activities in their community; caregivers' knowledge of childhood illness danger signs; household decision-making; and a module for each major childhood illness: fever, diarrhea, and fast breathing. The baseline questionnaire was also used at endline, but two questions were added to each illness module to gather information about reasons caregivers did not seek care at all or did not seek care from an HSA. The questionnaire was translated into the national language, Chichewa, and pretested during the enumerator and supervisor training. The survey took approximately one hour to administer in each household.

The HSA survey questionnaire contained eight sections, four of which were relevant to this study: HSA background, supervision, medicine and supplies, and iCCM activities and register review. The questionnaire was translated to Chichewa and pretested alongside the household survey questionnaire. The survey took approximately 30 minutes to administer to each HSA.

Data collection and analysis

Both household surveys and the HSA survey were conducted using paper questionnaires. All data were double-entered into CSPro (US Census Bureau, Suitland, Maryland, USA), cleaned, and imported into Stata version 14 (StataCorp LLC, College Station, Texas, USA) for analysis. The analyst further cleaned and coded the Stata data files for analysis and calculated point estimates and 95 percent confidence intervals for background, programme performance, and implementation strength indicators. Household survey indicators were calculated for baseline and endline, accounting for cluster effects. To test for statistically significant changes in indicators between baseline and endline, the analyst used a Pearson χ^2 test; all outcomes of interest were binary or categorical variables. Changes with p-values less than 0.05 were deemed statistically significant.

The household and HSA survey data were combined to also explore the relationship between iCCM access and caregiver perceptions of HSAs, care-seeking, and treatment coverage existed at endline. We classified the survey clusters as having limited or no access, moderate access, or high access to iCCM as follows: clusters with limited or no access did not have an HSA providing iCCM services or had an HSA who did not meet the MOH definition of functional (ie, managed at least one sick child case in past month and operated a village clinic at least two days per week); clusters with moderate access had an HSA who met the MOH definition of functional; and clusters with high access had an HSA who managed at least one sick child case in past month, operated a village clinic at least five days per week, and resided in catchment area.

RESULTS

Description of the sample

There were 1260 total cases of illness among 807 sick children in the baseline survey, and 1447 total cases of illness among 873 sick children in the endline survey (**Table 1**). There were 720 primary caregivers of sick children interviewed at baseline, and 783 primary caregivers of sick children interviewed at endline. The characteristics of the sick children and caregivers included in the baseline and endline surveys were similar, but at endline more children had fever in the two weeks preceding the survey (70%) compared to baseline (60%), and a larger percentage of caregivers were married at baseline (85%) compared to endline (75%).

Table 1. *Characteristics of sick children and their caregivers included in the surveys*

Child characteristic	Baseline % (95% CI)	Endline % (95% CI)	P-value
Sex of sick children included in survey:			
Male, %	51.4 (47.7-55.2)	49.8 (46.7-52.9)	0.491
Female, %	48.6 (44.8-52.3)	50.2 (47.1-53.3)	
Age (months) of sick children included in survey:			
2-11, %	22.1 (19.1-25.7)	22.1 (19.5-25.0)	0.724
12-23, %	24.7 (21.7-27.8)	24.6 (22.1-27.3)	
24-35, %	22.7 (19.9-25.7)	20.3 (17.5-23.4)	
36-47, %	17.2 (14.9-19.9)	20.3 (17.5-23.4)	
48-59, %	13.3 (10.7-16.3)	14.8 (12.6-17.3)	
Two-week history of illness of sick children included in survey:			
Had fever, %	59.9 (56.4-63.2)	70.7 (66.9-74.2)	<0.001
Had diarrhea, %	46.5 (43.7-49.2)	46.1 (43.3-48.9)	0.811
Had cough with difficult or fast breathing, %	58.5 (55.4-61.6)	60.0 (56.6-63.3)	0.461
Average number of illnesses, N	1.6	1.8	
Total number of sick children included in survey	**807**	**873**	
Cases of illness among sick children included in survey:			
Fever, N	455	571	
Diarrhea, N	364	387	
Cough with difficult or fast breathing, N	441	489	
Total number of sick child cases included in survey	**1260**	**1447**	
Caregiver characteristic:			
Age (years):			
15-24	35.8 (32.7-39.1)	40.2 (36.4-44.2)	0.306
25-34	44.3 (40.6-48.1)	40.0 (36.7-43.4)	
35-44	15.6 (13.3-18.1)	15.7 (13.2-18.6)	
45-76	4.3 (2.9-6.4)	4.1 (2.7-6.2)	
Mean age (years)	29	28	
Highest level of education:			
None	14.4 (11.1-18.6)	12.1 (9.5-15.4)	0.063
Primary,≤4 years	32.2 (28.4-36.3)	36.0 (31.8-40.5)	
Primary,≥5 year	43.5 (38.6-48.5)	39.1 (34.3-44.1)	
Secondary or higher	9.9 (7.6-12.7)	12.8 (10.2-15.8)	
Marital status:			
Currently married	84.9 (81.1-88.0)	75.4 (71.4-78.9)	<0.001
Not married but living with partner	3.8 (2.2-6.4)	9.2 (6.4-13.1)	
Not in union	11.4 (8.9-14.5)	15.5 (13.1-18.1)	
Total number of caregivers	**720**	**783**	

On average, caregivers reported that they lived between 9 and 10 km from the nearest health facility, and the majority of caregivers reported walking to the health facility in both surveys. It took caregivers approximately two hours, on average, to reach the nearest health facility at both baseline and endline, regardless of whether they walked or traveled by other means.

iCCM care-seeking and treatment coverage

The household survey analysis resulted in a mix of positive and negative trends (**Tables 2 to 4**). Caregiver awareness of the presence of the iCCM-trained HSA in their community was high at both baseline (90%) and endline (83%) but showed a downward trend over the project period ($P < 0.05$) (**Table 2**). Of those aware of an iCCM-trained HSA in their community, only one-third knew the HSA's role (ie, could name two or more curative services that the HSA performs) at both baseline and endine. In addition, perceptions of HSAs as trusted health care providers (82% at baseline and 70% at endline) who are convenient sources of care (60% at baseline and 47% at endline) and providers of quality services (68% at baseline and 58% at endline) all decreased over the project period ($P < 0.01$). Among caregivers who sought care from an HSA for at least one illness, there was no change in the percentage who found the HSA at first visit (approximately 85% at both baseline and endline). Seeking care from an appropriate health care provider remained consistent over the project period (66% at baseline and 70% at endline), but the percentage of children taken to an HSA increased from 26% at baseline to 33% at endline among all cases of illness and from 30% at baseline to 41% at endline among cases of illness for which any care was sought.

Sick child assessment indicators showed improvement over the project period (**Table 3**). The percentage of febrile children who had blood drawn for malaria testing increased overall from 36% at baseline to 59% at endline, and among cases for which care was sought from an HSA, the percentage increased from 0% at baseline to 62% at endine ($P < 0.001$). At baseline, HSAs were providing presumptive malaria treatment; mRDTs were introduced during RAcE. The percentage of children with cough and difficult or fast breathing who had their respiratory rate assessed for fast breathing increased overall from 26% at baseline to 39% at endline, and from 30% at baseline to 56% at endline among cases for which care was sought from an HSA ($P < 0.001$).

The overall percentage of febrile children with confirmed malaria who received artemisinin-based combination therapy (ACT) treatment increased from 84% at baseline to 92% at endline ($P < 0.05$), but the percentage who received ACT

Table 2. Household survey results: caregiver knowledge, perceptions, and care-seeking

Indicator	Baseline % (95% CI)	Endline % (95% CI)	Baseline N	Endline N	P-value
Caregiver knowledge of iCCM HSA in their community					
% aware of iCCM HSA	90.0 (83.3-94.2)	83.4 (74.7-89.6)	720	783	**0.036**
% know the role of the iCCM HSA*	35.0 (29.6-40.9)	34.0 (28.7-39.7)	648	653	0.793
Caregiver perceptions of iCCM services					
% view HSAs as trusted health care providers*	82.3 (77.5-86.2)	70.3 (62.8-76.8)	648	653	**<0.001**
% believe HSAs provide quality services*	68.4 (63.7-72.7)	57.6 (52.3-62.7)	648	653	**<0.001**
% cite HSAs as a convenient source of treatment*	59.6 (52.5-66.3)	47.3 (39.9-54.8)	648	653	**0.005**
% found HSA at first visit	86.5 (79.3-91.5)	84.0 (78.2-88.4)	230	312	0.541
Sick child care-seeking†					
% sought care from an appropriate provider	65.6 (60.7-70.1)	70.0 (65.4-74.2)	1260	1447	0.074
% sought care from HSA as first source, all sick child cases	25.7 (20.2-32.1)	33.4 (27.1-40.3)	1260	1447	**0.028**
% sought care from HSA as first source, sought any care	30.1 (23.7-37.4)	40.5 (33.2-48.2)	1076	1194	**0.012**

HSA – health surveillance assistant, iCCM – integrated community case management
* Asked only of caregivers who states that there was an iCCM-trained HSA in their community.
†Denominator for these indicators is sick child cases, not caregivers.

Table 3. Household survey results: sick child assessment

Indicator	Baseline % (95% CI)	Endline % (95% CI)	Baseline N	Endline N	P-value
Sick child assessment, all illness cases					
% febrile children tested for malaria	35.6 (30.0-41.7)	59.0 (53.7-64.2)	455	471	**<0.001**
% febrile children who received the malaria test result	96.9 (92.6-98.7)	97.3 (95.0-98.6)	162	337	0.761
% children with cough and difficult or fast breathing who were assessed for fast breathing	25.6 (20.6-31.4)	38.5 (33.5-43.7)	441	489	**<0.001**
Sick child assessment by HSA at village clinic, sought care from HSA					
% febrile children tested for malaria	0	61.7 (52.7-70.0)	126	196	**<0.001**
% febrile children who received the malaria test result	0*	98.4 (93.3-99.6)	0	121	–
% children with cough and difficult or fast breathing who were assessed for fast breathing	29.6 (21.0-40.0)	55.8 (46.0-65.1)	98	147	**<0.001**

CI – confidence interval, HSA – health surveillance assistant
*There were no cases or number of cases was too small to calculate a percentage.

Table 4. *Household survey results: Sick child treatment*

INDICATOR	BASELINE % (95% CI)	ENDLINE % (95% CI)	BASELINE N	ENDLINE N	P-VALUE
Sick child treatment, all illness cases					
% confirmed malaria cases that received ACT*	84.4 (77.0-89.8)	92.4 (87.9-95.4)	122	238	**0.032**
% confirmed malaria cases that received ACT promptly*,†	57.4 (47.5-66.7)	59.2 (52.5-65.7)	122	238	0.747
% diarrhea cases that received both ORS and zinc	18.4 (13.8-24.1)	21.2 (16.9-26.3)	364	387	0.398
% diarrhea cases that received ORS	70.1 (64.4-75.1)	68.5 (63.2-73.3)	364	387	0.664
% diarrhea cases that received zinc	21.4 (16.8-26.9)	24.0 (19.1-29.8)	364	387	0.439
Sick child treatment by HSA, all illness cases					
% confirmed malaria cases that received ACT*	0.0	34.9 (25.6-45.4)	122	238	**<0.001**
% confirmed malaria cases that received ACT promptly*,†	0.0	25.2 (17.8-34.4)	122	238	**<0.001**
% diarrhea cases that received both ORS and zinc	7.1 (4.3-11.6)	10.6 (7.2-15.4)	364	387	0.183
% diarrhea cases that received ORS	27.8 (21.5-35.1)	30.2 (23.6-37.8)	364	387	0.533
% diarrhea cases that received zinc	8.2 (5.1-13.0)	11.1 (7.7-15.9)	364	387	0.263
Sick child treatment by HSA, sought care from HSA					
% fever cases that received ACT*	59.7 (51.2-67.7)	54.4 (45.2-63.2)	124	184	0.446
% fever cases that received ACT promptly*,†	52.4 (43.9-60.8)	38.6 (30.6-47.3)	124	184	**0.026**
% confirmed malaria cases that received ACT*	0‡	89.0 (79.1-94.6)	0	91	–
% confirmed malaria cases that received ACT promptly*,†	0‡	64.8 (53.8-74.5)	0	91	–
% diarrhea cases that received both ORS and zinc	22.2 (14.1-33.3)	27.4 (20.0-36.3)	117	146	0.421
% diarrhea cases that received ORS	82.9 (72.8-89.8)	76.7 (68.5-83.3)	117	146	0.320
% diarrhea cases that received zinc	24.8 (16.2-36.0)	28.8 (21.3-37.6)	117	146	0.525

CI – confidence interval, ACT – artemisinin-based combination therapy, ORS – oral rehydration solution, HSA – health surveillance assistant
* Includes only children 5-59 months old, per national malaria treatment protocol.
† "Promptly" indicates the same day or next day after the onset of fever.
‡There were no cases or number of cases was too small to calculate a percentage.

treatment the same or next day following the onset of fever (prompt ACT treatment) was slightly less than 60% at baseline and did not change over the project period (**Table 4**). The percentage of confirmed malaria cases treated by an HSA increased from 0% at baseline to 35% at endline ($P < 0.001$), and the percentage of confirmed malaria cases treated promptly by an HSA increased from from 0% at baseline to 25% at endline ($P < 0.001$). Among those who sought care from an HSA, the percentage of confirmed malaria cases treated by an HSA was 89% at endline, and the percentage treated by an HSA promptly was 65%. The percentage of febrile children who received ACT treatment from an HSA, among those who sought care from an HSA remained between 50% and 60% over the project period, but the percentage that received ACT treatment promptly decreased from 52% to 39% over the same period ($P < 0.05$).

Although care-seeking from an appropriate health care provider for children with diarrhea was 64% at baseline and 70% at endline, the percentage of children with diarrhea who received both oral rehydration solution (ORS) and zinc, as specified in the national treatment guidelines, was only 18% at baseline and 21% at endline, and the findings were similar among those who sought care from an HSA: 22% at baseline and 27% at endline.

Implementation strength

Forty-seven of 60 survey clusters (78%) had iCCM-trained HSAs available for interview. The remaining 13 clusters either had an HSA in the community who was not trained in iCCM, or the HSA who had been providing iCCM services in the community had passed away or had been transferred and not replaced. Among those interviewed, the median age was 36 years (range: 29-59 years), and 30% were female. The majority (62%) had completed form four; 32% had completed form two; and 6% had only a primary school education. Four of five (83%) reported residing in their catchment area, and of those who did not, 63% lived less than 30 minutes from their village clinic. It took 21% of HSAs two or more hours to travel from their village clinic to their supervisory health facility; 43% between one hour to just under two hours; and 36% less than one hour. Seventy-five percent of HSAs usually traveled this distance by bicycle, 19% walked and 6% used a motorbike.

Almost 90% of the HSAs interviewed met the Malawi MOH's definition of a functional HSA (**Table 5**). Only 26%, however, resided in their catchment area, provided iCCM services during the month preceding the survey, and operated their village clinic for at least five days per week. HSAs, on average, managed 43.5 sick child cases during the month preceding the survey. Gaps in availability of essential iCCM medicines and supplies were common; 60% of HSAs interviewed had all essential iCCM medicines and diagnostics in stock on the day of the survey, and 36% reported stockouts of essential iCCM supplies lasting 7 or more days in the month preceding the survey. In the three months preceding the survey, two-thirds of HSAs reported being supervised and just over half reported receiving clinical mentorship.

Table 5. *Implementation strength (N = 47 HSAs)*

INDICATOR	ENDLINE
HSA residency and functionality (%, 95% CI)	
% HSAs living in catchment area	83.0% (68.8-91.5%)
% functional HSAs, according to MOH criteria*	89.4% (76.2-95.7%)
% functional HSAs, according to stricter criteria†	25.5% (14.8-40.4%)
HSA activity levels	
# days HSAs report operating village clinic per week	Mean: 3.3 (±2.2)
	Median: 2.0 (range: 0-7)
# days HSAs report working from health facility in past month	Mean: 5.5 (±5.4)
	Median: 4.0 (range: 0-31)
# sick child cases HSAs treated in the past month	Mean: 43.5 (±38.9)
	Median: 37.0 (range: 0-220)
Medicine and diagnostics availability (%, 95% CI)	
% HSAs with all essential iCCM supplies‡ and functional timer in stock on day of survey	59.6% (44.6%-73.0%)
LA (1×6) (1 packet)	87.2% (73.7-94.3%)
LA (2×6) (1 packet)	78.7% (64.2-88.4%)
mRDT (2 tests)	89.4% (76.2-95.7%)
Amoxicillin (1 blister pack)	78.7% (64.2-88.4%)
ORS (3 sachets)	78.7% (64.2-88.4%)
Paracetamol (6 tablets)	89.4% (76.2-95.7%)
Zinc (10 tablets)	83.0% (68.9-91.5%)
Eye antibiotic ointment (1 tube)	68.1% (53.0-80.1%)
Timer (1 functional)	87.2% (73.7-94.3%)
% HSAs reporting no stockouts of essential iCCM supplies‡ lasting 7 or more days in past month	63.8% (48.8-76.6%)
Supervision	
% HSAs supervised, including register review, during the past 3 months	66.0% (50.9-78.4%)
% HSAs mentored, including clinical observation, during the past 3 months	55.3% (40.5-69.2%)

MOH – Ministry of Health, CI – confidence interval, LA – lumenfantrine artesunate, ORS – oral rehydration solution, mRDT – malaria rapid diagnostic test, HSA – health surveillance assistant
*(1) have provided iCCM services in past month, and (2) report operating village clinic for at least two days per week
†(1) reside in their catchment area, (2) have provided iCCM services in past month, (3) report operating village clinic for at least five days per week.
‡LA, mRDTs, amoxicillin, ORS, and zinc.

The survey data showed that caregivers were more likely to have sought care from an HSA during the two weeks preceding the survey if the HSA in their community had ACTs in stock on the day of the survey (52%) compared to HSAs who did not have ACTs in stock (16%) ($P < 0.001$). We did not find similar relationships between care-seeking and any other iCCM medicines or supplies.

Twenty percent of clusters were classified as having high access to iCCM; 50% moderate access, and 30% limited or no access. We found significant differences between clusters with limited or no access to iCCM and those with moderate or high access (**Table 6**). Differences did not exist, however, between clusters with moderate access and high access. For example, only one quarter of caregivers in clusters with limited or no access to iCCM viewed HSAs as convenient sources of care, whereas more than half of caregivers in clusters with moderate or high access found HSAs to be convenient. Furthermore, only 13% of sick child cases were brought to an HSA as a first source of care in clusters with limited or no access to iCCM, but approximately 40% of sick child cases were brought to an HSA as a first source of care in clusters with moderate or high access to iCCM.

DISCUSSION

The household survey findings showed that there were population-level improvements over the project period. At endline, a greater proportion of caregivers took their sick children to HSAs for treatment; a greater proportion of children with fever were assessed for malaria and, in turn, received ACTs only if they were confirmed to have malaria; and a greater proportion of children with cough and difficult or fast breathing were assessed for high respiratory rate for their age.

Care-seeking from an appropriate provider, however, did not increase over the project period; the increase in care-seeking from HSAs was offset by a decrease in care-seeking from other health care providers. A 2013-2014 national-level evaluation of Malawi's iCCM programme also found no change in care-seeking from an appropriate provider as iCCM was introduced in Malawi, noting (1) that care-seeking had increased substantially for malaria, pneumonia, and diarrhea during the years just prior to the introduction of iCCM, and (2) that although care-seeking from HSAs increased during the evaluation period, care-seeking from public health facilities decreased in parallel [8].

Other studies of established iCCM programmes in sub-Saharan countries found variable results related to care-seeking. In Rwanda, a study comparing national-level data from the health management information system for a

Table 6. *Select household survey results by iCCM access*

INDICATOR	iCCM ACCESS*			P-VALUE
	Limited/none % (95% CI)	Moderate % (95% CI)	High % (95% CI)	
Caregiver perceptions of iCCM services				
% know the role of the iCCM HSA†	22.9 (15.4-32.6)	36.4 (29.7-43.8)	42.8 (29.9-56.7)	0.032
% view HSAs as trusted health care providers†	45.8 (36.9-55.0)	78.4 (70.8-84.5)	82.4 (57.3-94.3)	0.001
% believe HSAs provide quality services†	44.7 (36.1-53.6)	61.5 (55.0-67.7)	64.9 (53.3-75.0)	0.005
% cite HSAs as a convenient source of treatment†	24.6 (16.2-35.4)	58.8 (49.0-68.0)	52.8 (37.6-67.5)	<0.001
% found HSA at first visit	81.6 (66.8-90.7)	81.8 (73.6-87.9)	90.8 (83.0-95.2)	0.169
Number of caregivers	236	386	161	
Sick child care-seeking‡				
% sought care from an appropriate provider	62.9 (54.5-70.6)	75.1 (68.6-80.7)	68.1 (60.5-74.9)	0.030
% sought care from HSA as first source, all sick child cases	13.0 (8.7-19.1)	43.5 (34.3-53.3)	38.9 (26.4-53.1)	<0.001
% sought care from HSA as first source, sought any care	16.2 (10.7-23.7)	51.8 (41.4-62.0)	47.9 (34.0-62.2)	<0.001
Sick child treatment				
% diarrhea and confirmed malaria cases treated correctly by any provider	34.2 (27.3-41.9)	36.3 (29.8-43.2)	36.4 (27.9-45.8)	0.905
% diarrhea and confirmed malaria cases treated correctly by an HSA	4.9 (1.3-17.2)	20.3 (14.0-28.6)	22.3 (12.5-36.6)	0.028
% diarrhea and confirmed malaria cases treated correctly by an HSA, sought care from HSA	27.3 (9.9-56.2)	43.1 (34.0-52.6)	47.2 (29.3-65.9)	0.421
Number of sick child cases	437	712	298	

HSA – health surveillance assistant, CI – confidence interval, iCCM – integrated community case management
*Limited/none: no HSA providing iCCM services in cluster or HSA does not meet MOH definition of functional; moderate: HSA managed at least one sick child case in past month and operates village clinic at least 2 d/week (met MOH definition of functional); high: HSA managed at least one sick child case in past month, operates village clinic at least 5 d/week, and resides in catchment area.
†Asked only of caregivers who stated that there was an iCCM-trained HSA in their community.
‡Denominator for these indicators is sick child cases, not caregivers.

period just prior to the start of iCCM implementation and a period one year later found a decrease in sick child visits to health facilities [9]. During the same period, the number of pneumonia and diarrhea treatments by CHWs increased; however, the study did not look at overall care-seeking from an appropriate provider [9]. In Uganda, an evaluation of iCCM in eight districts showed the proportion of CHW-provided sick child treatments increased while the proportion of facility-provided treatments decreased, but the total number of treatments provided by both CHWs and facilities increased [10]. A randomized control study in the Oromia region of Ethiopia found that though good quality iCCM services were available through health posts, the majority of caregivers did not use iCCM services and levels of care-seeking outside the homes remained low two years after iCCM was introduced [11,12]. Another evaluation comparing areas with iCCM and areas without iCCM in Mozambique found that most caregivers used iCCM services if they were available in their community, rather than seek care from a health facility and that overall levels of care-seeking were higher in areas with iCCM services [13]. These results indicate that factors influencing health care-seeking behaviour must be investigated while also having a thorough understanding of the local context, including community demand and need vis-à-vis the design of the iCCM programme.

In Malawi, the household surveys indicated that majority of caregivers lived far – two hours on average – from the nearest health facility. Furthermore, health facility staff can see 200 to 300 patients per day in Malawi, which can mean long wait times and overburdened staff who have little time to spend with individual patients. Increased care-seeking from well-trained, well-supplied, and available HSAs, therefore, benefits not only sick children and their caregivers but also facility staff.

Findings from the household surveys that merit further investigation include the proportion of caregivers who seek care from HSAs and caregiver perceptions of HSAs. Less than half of sick child cases in iCCM-eligible areas were brought to an HSA for care at endline. Seeking care at public health facilities was just as common as seeking care from HSAs in the surveyed HTRAs. Furthermore, among cases of illness for which care was not sought from an HSA at endline, the majority of caregivers reported a preference for a provider other than an HSA. The household survey did not capture reasons for caregiver provider preferences.

Caregiver perceptions of HSAs as trusted sources of high-quality, convenient care decreased over the project period, and perceptions of HSAs a convenient sources of care at endline were particularly low (47%). Perceptions of HSAs were notably more positive in clusters with moderate or high access to iCCM services but still indicated room for improvement, particularly around providing convenient, high-quality care.

HSA availability likely played a large part in the care-seeking and HSA perception results. HSA survey results indicated that iCCM services were not regularly available in many HTRAs. At endline, iCCM-trained HSAs were not found in almost one quarter of surveyed clusters. Because of numerous HSA post vacancies, RAcE project activities could not be implemented in all targeted iCCM-eligible areas as planned, and as of March 2017, the government had suspended new HSA recruitment due to lack of funds [14]. HSA posts were vacant for a variety of reasons including promotions, transfers, retirement, and deaths. Other HSAs were usurped by health facilities to assist with their heavy workloads or became data clerks at health facilities. Some district managers did not allow HSAs who were not residents of their catchment areas to attend iCCM trainings or to provide iCCM services.

HSA residency has been a long-standing issue in Malawi's iCCM programme. HSAs are centrally recruited and may be assigned to a district other than where they are from or where their family lives, which has been reported to negatively affect HSA retention and availability within their assigned communities [6]. HSAs who do not reside in their catchment areas often live elsewhere because suitable accommodations are not available, they have spouses who work in market towns or live with their families [6,15]. A national cellphone survey of HSAs in Malawi found that only 70% of HSAs lived in their catchment areas [4], a result similar to our findings when clusters without HSAs providing iCCM services are included. In one study about HSA selection and assignment, researchers found that limited village clinic hours, which result from the numerous other responsibilities that HSAs have, were most pronounced among communities that have non-resident HSAs [1].

HSA availability is also affected by their tremendous workload. HSAs are officially responsible for performing 262 tasks, of which iCCM-related tasks are just a small proportion [7]. This is large number of tasks in and of itself, but a recent HSA workload analysis found that HSAs were actually being assigned more than 500 tasks [7]. The analysis also showed that 42% of an HSA's official tasks were added through task-shifting guidelines implemented in 2014 and that 21% of tasks could be shifted to others at the community level [7].

Most HSAs surveyed were functional, according to the MOH definition, but only one in four were living in their catchment area, actively providing iCCM services during the month preceding the survey and operating their village clinic at least five days a week. Therefore, across all surveyed clusters, 70% of the target population had access to an HSA providing iCCM at least 2 days per week, but only 20% had access to a resident HSA providing iCCM at least 5 days per week.

Although HSAs spend a limited amount of time operating their village clinics on a weekly basis and a sizable proportion of caregivers do not seek care from HSAs, HSAs are being accessed for treatment. On average HSAs saw more than 10 cases per week or 44 cases per month, which is similar to findings from another study conducted in Malawi [4].

Stockouts of essential iCCM supplies may have also affected caregivers' perceptions of HSAs, and consequently, care-seeking from HSAs. Despite programme support through RAcE and supply chain support tools such as c-Stock, HSAs still experienced shortages of iCCM medicines and supplies that limited their ability to provide high-quality care. A previous study acknowledged that limited district budgets and the inability to adequately forecast also contributed to iCCM programme stockouts in Malawi [1]. RAcE field monitoring data showed that health facilities used iCCM medicines meant for village clinics, particularly amoxicillin dispersible tablets, which were not being procured by the government. Others have also reported that iCCM supplies have been used by health facility staff in Malawi [14]. Efforts to identify and address supply chain management system issues at facility and HSA levels are needed.

Both the national iCCM evaluation and the RAcE HSA survey found supervision and clinical mentorship levels to be below the 80% MOH targets. Distances to HSAs' village clinics and transportation gaps are key barriers [16]. Numerous attempts have been made to address these issues with limited sustained success, but the MOH is currently developing an integrated approach to HSA supervision so that supporting HSAs is less demanding of over-stretched facility staff and more efficient [14]. More regular, high-quality supervision and mentorship could lead to better case management, which could in turn affect caregivers' perceptions of HSAs and care-seeking from HSAs. The quality of supervision provided to HSAs, however, is unknown and should be assessed; one study suggested that improving the quality of supervision had greater impact on quality of care than increasing only the frequency [17].

The household survey results also showed some suboptimal treatment patterns. Most notably HSA treatment of diarrhea with both ORS and zinc was low at baseline and did not improve during the project. Provision of zinc was the limiting factor in providing appropriate treatment; approximately two and a half times as many diarrhea cases received ORS compared zinc, regardless of source of care. The HSA survey showed, however, that most HSAs had zinc in stock at the time of the survey, and few reported stockouts of a week or longer in the month before the survey. The reasons for low provision of zinc by HSAs are unclear, but the trend likely went unnoticed by routine iCCM programme monitoring because the HSA monthly reporting forms do not include separate fields to indicate treatment with zinc and ORS. Further qualitative follow-up with HSAs, health facility staff, and community members is needed to understand the barriers to appropriate diarrhea treatment.

Moderate access to iCCM services was associated with increased care-seeking from HSAs, increased correct treatment of sick child cases by HSAs, and more positive perceptions of services provided by HSAs compared to areas with limited or no access. Areas with high access to iCCM did not show further improvements above areas with moderate access. These findings suggest that although HSAs are used by caregivers if they are available, as the iCCM programme is currently implemented, increasing the number of days HSAs spend in their village clinics may not lead to increased care-seeking from HSAs and treatments provided by HSAs that one might expect. This is not to say, however, that HSAs should not be more consistently available to provide iCCM services in their communities, but that this change alone may not be sufficient to improve child health outcomes. Opportunities exist to improve this and other aspects of the iCCM programme, and the MOH is working on some of these aspects.

Based on learning from the RAcE project, the MOH rolled out new HSA supervision tools and training materials and has recruited and trained additional HSA supervisors. The MOH plans to expand these efforts throughout the country and also to orient health center staff so that they can provide better supervision and support to the iCCM programme. The MOH has also developed a National Community Health Strategy [18] that aims to make community-level services more accessible and improve community awareness and demand for iCCM services and national guidelines to clarify the roles and responsibilities of HSAs and other community-level cadres who perform health-related work [7].

The MOH and its development partners could also strengthen the iCCM programme by filling more HSA posts, training and supporting more existing HSAs to provide iCCM services, ensuing iCCM supplies are more consistently available, and reducing HSAs' workloads. The current workloads of HSAs, particularly those providing iCCM, is not appropriately aligned with their levels of compensation and support. Further, HSA workloads fluctuate in sub-national areas according to needs of donor-funded projects. The MOH should consider revising HSA job descriptions to account for evidence-based needs, effectiveness of interventions, and capacity of HSAs to deliver services effectively and with greater availability to communities.

Limitations of the study

First, the household surveys provide estimates for the four RAcE project districts as a whole; they were not powered to provide district-specific estimates. Second, RAcE project activities were not implemented in all iCCM-eligible areas of the project districts because several HSA posts were vacant or did not have HSAs trained in iCCM and operating a village clinic. Third, the sampling frame was based on census EAs, which did not align perfectly with HTRAs, so some EAs included in the sampling frame may have included areas not eligible for iCCM, or an active iCCM-trained HSA may have been serving only a subset of an EA at the time of the endline survey. Lastly, caregiver recall of malaria diagnostic testing has been shown to be poor, which could have affected the malaria assessment and treatment indicators calculated [19].

CONCLUSIONS

Availability of well-equipped and supported HSAs is critical to provision of iCCM services in eligible communities. Additional qualitative research is needed to examine the challenges and to inform potential solutions. Malawi's mature iCCM programme has a strong foundation and the potential for improvement to strengthen the continuity of care from communities to facilities and to ultimately improve child health outcomes.

Acknowledgments: *We thank the staff of Save the Children Malawi, the RAcE Malawi grantee, and the Malawi National Statistic Office for their contributions to the RAcE household and HSA surveys. We also thank Tiyese Chimuna of UNICEF for her inputs to this manuscript.*

Ethical approval: *Both the household and health surveillance assistant survey protocols received ethical approval from Save the Children's Ethics Review Committee and Malawi's National Health Sciences Research Committee. The household survey also received approval from ICF's Institutional Review Board.*

Disclaimers: *The opinions expressed in this manuscript are those of the authors and do not necessarily reflect the views of the World Health Organization or Global Affairs Canada.*

Funding: This study was supported by the World Health Organization's Rapid Access Expansion programme funded by Global Affairs Canada.

Authorship contributions: *KZ conceptualized the study and drafted the manuscript. TG, DP, HN, EC, and SS provided critical reviews and content edits on manuscript drafts.*

Competing interests: *The authors completed the Unified Competing Interest form at www.icmje.org/coi_disclosure.pdf (available upon request from the corresponding author), and declare no conflicts of interest.*

References

1 Nsona H, Mtimuni A, Daelmans B, Callaghan-Koru JA, Gilroy K, Mgalula L, et al. Scaling up integrated community case management of childhood illness: update from Malawi. Am J Trop Med Hyg. 2012;87:54-60. Medline:23136278 doi:10.4269/ajtmh.2012.11-0759

2 World Health Organization, United Nations Children's Fund. Joint Statement: Integrated Community Case Management (iCCM). Geneva and New York: United Nations Children's Fund, 2012.

3 Fullerton J Sr, Auruku A. USAID Malawi Community Case Management Evaluation: Global Health Technical Assistance Project. Washington DC: 2011.

4 Heidkamp R, Hazel E, Nsona H, Mleme T, Jamali A, Bryce J. Measuring implementation strength for integrated community case management in Malawi: Results from a national cell phone census. Am J Trop Med Hyg. 2015;93:861-8. Medline:26304921 doi:10.4269/ajtmh.14-0797

5 Rodriguez DC, Banda H, Namakhoma I. Integrated community case management in Malawi: an analysis of innovation and institutional characteristics for policy adoption. Health Policy Plan. 2015;30 Suppl 2:ii74-83. Medline:26516153 doi:10.1093/heapol/czv063

6 Zembe-Mkabile WZ, Jackson D, Sanders D, Besada D, Daniels K, Zamasiya T, et al. The 'community' in community case management of childhood illnesses in Malawi. Glob Health Action. 2016;9:29177. Medline:26823049 doi:10.3402/gha.v9.29177

7 Government of Malawi. Role Clarity Guidelines for Community Health Workers 2017-2022. In: Health Mo, editor. 2017.

8 Amouzou A, Kanyuka M, Hazel E, Heidkamp R, Marsh A, Mleme T, et al. Independent evaluation of the integrated community case management of childhood illness strategy in Malawi using a national evaluation platform design. Am J Trop Med Hyg. 2016;94:574-83. Medline:26787158 doi:10.4269/ajtmh.15-0584

9 Mugeni C, Levine AC, Munyaneza RM, Mulindahabi E, Cockrell HC, Glavis-Bloom J, et al. Nationwide implementation of integrated community case management of childhood illness in Rwanda. Glob Health Sci Pract. 2014;2:328-41. Medline:25276592 doi:10.9745/GHSP-D-14-00080

10 Mubiru D, Byabasheija R, Bwanika JB, Meier JE, Magumba G, Kaggwa FM, et al. Evaluation of integrated community case management in eight districts of central Uganda. PLoS One. 2015;10:e0134767. Medline:26267141 doi:10.1371/journal.pone.0134767

11 Amouzou A, Hazel E, Shaw B, Miller NP, Tafesse M, Mekonnen Y, et al. Effects of the integrated community case management of childhood illness strategy on child mortality in Ethiopia: a cluster randomized trial. Am J Trop Med Hyg. 2016;94:596-604. Medline:26787148 doi:10.4269/ajtmh.15-0586

12 Shaw B, Amouzou A, Miller NP, Tsui AO, Bryce J, Tafesse M, et al. Determinants of utilization of health extension workers in the context of scale-up of integrated community case management of childhood illnesses in Ethiopia. Am J Trop Med Hyg. 2015;93:636-47. Medline:26195461 doi:10.4269/ajtmh.14-0660

13 Guenther T, Sadruddin S, Finnegan K, Wetzler E, Ibo F, Rapaz P, et al. Contribution of community health workers to improving access to timely and appropriate case management of childhood fever in Mozambique. J Glob Health. 2017;7:010402. Medline:28400951 doi:10.7189/jogh.07.010402

14 ICF. The Sustainability of Integrated Community Case Management in Malawi: A Synthesis Report. 2017.

15 Norwegian Agency for Development Cooperation. Local Perceptions, Participation and Accountability in Malawi's Health Sector. Oslo, Norway: Norad, 2013 February 2013. Report No.

16 Callaghan-Koru JA, Gilroy K, Hyder AA, George A, Nsona H, Mtimuni A, et al. Health systems supports for community case management of childhood illness: lessons from an assessment of early implementation in Malawi. BMC Health Serv Res. 2013;13:55. Medline:23394591 doi:10.1186/1472-6963-13-55

17 Hill Z, Dumbaugh M, Benton L, Kallander K, Strachan D, ten Asbroek A, et al. Supervising community health workers in low-income countries–a review of impact and implementation issues. Glob Health Action. 2014;7:24085. Medline:24815075 doi:10.3402/gha.v7.24085

18 Malawi GotRo. National Community Health Strategy 2017-2022. 2017.

19 Maternal and Child Health Integrated Program (MCHIP). Indicator Guide for monitoring and evaluating integrated community case management. 2013.

Home visits by community health workers for pregnant mothers and newborns: coverage plateau in Malawi

Tanya Guenther[1]*, Humphreys Nsona[2], Regina Makuluni[3], Mike Chisema[3], Gomezgani Jenda[4], Emmanuel Chimbalanga[5], Salim Sadruddin[6]

[1] Abt Associates, Dili, Timor-Leste
[2] IMCI unit, Ministry of Health, Lilongwe, Malawi
[3] District Health Office, Ntcheu, Malawi
[4] Save the Children Malawi, Lilongwe, Malawi;
[5] Management Sciences for Health (MSH), Lilongwe, Malawi
[6] World Health Organization, Geneva, Switzerland
* At the time this paper was first drafted, Ms. Guenther was employed by Save the Children, USA.

Background Home visits by community health workers (CHWs) during pregnancy and soon after delivery are recommended to improve newborn survival. However, as the roles of CHWs expand, there are concerns regarding the capacity of community health systems to deliver high effective coverage of home visits. The WHO's Rapid Access Expansion (RAcE) program supported the Malawi Ministry of Health to align their Community-Based Maternal and Newborn Care (CBMNC) package with the latest WHO guidelines and to implement and evaluate the feasibility and coverage of home visits in Ntcheu district.

Methods A population-based survey of 150 households in Ntcheu district was conducted in July-August 2016 after approximately 10 months of CBMNC implementation. Thirty clusters were selected proportional-to-size using the most recent census. In selected clusters, five households with mothers of children under six months of age were randomly selected for interview. The Health Surveillance Assistants (HSAs) providing community-based services to the same clusters were purposively selected for a structured interview and register review.

Results Less than one third of pregnant women (30.7%; 95% confidence interval CI = 21.7%-41.5%) received a home visit during pregnancy and only 20.7% (95% CI = 13.0%-29.4%) received the recommended two visits. Coverage of postnatal visits was even lower: 11.4% (95%CI = 6.8%-18.5%) of mothers and newborns received a visit within three days of delivery and 20.7% (95%CI = 12.7%-32.0%) received a visit within the first eight days. Reaching newborns soon after delivery requires timely participation of the family and/or health facility staff to notify the HSA – yet only 42.9% (95% CI = 33.4%-52.9%) of mothers reported that the HSA was informed of the delivery. Coverage of postnatal home visits among those who informed the HSA was significantly higher than among those in which the HSA was not informed (46.7% compared to 1.3%; $P = 0.00$). Most HSAs had the necessary equipment and supplies and were active in CBMNC: 83.9% (95% CI = 70.2%-97.6%) of HSAs had pregnancy home visits and 77.4% (95% CI = 61.8%-93.0%) had postnatal home visits documented in their registers for the previous three months.

Conclusions We found low coverage of home visits during pregnancy and soon after delivery in a well-supported program delivery environment. Most HSAs were conducting home visits, but not at the level needed to reach high coverage. These findings were similar to previous studies, calling into question the feasibility of the current visitation schedule. It is time to re-align the CBMNC package with what the existing platform can deliver and identify strategies to better support HSAs to implement home visits to those who would benefit most.

In Malawi, 15 000 (42%) of the estimated 36 000 under-five deaths in 2016 occurred in the first month of life [1]. The majority of these deaths are due to preventable and/or treatable causes, namely complications at birth, complications of prematurity, and infection [1]. Close to three-quarters of newborn deaths occur within the first week of delivery and this period is of great risk for mothers as well [2,3]. Prompt health checks for recently delivered women and newborns in the community can facilitate timely identification and management of complications as well as improve uptake of recommended newborn care practices [2-5].

In 2009, the World Health Organization (WHO) and the United Nations International Children's Emergency Fund (UNICEF) released a joint statement encouraging governments in low-income countries to introduce postnatal home visits for newborns to reduce mortality, including at least two visits within the first week after delivery with the first visit occurring within 48 hours of birth [3]. These recommendations were based on several studies in high mortality settings in Bangladesh, India and Pakistan that had shown promising results on a small scale under research conditions [6-8]. Building on the release of the joint statement and subsequent 2013 WHO guidance on postnatal care, countries started developing policies and programs and by 2016 more than 50 countries had a policy promoting home visits for newborns [9,10]. However, experience of implementing postnatal home visits within existing government systems at scale has shown major challenges to reaching high coverage of postnatal home visits [5,11,12]. A recent review of postnatal home visits in 11 countries in Africa and Asia that operated programs at scale found that for most countries, coverage of a postnatal home visit within 48 hours was below 10% and no country achieved greater than 20% [11].

Malawi was an early adopter of pregnancy and postnatal home visits as part of its strategy to reduce maternal and newborn mortality. Starting in 2007, the Ministry of Health (MOH), in partnership with Save the Children in Malawi (SC), UNICEF, WHO and other partners, designed and piloted a Community Based Maternal and Newborn Care (CBMNC) package delivered through CHWs referred as Health Surveillance Assistants (HSAs). The HSAs were trained to conduct three home visits during pregnancy (one per trimester) and three postnatal home visits within the first eight days of delivery (Day 1, Day 3 and Day 8). The CBMNC package was piloted in three districts (Chitipa, Dowa and Thyolo) starting in 2008 with support from Saving Newborn Lives (SNL), a project of SC. By 2011, the package was scaled up to 17 districts and 1781 HSAs had been trained in CBMNC with support from UNICEF, WHO, United States Agency for International Development (USAID) and Norwegian Church. Evaluation in the three pilot districts found that 36% of women received one or more home visits during pregnancy and 11% of newborns received a postnatal home visit within the first three days, and that mothers and babies in the richest quintile were more likely to receive home visits [5,13]. Despite the low coverage, an economic analysis indicated that the program would be cost-effective if coverage could be improved by increasing activity levels of HSAs [14]. In 2014, SC Malawi, under the WHO's integrated Community Case Management (iCCM) Rapid Access Expansion (RAcE) program, supported the Malawi MOH to design, implement and evaluate a revised CBMNC package in Ntcheu district. In this paper, we present an evaluation of the coverage of CHW home visits during pregnancy and postnatal period and explore household and CHW factors associated with coverage of home visits.

EVALUATION SETTING AND DESIGN

In 2014, the CBMNC package was revised to align with the *WHO Caring for the newborn at home* package [15]. The Integrated Management of Childhood Illness (IMCI) unit of the MOH led the consultative process that included members of the Reproductive Heath Directorate of the MOH and other implementing partners, with financial and technical support from WHO and SC Malawi through the RAcE program. Under the revised CBMNC package, the number of home visits during pregnancy was reduced from three to two, while the number of recommended postnatal home visits remained the same (three visits within the first eight days). During pregnancy home visits, HSAs convey messages regarding the importance of antenatal care and refer women to the health facility for antenatal care, preparing for facility delivery, and recognition and care-seeking for danger signs. During postnatal home visits, scheduled

for Day 1 (within 24 hours of delivery), Day 3 and Day 8, the HSAs assess
the mother and baby for signs of illness and refer them to an appropriate
facility, if required, weigh the baby, and help the mother with early and
exclusive breastfeeding and keeping the baby warm. Further details on the
timing and tasks of each HSA home visit are given in Table S1 in the **Online
Supplementary Document**.

Implementation of CBMNC in Ntcheu district

The revised CBMNC package was introduced in Ntcheu district. Ntcheu
district was selected by the MOH as it was an area where the RAcE iCCM
program was well-established, had a strong district health office, and was
the site for a linked operations research study testing the feasibility of outpatient management of possible serious bacterial infections in infants under
two months of age. Ntcheu is located in central Malawi, along the border
with Mozambique, and had an estimated population of 588 038 and 24 835
expected births in 2016 [16]. All HSAs in the district were targeted for training in the package. The CBMNC training was six days and delivered under
the leadership of the Ntcheu district maternal and newborn coordinator by
nationally recognized trainers who had completed a 'training of trainers'
course. A total of 299 HSAs were trained between September 2015 and May
2016 through 12 sessions with between 24 and 30 participants per session.
Most HSAs (85%; 253/299) had completed training by December 2015. Senior
HSAs/Cluster Supervisors as well as district staff were expected to supervise HSAs in CBMNC and they were trained on the package together with
HSAs. However, focused training on supervision of CBMNC and provision
of supervision checklists for CBMNC were not provided to senior HSAs until
November 2016 (after the evaluation). The HSAs were equipped with weigh-
ing scales, thermometers, respiratory rate timers, counseling cards, referral
slips and registers to document home visits, and monthly reporting forms.
Overall, 36 of the 38 health facilities in Ntcheu were providing CBMNC services following the training, with the majority having all associated HSAs
trained in the package, except for the district hospital catchment areas where
about half of the HSAs completed CBMNC training.

Data collection methods

A cross-sectional, population-based household survey was conducted in
August 2016 after approximately 10 months of implementation to capture
coverage of home visits and maternal and newborn care practices in the pro-

gram area. A survey of HSA serving the selected household survey clusters was implemented alongside the household survey to help understand HSA background characteristics, activity levels and program support in terms of supervision and supplies and birth notification.

Sampling

Household survey

A target sample size of 144 mothers of infants under six months of age was calculated for the primary outcome of home visit coverage for mothers and newborns, assuming 80% power, 90% confidence interval, a design effect of 2.0, and a coverage value 40%. Two-stage sampling methodology was used in which 30 clusters of five households were selected for a total of 150 households. Census enumeration areas (EAs) were used to define survey clusters and were selected proportional-to-size using the most recent census (2008). The listing of all EAs for Ntcheu district was obtained from the Malawi National Statistics Office (NSO).

Within selected clusters, all households were listed and a screening questionnaire administered to determine ages of all usual members of the household to identify eligible households with one or more caregivers of infants under six months. This age group was selected to ensure potential exposure to the CBMNC intervention during pregnancy and post-delivery. Households in which an adult representative was not home during the initial contact were revisited once before being considered unavailable. Following the listing, ineligible households were removed and five households with an eligible caregiver were randomly selected for interview. Interviewers administered the questionnaire to the eligible caregiver in selected households; in the case where there were more than one eligible caregiver present in a single household, one was randomly selected.

HSA survey

The HSAs providing services to the same 30 clusters sampled for the household survey were purposively selected for an interview using the HSA questionnaire. The objective of the HSA survey was to gain a better understanding of the HSAs' background characteristics, activity levels, and support and supervision to help interpret the results of the household survey. As HSA catchment areas did not align with the census enumeration areas, it was possible that more than one HSA was associated with a given cluster. In such cases, one HSA was randomly selected for interview.

Data collection

The household questionnaire was developed based on a 2011 household survey to evaluate the earlier CBMNC program implemented under the SNL project, with further updates made based on the latest Demographic and Health Survey (DHS) model women's questionnaire Phase 7 [17]. The questionnaire included four sections: 1) maternal background characteristics, 2) exposure to CBMNC interventions, 3) antenatal, delivery and newborn care, and 4) sick newborn care. Similarly, the HSA survey questionnaire was developed based on the 2011 SNL evaluation questionnaire for HSAs. The questionnaire captured HSA background characteristics, training and knowledge of newborn health, newborn health materials and supplies (observation-based), activity levels based on HSA report and register review, and supervision. Both questionnaires were translated into Chichewa and back-translated independently into English to check the accuracy of the translation. Questionnaires were pre-tested in Chichewa by NSO during the data collection training and minor modifications were made to finalize the survey tools.

The survey was implemented by NSO, with technical support from ICF International and SC. The CMBNC evaluation in Ntcheu was nested within a larger evaluation of the iCCM program, which was conducted in the four original RAcE districts (Ntcheu, Mzimba North, Dedza and Ntchisi). Data collectors were full-time NSO staff with experience conducting national household surveys. Data collectors and supervisors were trained by NSO for eight days, including two days of field practice. The training covered an overview of the RAcE project, interviewer roles and responsibilities, household and respondent selection, administering informed consent, question-by-question review of the data collection tools, mock interviews and data quality checks.

Data collection was carried out in August 2016 by nine survey teams of three interviewers each, with one team assigned to CBMNC in Ntcheu district. Each team was led by a supervisor trained to monitor and support the data collectors, review completed questionnaires, and oversee household listing and sampling. Technical staff from ICF International provided support for the last week of training and the first week of data collection. Staff from NSO and SC Malawi monitored data collection regularly throughout the data collection period.

Data management and analysis

Data were double-entered into CSPro (United States Census Bureau, Washington DC, USA) by data entry clerks trained and supervised by NSO. Data supervisors ran CSPro quality checks cluster by cluster to identify discrepancies. Discrepancies were resolved by checking the paper questionnaire to determine the correct value. After data were cleaned, NSO removed all direct identifiers and shared the data set for analysis. Data were analyzed using Stata IC 14.2 (StataCorp; USA, College Station, Texas, USA). Frequencies and 95% confidence intervals were calculated for the household survey and HSA indicators. Household survey indicators included coverage and content of pregnancy and postnatal home visits. HSA survey indicators included proportion of HSAs conducting pregnancy and postnatal home visits in the last three months before the survey, the mean number of visits made during this period, supervision coverage and availability of CBMNC supplies and equipment. Confidence intervals for household survey indicators were adjusted for clustering. As the small sample size precluded multivariate analysis, we performed bivariate analysis to assess the association of selected covariates on coverage of postnatal home visits. Covariates assessed included pregnancy home visits (yes or no), HSA birth notification (yes or no), maternal education (Less than Form 3; Form 3 or higher) and maternal age (<25 years; 25 years or older) and were selected based on previous studies and considering sample size limitations [18]. Associations with P-values of <0.05 were considered statistically significant.

Ethical considerations

The survey received ethical approval from the National Health Sciences Research Committee (NHSRC # 16/7/1617) of the MOH in Malawi, the ICF International Institutional Review Board and SC's Ethics Review Committee. All participants provided informed oral consent, which interviewers documented on the survey tools.

RESULTS

Household survey findings

Interviews were completed with 140 mothers of children under six months of age. **Table 1** provides an overview of characteristics of mothers and babies included in the survey. The mean age of mothers was 26.1 years (standard deviation SD: 6.7; range 17-43 years); 23.6% of mothers were under 20 years of age and 12.1% were older than 35. Most mothers had attended at least primary level education, but only 17.9% had reached secondary or higher education. The child's mean age was 2.8 months, and 35.0% of the sample was under two months of age. Most mothers (77.1%; 95% CI = 68.7-83.8) reported receiving at least one ANC visit from a medically skilled provider and nearly all women (97.9%; 95% CI = 93.5-99.3) reported delivering at a health facility.

Coverage and content of home visits: Less than one-third of mothers reported receiving one or more home visits by an HSA during pregnancy and one-fifth received the recommended two or more visits (**Table 1**). Most visits took place after the first trimester. Among those receiving a home visit, 38.1% (95% CI = 23.3-55.5) reported that their husband/partner was present for at least one of the home visits. Most women (86.0%; 95% CI = 65.5-95.2) who received a pregnancy home visit reported receiving at least two priority messages. The most commonly cited areas of counselling (unprompted) from HSAs included maternal nutrition during pregnancy, facility delivery, danger signs during pregnancy, and birth preparations (emergency saving, emergency transport, clothing for baby, etc). About 83.7% (95% CI = 63.5-93.8) of mothers who received a pregnancy home visit indicated the HSA counselled them to inform him or her of the birth as soon as possible after delivery.

An estimated 20.7% (95%CI = 12.7-32.0) of mothers and newborns received a postnatal home visit by an HSA within eight days of delivery and 11.4% (95% CI = 6.8-18.5) received a visit within three days (**Table 2**). Only 7.1% (95% CI = 3.5-13.9) received two or more home visits from an HSA within

Table 1. *Background characteristics of mothers and babies included in the household survey (N = 140)*

BACKGROUND CHARACTERISTICS	NUMBER	PERCENT
Mothers		
Age (years):		
<20	33	23.6
<20-24	39	27.9
≥25 y and older	68	48.6
Highest level school attended:		
None	11	7.9
Primary	104	74.3
Secondary or higher	25	17.9
Highest level completed education:		
Level 3 or less	98	70.0
Higher than level 3	42	30.0
Babies		
Age (months):		
<2	49	35.0
2-5	91	65.0
Sex:		
Male	78	55.7
Female	62	44.3

Table 2. *Coverage and content of HSAs home visits during pregnancy and within the first week of delivery*

INDICATOR	DE-NOMI-NATOR	RESULT (%)	95% CI
Pregnancy home visits coverage:			
Woman received at least one home visit during pregnancy from HSA	140	30.7	21.7-41.5
Woman received two or more home visits during pregnancy from HSA	140	20.0	13.0-29.4
Timing of first home visit during pregnancy:			
First trimester (1-3 months)	43	14.0	–
Second trimester (4 to 6 months)	43	58.1	–
Third trimester (7 to 9 months)	43	27.9	–
Pregnancy home visit content (among those receiving visit):			
HSA counselled on at least two priority messages during pregnancy* *(antenatal care, danger signs, skilled/facility delivery, birth planning, immediate newborn care)*	43	86.0	65.6-95.2
HSA counselled woman to inform/him or her of delivery	43	83.7	63.5-93.8
Postnatal home visits coverage:			
Mothers/newborns received at least one home visit from an HSA within eight days of delivery	140	20.7	12.7-32.0
Mothers/newborns who received two or more home visits from an HSAs within eight days of delivery	140	7.1	3.5-13.9
Mothers/newborns who received at least one home visit from an HSA within three days of delivery	140	11.4	6.8-18.5
Postnatal home visit content (among those receiving visit):			
Newborn received all four recommended actions during HSA postnatal visit[†] *(check cord, temperature, counsel on newborn danger signs, weigh baby)*	29	75.9	54.2-89.7
Mother received all three recommended actions during postnatal home visit[†] *(counsel on maternal danger signs, observe breastfeeding, discuss family planning)*	29	86.2	66.6-95.1

HSA – Health Surveillance Assistant, CI – confidence interval
*Question was unprompted.
†Question was prompted for each action.

the first week. The majority of newborns and mothers who received a postnatal home visit within eight days received all of the priority actions that HSAs were trained to provide as part of the postnatal home visits.

Factors associated with postnatal home visits coverage

Table 3 presents the results of a bivariate analysis to explore the association between pregnancy home visits, HSA birth notification, maternal age and maternal education on receipt of a postnatal home visit within eight days after

Table 3. *Bivariate analysis of the association between coverage of a postnatal home visit within eight days after delivery and selected covariates*

Variable	Denominator	Received postnatal home visit within 8 d (%)	P-value
Received pregnancy home visit:			
Yes	43	44.2	0.00
No	97	10.3	
Informed HSA of birth:			
Yes	60	46.7	0.00
No	80	1.3	
Maternal education (highest completed):			
Level 3 or less	98	21.4	0.75
Higher than Level 3	42	19.1	
Maternal age (years):			
<25	72	23.5	0.42
25 or older	68	18.1	

HSA – Health Surveillance Assistant

delivery. Women who received a home visit during pregnancy and women who reported the HSA had been informed of the birth were significantly more likely to receive a postnatal home visit in the first week of delivery. About 42.9% (95% CI = 33.4-52.8) of mothers reported that the HSA had been informed of the birth. Birth notification was significantly higher among those who received a pregnancy home visit than those who did not (74.4% vs 28.9%; $P = 0.00$). Communication to the HSA about the birth was in most cases (76.7%) made by an immediate family member (husband, mother, mother-in law) or other family member visiting the HSA in person or by the community action group (20.0%), with only 3.3% connections made by facility staff. Coverage of postnatal home visits among those who informed the HSA after delivery was 46.7% compared to 1.3% among those in which the HSA was not informed. Coverage of postnatal home visits did not vary significantly with maternal age or education level.

HSA survey findings:

Interviews were completed with 33 HSAs from Ntcheu district, of which 31 had completed CBMNC training and were administered the full questionnaire. Most of the sampled HSAs were male (71.0%) and they ranged in age from 30 to 59 years, with close to two-thirds under the age of 40 (**Table 4**). While nearly all (96.8%) HSAs had completed Form 2 education, just over half had obtained their Malawi School Certificate of Education (Form 4). Three-quarters of HSAs

Table 4. *Background characteristics of HSAs trained in CBMNC (N = 31)*

BACKGROUND CHARACTERISTICS	NUMBER	PERCENT
Age:		
<40 y	20	64.5
40 y or older	11	35.5
Sex:		
Male	22	71.0
Female	9	29.0
Highest level of education:		
Less than Form 4	14	45.2
Form 4 or higher (Malawi School Certificate of Education)	17	54.8
Resident in catchment area:	**23**	**74.2**
Travel time from village to health facility:		
Less than 30 min	8	25.8
30 min to less than one hour	9	29.0
One hour to less than two hours	11	35.5
Two or more hours	3	9.7

HSA – health surveillance assistant; CBMNC – community-based maternal newborn care

resided in their catchment areas. The main modes of transportation were bicycles (65%) or walking (23%). Just over half of the HSAs (54.8%) reported it took less than one hour to reach the nearest health facility and 35.5% took between one and two hours and 9.7% took two hours or more. For those not living in their catchment areas, 74.2% reported they could reach their village clinic within 30 minutes.

CBMNC activity levels and functionality

Register reviews revealed that 83.9% (95% CI = 65.4-93.5) of HSAs had conducted at least one pregnancy home visit and 77.4% (95% CI = 58.4-89.3) had conducted one or more postnatal home visits in the three months before the survey (corresponding to the period of May to June 2016) (**Table 5**). On average, HSAs conducted 7.9 pregnancy home visits and 4.7 postnatal home visits over the three-month period (total of 12.6 home visits). HSAs resident in their communities conducted more home visits on average (13.1 compared to 11.3), however the difference was not statistically significant due to the small sample size. Overall, 83.9% (95% CI:65.4-93.5) of HSAs were considered 'functional' for CBMNC, with evidence of conducting pregnancy or post-natal home visits in the past three months according to register review and submitting a report on CBMNC activities in the past month.

Table 5. *HSA pregnancy and postnatal home visit activity levels and supports for CMBNC (N = 31)*

INDICATOR	RESULT	95% CI
HSA activity levels (based on register review over last three months):		
Pregnancy home visits:		
Percent of HSAs who conducted at least one pregnancy home visit in last three months	83.9	65.4-93.5
Percent of HSAs who conducted at least one follow-up pregnancy home visit in last three months	64.5	45.5-79.9
Mean number of pregnancy home visits	*7.9*	*5.6-10.3*
Mean number of pregnancy follow-up visits	*2.3*	*1.3-3.3*
Postnatal home visits:		
Percent of HSAs who conducted at least one postnatal home visit in last three months	77.4	58.4-89.3
Percent of HSAs who conducted at least one follow-up postnatal home visit in last three months	45.2	28.0-63.5
Mean number of postnatal home visits	*4.7*	*2.6-6.9*
Mean number of postnatal follow-up visits	*1.9*	*0.63-3.1*
Home visits overall:		
Percent of HSAs who conducted at least one home visit (pregnancy or post-natal) in the last three months	87.1	68.9-95.4
Mean number of home visits (pregnancy and postnatal)	*12.6*	*9.0-16.3*
Levels of supervision and material support for CBMNC:		
Supervision:		
Percent of HSAs who received at least one supervision visit for newborn health in the last three months	12.9	4.6-31.1
Equipment and supplies:		
Percent of HSAs with all four essential newborn commodities for CBMNC available and functional on day of assessment (*scale, thermometer, timer and counseling materials*)	83.9	65.4-93.5
Percent of HSAs with all CBMNC supplies and equipment available and functional on day of assessment (*all above plus register, CMBNC manual, referral slips and pregnancy listing notebook*)	16.1	2.4-29.8

HSA – health surveillance assistant, CBMNC – community-based maternal newborn care. CI – confidence interval

Supervision, support and birth notification

Only a small number of HSAs (12.9%; 95% CI = 4.6-31.1) reported at least one supervision visit specific to newborn health in the past three months (**Table 5**). The supervision visits were conducted by senior HSAs (2/4) and SC staff (2/4). An estimated 83.9% (95% CI = 95% CI = 65.4-93.5) of HSAs were observed to have the essential newborn commodities for CBMNC (scale, thermometer, timer and counseling materials) at the time of the interview, but only 16.1% (95% CI = 2.4-29.8) had all eight items assessed. Newborn referral slips and exercise books for pregnancy listing had the lowest availability (29.0% and 54.8% respectively). Nearly all HSAs (96.8%; 95% CI = 78.4-99.6) reported being notified of births and three-quarters (74.2%; 95% CI = 55.1-87.1) indicated they were notified of the birth within three days. Family members (61.3%; 95% CI = 42.4%-77.3%), village health committees (35.8%; 95%: 20.1-54.5) and village leaders (19.4%; 8.5-38.1) were the most commonly mentioned sources of birth notification. Only 12.9% (95% CI = 4.6-31.1) of HSAs mentioned that health facility staff notified them – an important missed opportunity given that nearly all births occurred at health facilities.

DISCUSSION

Our evaluation found low coverage of home visits by HSAs during pregnancy and the early postnatal period. Only about one-third of women received a home visit during pregnancy and few received the recommended two visits during pregnancy. Coverage of postnatal visits was even lower, with about one in five mothers and newborns receiving a visit within the first eight days (and less than one in 10 within three days of delivery). These low coverage levels are similar to those reported in the 2011 evaluation of the pilot CBMNC program in three districts (Thyolo, Dowa and Chitipa) [13,14,18]. Other similar findings included the importance of birth notification in facilitating postnatal visits and that women reached during pregnancy were more likely to receive postnatal home visits [18].

This evaluation also captured information from HSAs serving the clusters that were sampled in the household survey, which revealed that the majority of HSAs trained in CBMNC were well-equipped (with the exception of newborn referral slips) and most had documented evidence in their registers of providing pregnancy and postnatal home visits during the three months before the survey. However, activity levels were well below what would be required to achieve high coverage. Assuming the average HSA's catchment population of 2000 and a crude birth rate of 42/1000, one would expect about 84 pregnancies/ births per year [16]. According to the CBMNC schedule of two home visits during pregnancy and three home visits in the first eight days after delivery, each HSA would need to conduct a minimum of 168 pregnancy home visits and 252 postnatal home visits per year (420 total), translating into approximately 35 home visits per month or 105 per quarter. In contrast, HSAs were conducting about 12-13 home visits per quarter, which tracks quite well with the observed coverage levels. We found that HSAs who resided full-time in their communities conducted more home visits than those who lived elsewhere, however the results were not statistically significant due to the small sample size. The evaluation of the CBMNC pilot also reported higher CBMNC activity levels among resident HSAs [18]. As HSAs assigned to more remote, poorer communities are less likely to reside full-time at their site, this can bias coverage toward wealthier communities, despite the intent of community-based programs to help address inequities in access to health care [13]. While we were unable to assess coverage by socioeconomic status, earlier studies of CBMNC suggest that that households in the wealthiest quintile are slightly more likely than those in the poorer quintiles to receive home visits, in part because of the underlying disparities in access to a resident HSA [13].

Supervision of HSAs for the CBMNC component was very low. Only a handful of HSAs had received any supervision specific to the newborn package; these low levels could be due the senior HSAs only receiving formal supervision training for CBMNC in November 2016 (after the evaluation). Analysis of supervision coverage and supply chain supports for other community-based programs such as iCCM are mixed. The HSAs interviewed as part of the evaluation of the larger iCCM program implemented through RACE reported much higher levels of supervision, with two-thirds of the HSAs reporting supervision for iCCM in the last three months [19]. However, other studies of program support for iCCM found lower levels of supervision (38% supervision coverage in last three months) and breaches in supply chain management, suggesting that sustaining consistent levels of program support for HSAs to deliver community-based activities remains a persistent challenge for the MOH and partners [20]. Going forward, it will be possible to conduct CBMNC supervision jointly with iCCM, although adjustments may be required as current supervision approach for CBMNC involves visiting the mothers in their own households and may not be feasible in most cases.

The household survey and HSAs findings taken together highlight the limited role health facilities are presently playing in helping to link HSAs to recently delivered mothers and their newborns. Given that nearly all births occurred at health facilities, this is a critical missed opportunity. Further efforts should be made to explore feasible options for facilities to notify HSAs of births in their catchment areas; it could be possible to have senior HSAs coordinate with the clinical staff involved in post-natal discharge to identify which HSAs serves the catchment area where the family is from before they leave to go home. At the community level, families and other community members may also be mobilized to help alert HSAs that a birth has taken place. Women who reported that an HSA was notified of the birth were more likely to receive a postnatal home visit; however, about half of these women still did not receive a postnatal home visit. This suggests that other barriers play an important role that needs to be further explored.

Despite revisions to the CBMNC package, including a somewhat reduced schedule of home visits, the performance of the CBMNC program appears to have reached a coverage plateau at a very low level, particularly for postnatal home visits. Even if efforts are successful in strengthening linkages between facilities and families and notification of HSAs is improved, it is unlikely that HSAs would be able to conduct home visits at the level required to achieve high coverage. A costing analysis found that it took an HSA 1.5 hours on average to conduct a CBMNC home visit, including time for preparation, travel and interaction with the family [14]. In addition to their role in CBMNC, HSAs are officially responsible for a wide range health and sanitation tasks at community and facility levels – estimated to be more than 250 [19,21]. These tasks include delivery of life-saving interventions such as supporting immunization outreach and providing assessment and treatment for childhood illness, and increased time spent on home visits could be a trade-off with other important health interventions. These struggles are not unique to Malawi, with many other countries failing to reach high coverage of home visits despite strong program support [11]. In addition, large scale evaluations of the coverage of other community-based interventions delivered through HSAs, such as iCCM, have also reported lower than expected coverage despite relatively strong implementation [22]. Given this reality, it is worth revisiting the feasibility of the CBMNC package in its current form and exploring options to focus on reaching those at greatest risk – such as first time mothers, women who have given birth to preterm or small babies, and women who deliver outside a health facility – and investigating opportunities to shift some components such as counselling to other community-based volunteers more likely to reside full-time in the community and have greater access to families [11,12]. Although the 2015-2016 DHS survey showed that more than 90% of deliveries in Malawi occurred at facilities and about three-quarters of mothers stayed in facility at least one to two days following delivery, just 44.6% of mothers who delivered at facility reported receiving a PNC check within two days [23]. For newborns, the results were similar, but slightly higher: 63.1% of babies born in facility received PNC within two days [23]. These findings imply that further efforts should be placed to improve the coverage and quality of these facility-based postnatal contacts with mothers and newborns [12]. Further investigations should be carried out to explore the potential for HSAs, who already spend considerable time at health facilities, to support facility staff to provide aspects of postnatal care and counselling at health facilities as well as in the community.

Limitations

Our evaluation had some important limitations. The CBMNC program had been implemented for a short period of time, with most HSAs completing training nine to 12 months prior to the survey, but a small number of HSAs were trained only five months prior to the survey. Although the design restricted the sample to infants under six months of age to maximize potential exposure to CBMNC, some women in our sample may have completed their pregnancy before HSAs were providing home visits, potentially underestimating coverage of home visits during pregnancy. Another limitation to the study is survival bias, since only mothers with a live birth were sampled for our study and women who experienced stillbirth or early infant death and may have had lower levels of care would have been excluded; however the effect of this would be fairly small and tend to bias the sample toward higher coverage (and coverage was found to be quite low). The sampling approach for the household survey defined clusters using census enumeration areas, which did not perfectly align with HSA catchment areas. This may have resulted in some clusters without access to a trained HSA. Indicators on coverage of postnatal contact and coverage relied on maternal recall using a complex series of questions similar to the DHS and MICS survey questionnaires on postnatal care and thus are subject to recall bias and measurement error [24]. However, studies show that most mothers are able to recall interactions with health providers and specific interventions received if the questions are adequately prompted and the actions notable (eg, required asking a question or use of equipment) [25]. Additionally, the small sample size in the household survey resulted in relatively large confidence intervals around some estimates and limited our ability to conduct multivariate analysis of factors associated with coverage of postnatal home visits or assess equity. Similarly, the small number of HSAs interviewed precluded disaggregated analysis to better understand factors associated with HSA activity levels and we did not capture information on workload or how HSAs spent their time. Finally, the evaluation was conducted in a single district of Malawi, and an evaluation of the previous CBMNC package in multiple districts found considerable variation in coverage of home visits and as such it unknown how generalizable the current results are to other districts implementing CBMNC interventions [14]. As the revised CBMNC package has continued to be rolled out across Malawi, further studies covering multiple districts and employing mixed methods could provide valuable information on factors driving performance and inform community and facility-based strategies to optimize care for mothers and babies in Malawi.

CONCLUSIONS

We found low coverage of home visits by HSAs during pregnancy and soon after delivery in a well-supported program delivery environment. Most HSAs were conducting home visits, but not at the level needed to reach high coverage. These findings were similar to previous studies, calling into question the feasibility of the current visitation schedule in the CBMNC package. It is time to re-align the CBMNC package with what the existing platform can deliver and identify strategies to support HSAs to implement home visits. Options for exploration include targeting home visits to those at greatest risk (first time mothers, women who have previously given birth preterm babies, women who deliver outside facility), supporting health facility staff to improve birth notification and engaging communities to increase demand and define locally appropriate solutions. Targeted efforts are also needed to improve the coverage and quality of essential interventions through the existing high level of facility-based prenatal and postnatal contacts with women and their babies in Malawi.

Acknowledgments: *The authors acknowledge the contribution of the Malawi National Statistics Office, who led data collection and data management efforts. We also thank all the survey supervisors, enumerators, and data entry clerks. We acknowledge the staff from ICF International, namely Kirsten Zalisk and Deborah Prosnitz, for their technical support throughout the design, implementation and data analysis phases. The opinions expressed are those of the authors and do not necessarily reflect the views of Save the Children or the World Health Organization.*

Funding: *This work was supported by the World Health Organization's Rapid Access Expansion Program (RAcE) funded by Global Affairs Canada.*

Authorship contributions: *TG, SS, EC, and HN designed the evaluation. EC, GJ, and RM participated in data quality monitoring. TG and SS conceptualized the analysis and TG analyzed the data. TG and SS wrote the manuscript and all authors reviewed the manuscript drafts and provided inputs.*

Competing interests: *The authors have completed the ICMJE Competing Interest form at www.icmje.org/coi_disclosure.pdf (available on request from the corresponding author) and declare no conflict of interest.*

Additional Material
Online Supplementary Document

References

1 UNICEF. Levels and trends in child mortality. 2017 Report. Estimates Developed by the UN Interagency Group for Child Mortality Estimation. Available: http://www.childmortality.org/2017/files_v21/download/IGME%20report%202017%20child%20mortality%20final.pdf. Accessed: 25 January 2018.

2 Oza S, Cousens SN, Lawn JE. Estimation of daily risk of neonatal death, including the day of birth, in 186 countries in 2013: a vital-registration and modelling-based study. Lancet Glob Health. 2014;2:e635-44. Medline:25442688 doi:10.1016/S2214-109X(14)70309-2

3 Mannan I, Rahman SM, Sania A, Seraji HR, Arifeen SE, Winch PJ, et al; Bangladesh Projahnmo Study Group. Can early postpartum home visits by trained community health workers improve breastfeeding of newborns? J Perinatol. 2008;28:632-40. Medline:18596714 doi:10.1038/jp.2008.64

4 Tripathi A, Kabra SK, Sachdev HP, Lodha R. Home visits by community health workers to improve identification of serious illness and care seeking in newborns and young infants from low- and middle-income countries. J Perinatol. 2016;36 Suppl 1:S74-82. Medline:27109094 doi:10.1038/jp.2016.34

5 Sitrin D, Guenther T, Waiswa P, Namutamba S, Namazzi G, Sharma S, et al. Improving newborn care practices through home visits: lessons from Malawi, Nepal, Bangladesh, and Uganda. Glob Health Action. 2015;8:23963. Medline:25843490 doi:10.3402/gha.v8.23963

6 World Health Organization. UNICEF. WHO-UNICEF Joint Statement on home visits for the newborn child: a strategy to improve survival. 2009. Available: http://apps.who.int/iris/bitstream/10665/70002/1/WHO_FCH_CAH_09.02_eng.pdf?ua=1&ua=1. Accessed: 25 January 2018.

7 Baqui AH, El-Arifeen S, Darmstadt GL, Ahmed S, Williams EK, Seraji HR, et al; Projahnmo Study Group. Effect of community-based newborn-care intervention package implemented through two service-delivery strategies in Sylhet district, Bangladesh: a cluster-randomised controlled trial. Lancet. 2008;371:1936-44. Medline:18539225 doi:10.1016/S0140-6736(08)60835-1

8 Kumar V, Mohanty S, Kumar A, Misra RP, Santosham M, Awasthi S, et al. Effect of community-based behaviour change management on neonatal mortality in Shivgarh, Uttar Pradesh, India: a cluster-randomised controlled trial. Lancet. 2008;372:1151-62. Medline:18926277 doi:10.1016/S0140-6736(08)61483-X

9 Bhutta ZA, Memon ZA, Soofi S, Salat MS, Cousens S, Martines J. Implementing community-based perinatal care: results from a pilot study in rural Pakistan. Bull World Health Organ. 2008;86:452-9. Medline:18568274 doi:10.2471/BLT.07.045849

10 WHO. (2013). WHO recommendations on postnatal care of the mother and newborn. Geneva: World Health Organization. Available: http://apps.who.int/iris/bitstream/handle/10665/97603/9789241506649_eng.pdf?sequence=1. Accessed: 2 May 2018.

11 McPherson R, Hodgins S. Postnatal home visitation: lessons from country programs operating at scale. J Glob Health. 2018;8:010422. Medline:29977530 doi:10.7189/jogh.08.010422

12 Care P. with a Focus on Home Visitation: A Design Decision-Aid For Policymakers And Program Managers April 2017. Available: https://www.healthynewbornnetwork.org/hnn-content/uploads/PostnatalCarewithaFocusonHomeVisitation.pdf. Accessed: 2 May 2018.

13 Callaghan-Koru JA, Nonyane BA, Guenther T, Sitrin D, Ligowe R, Chimbalanga E, et al. Contribution of community-based newborn health promotion to reducing inequities in healthy newborn care practices and knowledge: evidence of improvement from a three-district pilot program in Malawi. BMC Public Health. 2013;13:1052. Medline:24199832 doi:10.1186/1471-2458-13-1052

14 Greco G, Daviaud E, Owen H, Ligowe R, Chimbalanga E, Guenther T, et al. Malawi three district evaluation: Community-based maternal and newborn care economic analysis. Health Policy Plan. 2017;32(suppl_1):i64-i74. Medline:28981762 doi:10.1093/heapol/czw079

15 WHO. (2015). Caring for the Newborn at Home. Geneva: World Health Organization. Available: http://apps.who.int/iris/bitstream/handle/10665/204273/9789241549295_FacilitatorNotes_eng.pdf?sequence=2. Accessed: 2 May 2018.

16 National Statistics Office Malawi. Population Projections Malawi. Malawi: National Statistics Office. 2008. Available: http://www.nsomalawi.mw/images/stories/data_on_line/demography/census_2008/Main%20Report/ThematicReports/Population%20Projections%20Malawi.pdf. Accessed: 2 May 2018.

17 Measure Evaluation. Demographic and Health Survey Model Women's Questionnaire. March 2016. Available: https://www.dhsprogram.com/pubs/pdf/DHSQ7/DHS7-Womans-QRE-EN-07Jun2017-DHSQ7.pdf. Accessed: 2 May 2018.

18 Sitrin D, Guenther T, Murray J, Pilgrim N, Rubayet S, Ligowe R, et al. Reaching mothers and babies with early postnatal home visits: the implementation realities of achieving high coverage in large-scale programs. PLoS One. 2013;8:e68930. Medline:23874816 doi:10.1371/journal.pone.0068930

19 Zalisk K, Guenther T, Prosnitz D, Nsona H, Chimbalanga E, Sadruddin S. Achievements and challenges of implementation in a mature iCCM programme: Malawi case study. J Global Health. 2019;9:010802. doi:10.7189/jogh.09.010802

20 Callaghan-Koru JA, Gilroy K, Hyder AA, George A, Nsona H, Mtimuniet A, et al. Health systems supports for community case management of childhood illness: lessons from an assessment of early implementation in Malawi. BMC Health Serv Res. 2013;13:55. Medline:23394591 doi:10.1186/1472-6963-13-55

21 Government of Malawi. Role Clarity Guidelines for Community Health Workers 2017-2022. Lilongwe: Ministry of Health; 2017.

22 Amouzou A, Kanyuka M, Hazel E, Heidkamp R, Marsh A, Mleme T, et al. Independent evaluation of the integrated Community Case Management of Childhood Illness strategy in Malawi Using a National Evaluation Platform Design. Am J Trop Med Hyg. 2016;94:574-83. Medline:26787158 doi:10.4269/ajtmh.15-0584

23 National Statistical Office (NSO) [Malawi] and ICF. 2017. Malawi Demographic and Health Survey 2015-16. Zomba, Malawi, and Rockville, Maryland, USA. NSO and ICF.

24 Amouzou A, Mehra V, Carvajal-Aguirre L, Khan SM, Sitrin D, Vaz LM. Measuring postnatal care contacts for mothers and newborns: An analysis of data from the MICS and DHS surveys. J Glob Health. 2017;7:020502. Medline:29423179 doi:10.7189/jogh.07.020502

25 Hill Z, Okyere E, Wickenden M, Tawiah-Agyemang C. What can we learn about postnatal care in Ghana if we ask the right questions? A qualitative study. Glob Health Action. 2015;8:28515. Medline:26350434 doi:10.3402/gha.v8.28515

Barriers on the pathway to survival for children dying from treatable illnesses in Inhambane province, Mozambique

Karin Källander[1,2], Helen Counihan[1], Teresa Cerveau[2], Francisco Mbofana[3]

[1] Malaria Consortium London, UK
[2] Karolinska Institutet, Stockholm, Sweden
[3] Malaria Consortium Mozambique, Maputo, Mozambique
[4] Ministerio de Saúde, Maputo, Mozambique

Background Mozambique has one of the highest under-5 mortality rates in the world. Community health workers (CHWs) are deployed to increase access to care; in Mozambique they are known as agentes polivalentes elementares (APEs). This study aimed to investigate child deaths in an area served by APEs by analysing the causes, care seeking patterns, and the influence of social capital.

Methods Caregivers of children under-5 who died in 2015 in Inhambane province, Mozambique, were interviewed using Verbal Autopsy/Social Autopsy (VA/SA) tools with a social capital module. VA data were analysed using the WHO InterVA analytical tool to determine cause of death. SA was analysed using the INDEPTH SA framework for illnesses lasting no more than three weeks. Social capital scores were calculated.

Results 117 child deaths were reported; VA/SA was conducted for 115. Eighty-five had died from an acute illness lasting no more than three weeks, which in most cases could have been treated at community level; 50.6% died from malaria, 11.8% from HIV/AIDS, and 9.4% for each of diarrhoea and acute respiratory infections. In 35.3% the caregiver only noticed that the child was sick when symptoms of very severe illness developed. One in four children were never taken outside the home before dying. Sixteen children were first taken to an APE; of these 7 had signs of very severe illness. Caregivers who waited to seek care until the illness was very severe had a lower social capital score. The mean travel time to go to the APE was 2hrs 50min, which was not different from any other provider. Most received treatment from the APE, 3 were referred. The majority went to another provider after the APE; most to a health centre.

Conclusions The leading causes of death in children under-5 can be detected, treated or referred by APEs. Major care seeking delays took place in the home, largely due to lack of early disease recognition and late decision-making. Low social capital, distance to APEs and to referral facilities likely contribute to these delays. Increasing caregiver illness awareness is urgently needed, as well as stronger referral linkages. A review of the geographical coverage and scope of work of APEs should be conducted.

The last two decades have seen impressive progress in global health. There were 7.2 million fewer deaths globally of children under five in 2017 than there were in 2000, with half of the lives saved attributed to the gains made in preventing and treating pneumonia, diarrhoea, intra-partum related events, malaria and measles [1]. Malaria deaths alone fell by 62 percent between 2000 and 2015, largely as a result of increased efforts and a huge mobilisation of funding [2]. Progress, however, has been uneven, with the poorest and most vulnerable still being left behind, largely due to a lack of access to vital health services [3]. In many rural villages access to health facilities is limited. The majority of the 5.6 million children who die each year still die from illnesses that are easily preventable and treatable [4]. This is exacerbated by a global health worker shortage of over seven million – a figure which is expected to rise to nearly 13 million by 2035 [3,5]. As the international community mobilises towards realising the Global Goals for Sustainable Development, it is clear that more needs to be done in order to achieve universal health coverage and secure healthy lives for all by 2030.

Community-based primary health care (CBPHC) is a key mechanism to delivering health services to hard-to-reach and under-served communities. CBPHC involves using trained community health workers (CHWs), who may or may not be paid, to deliver health services to these communities. CHWs are provided with training, tools and medicines and supplies to deliver basic health services to the rural communities in which they live. This allows CBPHC programmes to reach into the heart of communities to tackle the major causes of childhood and maternal illness and mortality. In this way, CBPHC leverages greater efficiencies from health services and has the potential to address many of the remaining challenges in global health, becoming an essential vehicle in the achievement of the Global Goal on health.

CHWs have been a foundation for CBPHC in Mozambique since 1978; nationally referred to as *Agentes Polivalentes Elementares* (APEs) [6,7]. The APE programme faced many challenges and was severely disrupted by the 1977-1992 civil war. In particular, the lack of supervision and commodity supply systems resulted in the interruption of programme implementation in the mid-1990s [8]. In 2010, the Ministry of Health (MoH) launched a revitalization programme for the APEs and as of December 2016, 3524 APEs had been trained to conduct health-promotion activities and provide integrated community case management (iCCM) for malaria, pneumonia and diarrhoea for children aged 2-59 months. They also treat all age groups for malaria and diarrhoea, refer acute malnutrition cases, newborns, pregnant women with danger signs and register all births and deaths in their communities. In 2014, the services APEs provide were expanded to include family planning, pregnancy tracking, antenatal care, post-partum care, healthy child check-ups, as well as TB and HIV patient follow-up for treatment adherence counselling [9]. According to the MoH, 80% of the APE workload should be devoted to health promotion activities, including promoting the use of health services, and encouraging caregivers to bring the sick child in a timely manner for appropriate care [10]. Medicines for APEs are provided from the central medical stores (CMAM) through a kit system with funding from the World Bank, Global Fund and the President's Malaria Initiative. APEs receive a monthly stipend of 20 USD (1200 MZM in 2017). Oversight, training and support to APEs are provided by the province, district and health centre, with a designated APE supervisor at the nearest health centre providing direct supervision to 5-8 APEs.

While under five mortality in Mozambique, estimated at 79 per 1000 live births in 2015, has reduced by more than two-thirds from the rate in 1990, the mortality rate is still among the highest in the world. Due to an inadequate civil registration and vital statistics (CRVS) system, more than 2.5 million children are unregistered and the causes of over 300 000 deaths are unknown in the country [11]. As a result, the modifiable factors at the level of the household, community and health facility that could have prevented these deaths are also unknown. Risk factors for fatal outcomes in sick children include poor socioeconomic status, incomplete immunization schemes, malnutrition, late care seeking and inadequate treatment [4]. Yet cheap and effective tools exist for most childhood infections [12], many which are included in the kit used by the APEs in Mozambique. Lack of social capital, i.e, the (usually non-monetary) resources generated through social networking and involvement in community affairs (eg, sense of belonging, trust and influence) [13], has also shown to be associated with poorer health outcomes and behaviours [14,15]. While social capital as a concept is increasingly being used to help policy-makers and programmers understand how formal and informal networks within and among communities can foster better governance and accountability, as well as contribute to improvements in health, health financing and the equitable delivery of health services [13], it has never been explored in the context of understanding care seeking patterns for child deaths. This study used verbal and social autopsy methodology, combined with a short Social Capital Assessment Tool to investigate the biological causes of child death, care seeking preceding death and the structural (ie, community group membership, emotional/ economic support from individuals) and cognitive social capital (ie, trust, social harmony) in an area covered by APEs, to understand why children fall off the pathway to survival.

METHODS

Study design

A community-based investigation of child deaths in Inhambane province in Southern Mozambique was conducted. The target population included all families living in any of the non-urban 11 districts where an APE was serving their community (**Figure 1**). The total population of children 2-59 months in areas covered by APEs in Inhambane in 2015 was estimated at 62 475 children [16], with one APE serving a population of 2500-5000.

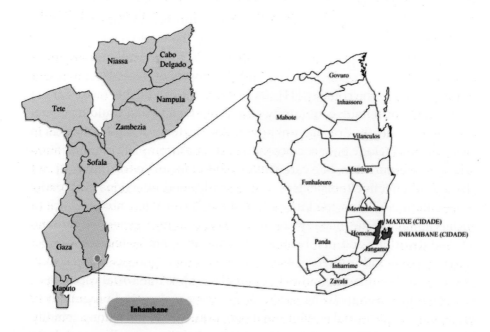

Figure 1. *Map of Mozambique, Inhambane province, and its districts. The red areas are the urban district of Maxixe and Inhambane City, which was excluded from the research.*

Before entering into the field, the study team spent time with the APEs and the community leaders explaining the study. Due to the nature of the research, a four-month mourning period was left between the death of the child and the interview. Family members were given enough time to read the participant information sheet and the key points were summarized verbally to all participants who could not read; all questions that arose were answered. Written informed consent of all participants was obtained; for those who could not read or write a fingerprint was requested. Participants were informed that the decision to participate was entirely voluntary and that the respondent could refuse to answer questions without any consequences.

Data collection

All of the 12 monthly reports submitted by 275 APEs serving 11 of the 12 districts in the province were collected for 1st January to 31st December 2015. From these, information on deaths in children 2-59 months were extracted and with the help of the APE who had submitted the data, together with the community leader, the deaths were verified and the households of these children located. One of the eight research assistants was responsible for investigating the circumstances of the deaths, from initial illness through to death, by interviewing the family to ascertain the sequence of events and their health-seeking behaviour.

A standard WHO verbal autopsy (VA) tool [17], the INDEPTH network (http://www.indepth-network.org/) social autopsy (SA) tool [18,19] and a simplified short social capital tool adapted from the World Bank [20] were programmed in CommCare [21] into a tablet based interview tool in Portuguese, which was used to interview caregivers of children who had died. The VA tool is designed to help determine probable causes of death in cases where there was no medical record or formal medical attention given, whereas the SA tool is designed to investigate the socio-cultural, behavioural and health systems factors that contribute to child deaths. The social capital tool was designed to create an understanding of the networks of relationships among people who live and work in a particular society, as low social capital has shown to have a negative impact on health outcomes [22]. For example, "groups and networks" included questions on the household member's participation in various types of social organisations; for "trust and vulnerability", questions considered if, in general, people can be trusted and if people can get emotionally or morally hurt; and for "collective action and cooperation", questions were asked about how members of a community supported each other in response to a crisis. It is important to note that no validated social capital tool existed at the time of this study and our questionnaire was drawn up from a combination of previous studies on antiretroviral therapy adherence [23] and from an integrated questionnaire for measurement of social capital by the World Bank [19].

The data collectors were hired at provincial level and conducted data collection under the supervision of the National Institute of Health (INS), the Ministry of Health APE Programme Manager, the Provincial Health Directorate (DPS), and Malaria Consortium. The seven-day training of the data collectors covered instructions on survey implementation, the use of tablets (Lenovo Tab4 8"; Lenovo, Morrisville, NC, United States) for data collection, the need for confidentiality and privacy, and interviewing techniques, and involved a combination of classroom teaching and role plays, followed by two days of field testing. The interview tools were in Portuguese, but interviewers were trained to do on-the-spot translation of questions into the local languages of the communities (Changana, Nyanja and Makhuwa). There was structured regular supervision in the field throughout the data collection period, and all questionnaires completed using the tablets were reviewed after the interview by the interviewers themselves and subsequently by the field supervisors on a daily basis. Checks and rules were built into the application to reduce missing data or data entry errors.

Data analysis

The CommCare application synchronised data with a server from which a data set was downloaded into Excel. The VA data were exported and integrated into the WHO InterVA-4 (v4.04) analytical tool to determine likely cause of death using the built in probabilistic models [24]. For those with an acute illness (<3 weeks) the SA data were analysed in STATA 13 (StataCorp, College Station, TX, US) and Microsoft Excel (Microsoft Inc, Seattle WA, USA), using the INDEPTH SA framework [19] to analyse common bottlenecks and delays to appropriate care.

Social capital was measured using two dimensions, namely structural and cognitive, and within those there were four different categories:

1. Number of groups: the number of groups or organisations to which the participant belonged (e.g. religious group, political club, etc.). One point was allocated per group, with a maximum score of four.
2. Trust: if the participant had trust in people in general. A score of zero was allocated for a negative response; five points was allocated for a positive response.

3. Vulnerability: If the participant felt that people in general can get hurt. A score of five was allocated for a negative response; zero points was allocated for a positive response.

4. Ability to borrow money from someone, including friends and relatives. Points were allocated from one to five, based on a Lickert scale (from 'certainly not' to 'certainly').

All the statistical analysis was descriptive: confidence intervals are reported where appropriate, on the basis of the standard error of a proportion. The main analysis included a description of the steps in the pathway to care seeking preceding the death, as well as the "three delays analytical model", as suggested in the literature [19,25,26]. An absolute total social capital score was calculated similar to the method by Kang et al [14], based on the responses to the questions listed above. The lowest possible score was 0 and the highest was 19. Bivariate regression using Student's t test was used to document the association between mean social capital score and key steps in the social autopsy pathways to care seeking.

Ethical considerations

Ethical approval was obtained by the bioethics committee of the National Institute of Health (CIBS-INS) in Maputo, Mozambique in October 2014 (356/CIBS-INS/2014 and 236/CNBS/2015). The survey was conducted in accordance with the principles of good practices and all information collected during the study was treated with strictest confidence. Personal data, particularly name, geographic information and contacts that were used to localise the household of the deceased, were kept separately from the data collection forms used by the research assistants, to protect privacy and ensure confidentiality.

RESULTS

Background characteristics

A total of 117 child deaths were extracted from the APE monthly reports, of which VA/SA were conducted for 115. Of these, 85 had died from an acute illness that had lasted less than three weeks and these were the ones included in the analysis. The majority (91.8%) of the deaths occurred at home (80.0%) or on the way to hospital (11.8%). Of the 85 deaths investigated, 52.9% were girls and 88.2% (75/85) were reported to normally sleep under a bed net. Half of the deaths occurred in children 12-59 months old (43/85; 50.6%), whereas

49.4% (42/85) occurred in infants (1-11 months). Of the 85 deaths investigated, 72 (84.5%) had information available for a social capital score (13 responded "don't know" to at least one of the questions). The mean total social capital score was 11.2 (range 1-19).

Cause of death

Malaria was the main cause of death (COD), accounting for 50.6% of deaths (43/85), followed by deaths related to HIV/AIDS (10/85; 11.8%), diarrhoeal diseases and acute respiratory infections (both 8/85; 9.4%). Nine children were also assigned a second possible COD, with meningitis/encephalitis (3/9) and malaria (2/9) being the main possible secondary causes (**Table 1**).

Table 1. *Causes of death in children under five (n = 85)*

1ˢᵀ CAUSE OF DEATH	No. (N = 85)	%
Malaria	43	50.6
HIV/AIDS* related death	10	11.8
Acute respiratory infection (including pneumonia)	8	9.4
Diarrhoeal disease	8	9.4
Epilepsy	5	5.9
Acute abdomen	3	3.5
Undetermined	3	3.5
Asthma	2	2.4
Congenital malformation	2	2.4
Sepsis (non-obstetric)	1	1.2
2ᴺᴰ CAUSE OF DEATH		
Meningitis and encephalitis	3	33.3
Malaria	2	22.2
Acute respiratory infection (including pneumonia)	1	11.1
HIV/AIDS* related death	1	11.1
Diarrhoeal disease	1	11.1
Acute abdomen	1	11.1

*Human immunodeficiency virus/Acquired immunodeficiency syndrome

Care seeking pathways preceding death

Figure 2 shows the pathways for care seeking that children followed before dying. In 36% (31/82; 3 did not know the status) of children the caregiver only noticed that the child was sick when symptoms of very severe illness had developed (stopped eating, unconscious or stopped moving). The majority (67/85; 78.8%) had received some form of treatment before dying, whereof 55.2% (37/67) were first treated with mainly herbal medicines at home before seeking outside

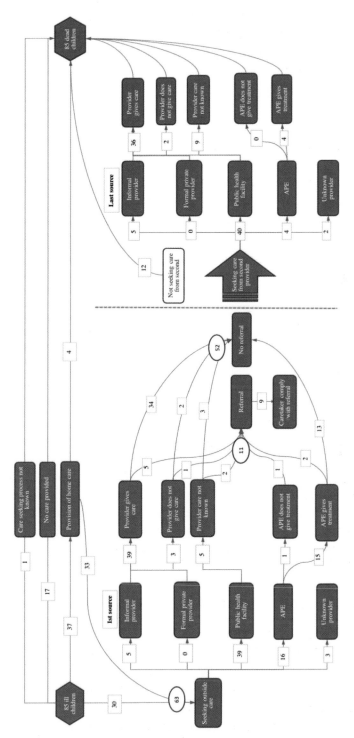

Figure 2. *Pathway of care seeking for 85 child deaths, showing the providers and provider actions for the first and last source of care sought.*

care (25/37; 67.6%). 75% (63/85) were taken outside the home for care before death; of the 21 (25.0%) children who were never taken outside the home, most of these (17/21) had not received any treatment before death. When asked why they had not sought any care for these children, caregivers answered that the child died suddenly before they were able to initiate care seeking (7/21; 33.3%), because they did not realise that the illness was serious (4/21; 19%), and various other reasons (10/21; 47.6%) (used medicines /herbs they had at home, parents were not at home, had no transport/registration card/money, thought the illness was related to a recent vaccination, or could not explain why).

Of children who were taken outside the home, 25.4% (16/63) were first taken to an APE, whereas 52.4% (33/63) (were taken to a health facility, 9.5% (6/63) to a hospital, 7.9% (5/63) to a traditional healer (and three were taken to an unspecified location. Of the children who were first taken to an APE, 43.8% (7/16) were reported to have had signs of very severe illness when the care-taker took the decision to seek care, whereas 56.3% (9/16) were moderately ill (ate poorly, sleepy or less active than normal). While the children who were first taken to a health facility were less often severely ill (30.3%) compared to those who first when to an APE, the difference was not significant ($P = 0.35$). None of the children were taken to the APE when they had mild illness (sick but eating normally, being alert and active). The mean time to walk to the APE as first provider was 2hr 50min, which was not significantly different com-pared to other providers ($P = 0.72$). All except one child received treatment from the APE; seven reportedly received an antimalarial, one paracetamol, and eight did not know the medicine. Three children who first went to an APE were referred to a health facility. There was no significant difference in referral rate between those who first went to an APE vs another provider ($P = 0.88$). The majority (12/16; 75%) of children who were first seen by an APE were taken to a second provider later in the illness; most to a health centre (9/16; 69.2%). Two children were taken back to the APE before dying. The mean time spent to get to the last provider was 3.12 hours (SD 5.84) and 33.9% of caregivers travelled by foot. A total of 16 (25.4%) of the children who sought outside care during the illness were hospitalised; there was no significant difference in hospitalisation rate between those who first went to an APE and those who went to other providers ($P = 0.64$).

Decision making in the household

Several questions were asked about the decision-making processes in rela-tion to different decisions taken in the household. In general, women (47.1%; 40/85) were significantly more often the ones in charge of decisions relating to routine decisions in the home (buying and selling food, daily activities in the home) than when big decisions were made (moving house, buying/selling or rebuilding the house, renting the land) (10.6%; 9/85) ($P < 0.0001$). For other decisions, such as whether to visit relatives or friends, to take a sick relative to a health facility, or take a sick child to a health facility or APE, on average 49.4% stated that this was decided by both the husband and the wife and none of these decisions were stated to involve women less than the men. On the contrary, more women were solely responsible for the decision to seek care for their sick children that men (22.3% vs 11.6%) ($P = 0.11$) and 96.5% (82/85) responded that do not need to seek permission from their husbands before seeking care from a health facility or APE for their sick child.

Social capital

Mean social capital scores for each of the pathway indicators are reported in **Table 2**. Out of the four categories included to form the score, the highest principal component eigenvector loadings were found for Vulnerability (0.61) and Trust (0.58), whereas Ability to loan money (0.41) and member of Number of groups (0.36) had less loading. The only indicator that was associated with social capital was the status of the child when the caregiver detected that the child was ill; caregivers who only detected the illness when the child had severe symptoms reported a significantly lower social capital score ($P = 0.0007$).

The three delays

The relative contribution of delays at the home, on the way to, or in the health facility was calculated (**Figure 3**). Most delays in the care-seeking process were caused by problems at home (44.5%). The second biggest contribution to delay (40.2%) was caused by problems at the health provider, whereas transport delays contributed to 15.2% of the total delay.

Delays in the home

31 (37.8%) of the 82 caregivers who gave information about the child's state had only realised that the child was ill when the condition was severe, and 21 (24.7%) were not taken out of the house for treatment. Some narratives on the reasons why caregivers did not seek care outside the home, or sought care late are provided in **Box 1**.

Table 2. *Pathway indicators and social capital score**

INDICATOR	NUMBER OF DEATHS	%	MEAN SOCIAL CAPITAL SCORE (SD)	95% CI	P-VALUE
Child status when caregiver detected that the child was ill:					
Mildly or moderately sick	46	64.8%	12.6 (3.9)	11.4, 13.7	0.0007‡
Severely sick	25	35.2%	9 (4.3)	7.2, 10.8	
Children who were treated at home:					
No	40	55.6%	11.2 (4.7)	9.7, 12.7	0.94
Yes	32	44.4%	11.3 (4.0)	9.8, 12.7	
Children who were neither treated in nor outside the home:					
No	57	80.3%	11.1 (4.2)	10.0, 12.2	0.43
Yes	14	19.7%	12.1 (5.2)	9.1, 15.2	
Caregivers waiting >1 day to seek care after recognising the symptoms:					
No	23	31.9%	10.7 (4.1)	8.9, 12.4	0.44
Yes	49	68.1%	11.5 (4.5)	10.2, 21.8	
Children who were taken outside the home for care:					
No	17	23.9%	13 (5.2)	10.3, 15.7	0.07
Yes	54	76.1%	10.7 (3.9)	9.7, 11.9	
Children whose caregiver waited >3 hours to seek care after decision had been taken:					
No	24	44.4%	11.6 (3.8)	10.0, 13.2	0.16
Yes	30	55.6%	10.1 (4.1)	8.6, 11.6	
Caregivers who delayed >2 hours to reach first provider:					
No	44	81.5%	10.8 (3.7)	9.6, 11.9	0.98
Yes	10	18.5%	10.8 (0.3)	7.0, 14.6	
Children who were taken to an informal first source of care:†					
No	49	94.2%	10.7 (4.1)	9.5, 11.8	0.58
Yes	3	5.8%	12 (3.5)	3.4, 20.6	
Children who were taken to an APE as first source of care:†					
No	40	74.1%	11.0 (4.1)	9.7, 12.3	0.54
Yes	14	25.9%	10.2 (3.7)	8.1, 12.3	
Cause of death – malaria:					
No	35	48.6%	11.5 (3.7)	10.2, 12.8	0.60
Yes	37	51.4%	11.0 (5.0)	9.3, 12.6	
Cause of death – HIV/AIDS:					
No	64	88.9%	11.3 (4.5)	10.1, 12.4	0.87
Yes	8	11.1%	11.0 (3.9)	7.7, 14.3	
Cause of death – ARI, including pneumonia					
No	65	90.3%	11.0 (4.4)	10.0, 12.1	0.26
Yes	7	9.7%	13 (4.3)	9.0, 17.0	
Cause of death – diarrhoea:					
No	65	90.3%	11.4 (4.6)	10.2, 12.5	0.38
Yes	7	9.7%	9.9 (1.8)	8.2, 11.5	

ARI – acute respiratory infection, APE – agentes polivalentes elementares
*The total number varies because of missing data (due to "don't know" answers) in both the pathway indicator and the social capital indicators.
†Out of the ones who were taken outside the home for care.
‡Significant at P<0.01 level.

Of children reported with moderate or severe disease, 34 (47.9%) delayed more than one day before seeking health care and 33 (57.9%) delayed more than three hours to act on the decision to go outside for care; the main reason being that they believed that the child had improved or the symptoms had stopped. Of the 11 children who were referred from at least one provider, only two did not adhere to the referral advice.

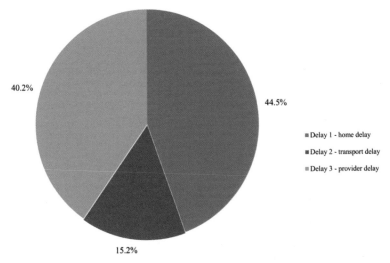

40.2%

44.5%

■ Delay 1 - home delay

■ Delay 2 - transport delay

■ Delay 3 - provider delay

15.2%

Figure 3. *Different types of delay preceding death of children.*

Box 1. *Sample of narratives for reasons why caregivers did not seek timely care outside the home*

Caregiver 1: "The child's parents had not given approval [to take the child for care] as they had already gone to Maputo [the capital of Mozambique].

Caregiver 2: "I lacked immediate transportation, and at the time [of the death] the APE was not available"

Caregiver 3: "When I got home from the field I found my child very ill and she died shortly after."

Caregiver 4: "I thought it was a simple fever that could resolve by itself."

Caregiver 5: "We thought that we could wait a little bit and take the child [for care] the next day, but he ended up losing his life that night."

Caregiver 6: "I thought the child was healthy."

Caregiver 7: "The mother of the child did not take the child to the health unit because she claimed that they would not see them there because they don't have a health card".

Caregiver 8: "Everything happened very fast and the baby died while we were getting ready to go to the hospital."

Caregiver 9: "Because I had no money to go for care."

Caregiver 10: "Because he had gone to the hospital on Friday to get the baby vaccinated and I thought the illness was vaccine-induced."

Delays due to transportation

Of the 63 children taken for care outside the home, 3 (5.3%) delayed more than three hours to act on the decision due to lack of transport, and 13 (21.0%) delayed more than two hours to reach the provider after having found a transport method. The majority (43/63; 68.3%) went by foot to the health provider. Of the two children who failed to adhere to referral neither were mentioned to have had difficulties in finding transport.

Provider delay

Most children (93.1%; 54/58 (5 missing data)) who sought care from at least one health provider received some kind of treatment, but 18 (31.0%) of them had to wait more than one hour to receive the treatment. Of the 11 children who were referred, 3 (27.3%) were referred because of lack of medicines or equipment.

The total delay score at home, transport or provider was calculated for each provider first seen, among the children who were taken outside for care before dying (**Table 3**). The home delay was significantly lower among the children who were first taken to an APE compared to other providers ($P = 0.02$) but was significantly higher among the children who were taken to a traditional healer ($P = 0.04$). The children who were taken to a health facility had a significantly higher transport delay score than other providers ($P = 0.004$), and the children who were taken to traditional healers had a significantly higher provider delay score ($P = 0.04$), whereas those who went to health facilities had a lower provider delay score.

DISCUSSION

In this study, we found that almost all the illnesses leading to the deaths in children younger than 5 years were preventable and treatable. The majority

Table 3. *Home, transport and provider delay score by first provider seen (N = 63)*

	HOME DE-LAY SCORE (MAX = 7) N (95% CI)	P VALUE*	TRANSPORT DELAY SCORE (MAX = 3) N (95% CI)	P VALUE	PROVIDER DELAY SCORE (MAX = 3) N (95% CI)	P-VALUE
APE	2.13 (1.61, 2.64)	0.02	0.13 (0.0, 0.31)	0.24	1.06 (0.93, 1.20)	0.19
Health facility	2.64 (2.34, 2.93)	0.77	0.42 (0.21, 0.64)	0.004	0.76 (0.54, 0.98)	0.03
Hospital	2.83 (1.80-3.87)	0.53	0	0.20	0.83 (0.40, 1.26)	0.75
Traditional healer	3.0 (1.48, 4.52)	0.04	0	0.25	1.4 (0.72, 2.08)	0.04

CI – confidence interval, APE – agentes polivalentes elementares
*Compared to the other three categories combined.

could also have been detected, treated or referred by community-based providers such as the APEs. Yet, many did not visit the APE during the child's illness, or reached when it was already too late for the APE to manage the child. The main contributors to death documented in this study included lack of caregiver awareness and recognition of illness symptoms, home care practices leading to delays in outside care seeking, and considerable distances between households and health facilities. While these factors have previously been established as key barriers to care for young children [27,28], several studies have suggested that these access barriers could be overcome through the introduction of integrated community case management (iCCM) delivered by community health workers (CHWs) [26,29]. However, in our study, we show that the same care seeking delays that caregivers experience when seeking care from distant health facilities also apply for families living in communities served by CHWs providing iCCM. The Mozambique APE programme is unique from other community based primary health care (CBPHC) programmes, in the sense that APEs do not have a fixed health post and that 80% of the time they are supposed to be conducting household visits; making it difficult for caregivers to know where and when to access the APE. With so few caregivers seeking care from an APE, and seeking care too late in the illness process, it is likely that APEs are simply not close enough to the households to be able to cover the access gap. The current APE strategy in Mozambique aims to expand the reach of care to the 20% of population who do not have access to a health facility, but as the strategy calls for 25 APEs per districts as a blanket recommendation, this can result in an APE:population ratio of 1:5000 or more, depending on the district. Hence, we recommend that a review of the geographical coverage of APEs, and the time they spend delivering curative services, should be conducted and that more APEs are deployed in areas where access is still problematic. Most delays happened at home, as a result of caregiver decision making processes or failure to recognise illness symptoms before the child was already severely ill (stopped eating/drinking, stopped moving, or unconscious). The lack of caregiver awareness of symptoms of malaria, pneumonia and diarrhoea, and of the potentially life-threatening nature of these conditions in a young child, has been documented previously [30-35]. In this setting, both parents are in charge of the decision to seek care for a sick child. Yet, while women do not need permission from their husbands to seek care, they may not have access to the cash that the care seeking process requires. While it may be logical to a poor and rural family to wait and hope for improvement in a febrile child before deciding to seek outside care, which often requires using sparse household savings, an untreated malaria infection can progress rapidly to convulsions, coma and death within

24 hours of symptom onset [36]. Instead, families have commonly reported resorting to herbal treatment as "first aid" for fever before seeking outside care [35,37], potentially delaying care seeking from a trained health provider. This practice was also common among the families of the deceased children in our study, including the children who were later taken to an APE for care. While household delays in care seeking have been documented for children seeking care from (often distant) health facilities and hospitals, it was unexpected to see that one in four children in our study never even left the home during the illness before they died.

Use of APEs among these children who later died was low, with only one of four first seeking care from their APE, and of these, most came late when the symptoms were already severe. More children with severe conditions were first taken to the APE than the facility, potentially because the APE was nearer than any other provider. None of the children had been taken to the APE at a stage when the illness symptoms were mild and still treatable by the APE with medicines that could be given at home; still, all but one child had received treatment from the APE. The low capacity of CHWs to recognise, manage and refer severe illness in children has been documented previously, with only about one third of children with severe illness being managed correctly and just over half being referred appropriately by health extension workers in Ethiopia [38]. The failure to recognise and act on signs of serious illness is also problematic in official primary care facilities, and a recent study showed that danger signs were missed in 43% of cases in Mali and in 39% in Uganda, and 45%-51% of patients who were seriously ill were not referred to a hospital in time [39]. These failures are in part due to insufficient training, feedback, and support for the staff at work, and it has been suggested that improvement is possible with introduction of better diagnostic tools to diagnose severe illness [40,41], along with local panel meetings to audit and improve health worker practices and work culture with feedback, education, and leadership [39].

The proportion who decided to seek care outside the home when the child was still moderately ill (ie, sick but not yet unmanageable by an APE) was significantly higher among families with a higher social capital score. While our results showed that a few components of social capital (eg, if the participant had trust in people in general and if the participant felt that people in general can get hurt) provided more loading to the principle component, they were not independently associated with the pathway indicators in binary analysis. However, social capital has been found important in promoting health globally, with associated effects on both health outcomes of people living with HIV/AIDS [15] and child nutritional status [14]. According to Ogden et al [13] the process of building social capital can support health policy and health system strengthening by creation of trust, norms of reciprocity, rights and sanctions across the health system and reaching into the community. Social capital can be accrued by groups of like-minded people within a community and is strengthened as those groups connect with other networks in pursuit of common goals. Our results support the call for further studies examining the possible linkage between child health seeking behaviours and social capital components. Depending on the available types and strengths of specific components of social capital (or the lack thereof), programme practitioners may be able to consider tailoring the caregiver-targeted health seeking programmes, eg, community empowerment interventions such as women's groups [42] or positive deviance [14], to effectively influence related behaviour changes.

The "three-delays" model has been used in previous studies to examine barriers to seeking care and preventing maternal and child mortality [19,26,29,43,44]. Children who die experience major delays of various kinds, largely due to lack of early recognition of the disease in the home and late decision-taking for outside care seeking. Distance to APEs and to referral facilities likely contributes to these delays, both for moderately and severely sick children. In this study, the main delays that prevented the children to receive health care in a timely manner are in line with other studies in fatal diseases in children in Guinea Bissau, United Republic of Tanzania and Uganda [19,26,29], where fatal outcomes were explained by factors related to the recognition of the disease and looking for late care (Delay 1), along with delays in receiving medication and lack of equipment and drugs from health providers (Delay 3). In our study, we found that home delays are less common among those who first sought care from an APE.

In the absence of routine civil registration and vital statistics (CRVS) systems, estimates suggest that one in two deaths go unrecorded globally every year in terms of medical causes [45]. We show in our study that as many as 92% of children died away from a hospital or health facility, and without a vital events registration system at community level, these deaths would largely go uncounted. With Mozambique now at the forefront of countries scaling up a national CRVS, the APEs could potentially play an important role in notifying the CRVS registrars about vital events in their catchment population. However, with only 117 deaths recorded the by 275 APEs in the year 2015, in a population with over 60 000 children under five-year olds and under-five mortality rate of 79 per 10 000 live births, we would have expected almost 10 times the number of deaths to have occurred. In order to support the successful scale up of the CRVS in Mozambique, the training and support of APEs in registration of all births and death in their catchment areas should therefore be seen as a priority.

A main limitation of verbal and social autopsy studies is that they are purely descriptive in nature and it is therefore not possible to determine any association between care seeking patterns and death. It has also been noted that social autopsy methodology does not sufficiently shed light on the details required to understand the complexities of decision making around care seeking for serious illnesses among mothers and babies [43]. Due to this complexity, standard SA tools only capture information on the acute illness phase and the first and last providers sought [19]. Still, there is a wide breadth and depth of existing social autopsy research in the recent literature and the methodology is seen as a powerful tool with the demonstrated ability to raise awareness, provide evidence in the form of actionable data and increase motivation at all levels to take appropriate and effective actions [39,43,46]. In a recent study by Willcox et al (2018), the authors took the death inquiry approach in Mali and Uganda a step further by adding a community intervention component; by using a panel of local health care workers and community representatives to review the investigation findings, formulate recommendations to address avoidable factors and, subsequently, oversee their implementation, an under five mortality reduction of 18%-27% was observed [39]. Further research is called for to optimise the implementation model for community-based death reviews, including verbal and social autopsy and other qualitative death inquiries, and actionable community-based response mechanisms. Linking these response mechanisms to other participatory community empowerment structures, such as village health clubs or women's groups, could potentially address not only the harmful delays in care seeking, but also be applied to strengthen social capital among families.

Another limitation of our study could be that we used the InterVA tool to provide us with the cause of death information; a software that has been praised for its automation, simplicity and cost and time saving aspects to VA analysis, but also questioned for its performance in relation to manual physician panel review and other automated methods like SmartVA and InSilicoVA [47]. However, at the time of planning this study InterVA was the only automated method that was available for use and that was fully aligned with the latest WHO VA tool. While this means that we could have misreported the cause of death in the children in our sample, the main purpose of our study was to investigate care seeking behaviour for acute illness, and cause of death was just one of many explanatory variables that we explored in our analysis.

As countries increase verbal autopsy surveillance, it is important to consider the best way to design sustainable systems for data collection [48], to also add on community-based death reviews to maximise their cost-effectiveness, and to make the method part of routine health service delivery. This could be achieved by investigating and reviewing only a sample of deaths, as many of the same issues frequently recur, and therefore the same recommendations may often be repeated [19,39]. As the tools used for automated analysis of VA data are constantly evolving and improving, and it is important that planners and researchers keep abreast with the latest recommendations that WHO publishes.

Finally, while social capital has been identified as a key determinant for health in the WHO Commission on Social Determinants of Health [49], its usefulness in the study of health outcomes has been questioned by some scholars, who argue that the social capital literature is 'gender and power blind' [50], that economic and social status are more important drivers to health [51], and that some conditions (like suicide) have higher rates among those most socially included [52]. While the theoretical and empirical links between social capital and health are still not resolved, it can still provide a useful framework for what constitutes health supporting environments, and gives guidance on how to achieve them [22]. Further research is needed to better understand how and why (or why not) different aspects of social capital are associated with different health outcomes, and a more detailed tool for measuring social capital should be developed that can map and mobilise social capital in local communities as a way of achieving community action for health promotion.

CONCLUSIONS

The leading causes of death in under-fives can be detected early, promptly treated or referred by APEs. Children who die experience major delays of various kinds, mainly at home, largely due to lack of early recognition of the disease and late decision-taking for outside care seeking. Distances to APEs and to referral facilities likely contribute to these delays, both for moderately and severely sick children. Efforts to increase caregiver awareness of illness in children are urgently needed, as well as stronger referral linkages with facility providers. A review of the geographical coverage of APEs, and the implications of the 80/20 time split for preventive/promotive vs curative services, should be conducted.

Acknowledgement: *We are grateful to all caretakers and community members who volunteered to share their experiences around the death of one of their children. We also thank the field workers for managing data collection, compilation and entering of the data. We are grateful to Guilhermina Maria Cremilde Fernandes for supporting the data collection and analysis.*

Funding: *The study was funded under the World Health Organisation (WHO) Rapid Access Expansion programme (RAcE).*

Author contributors: *KK conceptualised and designed the study protocol, conducted the analysis and interpretation, drafted and wrote the manuscript. HC participated in the design of the study, in the data interpretation, drafted and reviewed the manuscript. TC and FM participated in the design of the study protocol, supervised the data collection and drafted and reviewed the manuscript. All co-authors reviewed and approved the final version of the manuscript.*

Competing interests: *The authors have completed the Unified Competing Interest form at www.icmje.org/coi_disclosure.pdf (available on request from the corresponding author), and declare no conflicts of interest.*

References

1   Liu L, Oza S, Hogan D, Chu Y, Perin J, Zhu J, et al. Global, regional, and national causes of under-5 mortality in 2000-15: an updated systematic analysis with implications for the Sustainable Development Goals. Lancet. 2016;388:3027-35. Medline:27839855 doi:10.1016/S0140-6736(16)31593-8

2   World Health Organization. World Malaria Report 2016. Geneva: World Health Organization (WHO): 2016 www.who.int/malaria/publications/world-malaria-report-2016/report/en/.

3   Ambel AA, Andrews C, Bakilana AM, Foster EM, Khan Q, Wang H. Examining changes in maternal and child health inequalities in Ethiopia. Int J Equity Health. 2017;16:152. Medline:28830454 doi:10.1186/s12939-017-0648-1

4   United Nations Inter-agency Group for Child Mortality Estimation (UN IGME). Levels & Trends in Child Mortality: Report 2017, Estimates Developed by the UN Inter-agency Group for Child Mortality Estimation. New York: United Nations Children's Fund, 2017.

5   Global Health Workforce Alliance (GHWA) Secretariat and the World Health Organization. A Universal Truth: No Health Without a Workforce. Geneva: World Health Organization (WHO), 2014 www.who.int/workforcealliance/knowledge/resources/GHWA-a_universal_truth_report.pdf?ua=1.

6   Ali F, Mucache D, Scuccato R. Avaliação do Programa dos APEs. Maputo: Moçambique: Ministério da Saúde e Cooperação Suiça, 1994.

7   Ministério da saúde. Pontos Chave para a Implementação do Programa dos Agentes Polivalentes Elementares (APEs). Maputo, Moçambique: Direcção Nacional de Saúde Pública, Ministério da Saúde, 2010.

8   Succato R, Aly F, Mucache D, A. S. Relatório da Avaliação do Desempenho dos APEs. Maputo, Mocambique: Cooperação Suíça - Ministério da Saúde, 1994.

9   Ministério da saúde. Health sector strategic plan 2014-2019. Maputo: Ministry of health, Republic of Mozambique, 2014 http://www.nationalplanningcycles.org/sites/default/files/planning_cycle_repository/mozambique/mozambique_-_health_sector_strategic_plan_-_2014-2019.pdf.

10 Ministério da saúde. Programa de Revitalização dos Agentes Polivalentes Elementares. Maputo, Moçambique: Direcção Nacional de Saúde Pública, Ministério da Saúde, 2010.

11 World Health Organisation. Mozambique at forefront of improving population registration. 2017. Accessed.

12 Jones G, Steketee RW, Black RE, Bhutta ZA, Morris SS. How many child deaths can we prevent this year? Lancet. 2003;362:65-71. Medline:12853204 doi:10.1016/S0140-6736(03)13811-1

13 Ogden J, Morrison K, Hardee K. Social capital to strengthen health policy and health systems. Health Policy Plan. 2014;29:1075-85. Medline:24277736 doi:10.1093/heapol/czt087

14 Kang Y, Kim J, Seo E. Association between maternal social capital and infant complementary feeding practices in rural Ethiopia. Matern Child Nutr. 2018;14:1. Medline:28714283 doi:10.1111/mcn.12484

15 Mukoswa GM, Charalambous S, Nelson G. The association between social capital and HIV treatment outcomes in South Africa. PLoS One. 2017;12:e0184140. Medline:29121656 doi:10.1371/journal.pone.0184140

16 Instituto Nacional de Estatistica Mocambique. Projecções da População. 2018. Available: http://www.ine.gov.mz/estatisticas/estatisticas-demograficas-e-indicadores-sociais/projeccoes-da-populacao. Accessed: 9th May, 2018.

17 World Health Organization. Verbal autopsy standards: ascertaining and attributing cause of death. Geneva: WHO, 2016.

18 INDEPTH Network. INDEPTH Social Autopsy - Child. 2009. Available: http://www.indepth-network.org/sites/default/files/content/resources/files/New%20INDEPTH%20child%20SA%20tool.pdf. Accessed: 9th May, 2018.

19 Källander K, Kadobera D, Williams TN, Nielsen RT, Yevoo L, Mutebi A, et al. Social autopsy: INDEPTH Network experiences of utility, process, practices, and challenges in investigating causes and contributors to mortality. Popul Health Metr. 2011;9:44. Medline:21819604 doi:10.1186/1478-7954-9-44

20 Grootaert C, Narayan D, Nyhan Jones V, Woolcock M. Measuring Social Capital - An Integrated Questionnaire. Washington DC: World Bank, 2004.

21 Dimagi. CommCare. Available: [Archived by WebCite® at http://www.webcitation.org/6wrUb4GRO]. Accessed: January 30, 2018.

22 Eriksson M. Social capital and health–implications for health promotion. Glob Health Action. 2011;4:5611. Medline:21311607 doi:10.3402/gha.v4i0.5611

23 Binagwaho A, Ratnayake N. The role of social capital in successful adherence to antiretroviral therapy in Africa. PLoS Med. 2009;6:e18. Medline:19175286 doi:10.1371/journal.pmed.1000018

24 Nichols EK, Byass P, Chandramohan D, Clark SJ, Flaxman AD, Jakob R, et al. The WHO 2016 verbal autopsy instrument: An international standard suitable for automated analysis by InterVA, InSilicoVA, and Tariff 2.0. PLoS Med. 2018;15:e1002486. Medline:29320495 doi:10.1371/journal.pmed.1002486

25 Waiswa P, Kalter HD, Jakob R, Black RE, Social Autopsy Working Group. Increased use of social autopsy is needed to improve maternal, neonatal and child health programmes in low-income countries. Bull World Health Organ. 2012;90:403-A.

26 Waiswa P, Kallander K, Peterson S, Tomson G, Pariyo GW. Using the three delays model to understand why newborn babies die in eastern Uganda. Trop Med Int Health. 2010;15:964-72. Medline:20636527 doi:10.1111/j.1365-3156.2010.02557.x

27 Kiwanuka SN, Ekirapa EK, Peterson S, Okui O, Rahman MH, Peters D, et al. Access to and utilisation of health services for the poor in Uganda: a systematic review of available evidence. Trans R Soc Trop Med Hyg. 2008;102:1067-74. Medline:18565559 doi:10.1016/j.trstmh.2008.04.023

28   Rutebemberwa E, Kallander K, Tomson G, Peterson S, Pariyo G. Determinants of delay in care-seeking for febrile children in eastern Uganda. Trop Med Int Health. 2009;14:472-9. Medline:19222823 doi:10.1111/j.1365-3156.2009.02237.x

29   Källander K, Hildenwall H, Waiswa P, Galiwango E, Peterson S, Pariyo G. Delayed care seeking for fatal pneumonia in children aged under five years in Uganda: a case-series study. Bull World Health Organ. 2008;86:332-8. Medline:18545734 doi:10.2471/BLT.07.049353

30   Abbey M, Chinbuah MA, Gyapong M, Bartholomew LK, van den Borne B. Community perceptions and practices of treatment seeking for childhood pneumonia: a mixed methods study in a rural district, Ghana. BMC Public Health. 2016;16:848. Medline:27549163 doi:10.1186/s12889-016-3513-z

31   Deshmukh V, Lahariya C, Krishnamurthy S, Das MK, Pandey RM, Arora NK. Taken to Health Care Provider or Not, Under-Five Children Die of Preventable Causes: Findings from Cross-Sectional Survey and Social Autopsy in Rural India. Indian J Community Med. 2016;41:108-19. Medline:27051085 doi:10.4103/0970-0218.177527

32   Digre P, Simpson E, Cali S, Lartey B, Moodley M, Diop N. Caregiver perceptions and utilization of oral rehydration solution and other treatments for diarrhea among young children in Burkina Faso. J Glob Health. 2016;6:020407. Medline:27699000 doi:10.7189/jogh.06.020407

33   Källander K, Tomson G, Nsabagasani X, Sabiiti JN, Pariyo G, Peterson S. Can community health workers and caretakers recognise pneumonia in children? Experiences from western Uganda. Trans R Soc Trop Med Hyg. 2006;100:956-63. Medline:16455119 doi:10.1016/j.trstmh.2005.11.004

34   Mitiku I, Assefa A. Caregivers' perception of malaria and treatment-seeking behaviour for under five children in Mandura District, West Ethiopia: a cross-sectional study. Malar J. 2017;16:144. Medline:28390423 doi:10.1186/s12936-017-1798-8

35   Nsungwa-Sabiiti J, Peterson S, Pariyo G, Ogwal-Okeng J, Petzold MG, Tomson G. Home-based management of fever and malaria treatment practices in Uganda. Trans R Soc Trop Med Hyg. 2007;101:1199-207. Medline:17945320 doi:10.1016/j.trstmh.2007.08.005

36   Greenwood BM, Bradley AK, Greenwood AM, Byass P, Jammeh K, Marsh K, et al. Mortality and morbidity from malaria among children in a rural area of The Gambia, West Africa. Trans R Soc Trop Med Hyg. 1987;81:478-86. Medline:3318021 doi:10.1016/0035-9203(87)90170-2

37   O'Neill S, Gryseels C, Dierickx S, Mwesigwa J, Okebe J, d'Alessandro U, et al. Foul wind, spirits and witchcraft: illness conceptions and health-seeking behaviour for malaria in the Gambia. Malar J. 2015;14:167. Medline:25908392 doi:10.1186/s12936-015-0687-2

38   Miller NP, Amouzou A, Hazel E, Degefie T, Legesse H, Tafesse M, et al. Assessing the Quality of Sick Child Care Provided by Community Health Workers. PLoS One. 2015;10:e0142010. Medline:26551035 doi:10.1371/journal.pone.0142010

39   Willcox ML, Kumbakumba E, Diallo D, Mubangizi V, Kirabira P, Nakaggwa F, et al. Circumstances of child deaths in Mali and Uganda: a community-based confidential enquiry. Lancet Glob Health. 2018;6:e691-702. Medline:29773123 doi:10.1016/S2214-109X(18)30215-8

40   Keitel K, Kagoro F, Samaka J, Masimba J, Said Z, Temba H, et al. A novel electronic algorithm using host biomarker point-of-care tests for the management of febrile illnesses in Tanzanian children (e-POCT): A randomized, controlled non-inferiority trial. PLoS Med. 2017;14:e1002411. Medline:29059253 doi:10.1371/journal.pmed.1002411

41   McCollum ED, King C, Deula R, Zadutsa B, Mankhambo L, Nambiar B, et al. Pulse oximetry for children with pneumonia treated as outpatients in rural Malawi. Bull World Health Organ. 2016;94:893-902. Medline:27994282 doi:10.2471/BLT.16.173401

42 Prost A, Colbourn T, Seward N, Azad K, Coomarasamy A, Copas A, et al. Women's groups practising participatory learning and action to improve maternal and newborn health in low-resource settings: a systematic review and meta-analysis. Lancet. 2013;381:1736-46. Medline:23683640 doi:10.1016/S0140-6736(13)60685-6

43 Moyer CA, Johnson C, Kaselitz E, Aborigo R. Using social autopsy to understand maternal, newborn, and child mortality in low-resource settings: a systematic review of the literature. Glob Health Action. 2017;10:1413917. Medline:29261449 doi:10.1080/16549716.2017.1413917

44 Samuelsen H, Tersbol BP, Mbuyita SS. Do health systems delay the treatment of poor children? A qualitative study of child deaths in rural Tanzania. BMC Health Serv Res. 2013;13:67. Medline:23421705 doi:10.1186/1472-6963-13-67

45 Thomas LM, D'Ambruoso L, Balabanova D. Verbal autopsy in health policy and systems: a literature review. BMJ Glob Health. 2018;3:e000639. Medline:29736271 doi:10.1136/bmjgh-2017-000639

46 Kalter HD, Salgado R, Babille M, Koffi AK, Black RE. Social autopsy for maternal and child deaths: a comprehensive literature review to examine the concept and the development of the method. Popul Health Metr. 2011;9:45. Medline:21819605 doi:10.1186/1478-7954-9-45

47 Lozano R, Freeman MK, James SL, Campbell B, Lopez AD, Flaxman AD, et al. Performance of InterVA for assigning causes of death to verbal autopsies: multisite validation study using clinical diagnostic gold standards. Popul Health Metr. 2011;9:50. Medline:21819580 doi:10.1186/1478-7954-9-50

48 D'Ambruoso L, Boerma T, Byass P, Fottrell E, Herbst K, Kallander K, et al. The case for verbal autopsy in health systems strengthening. Lancet Glob Health. 2017;5:e20-1. Medline:27866775 doi:10.1016/S2214-109X(16)30332-1

49 CSDH. Closing the gap in a generation: health equity through action on the social determinants of health. Final Report of the Commission on Social Determinants of Health. Geneva: World Health Organization, 2008.

50 Gidengil E, O'Neill B. Removing rose colored glasses: examining theories of social capital through a gendered lens. In: O'Neill B GE, editor. Gender and social capital. New York NY: Routledge; 2006.

51 Muntaner C, Lynch JW, Hillemeier M, Lee JH, David R, Benach J, et al. Economic inequality, working-class power, social capital, and cause-specific mortality in wealthy countries. Int J Health Serv. 2002;32:629-56. Medline:12456119 doi:10.2190/N7A9-5X58-0DYT-C6AY

52 Kushner HI, Sterk CE. The limits of social capital: Durkheim, suicide, and social cohesion. Am J Public Health. 2005;95:1139-43. Medline:15933234 doi:10.2105/AJPH.2004.053314

Testing a simplified tool and training package to improve integrated Community Case Management in Tanganyika Province, Democratic Republic of Congo: a quasi-experimental study

Anne Langston[1], Alison Wittcoff[1], Pascal Ngoy[2], Jennifer O'Keefe[1], Naoko Kozuki[1], Hannah Taylor[1], Yolanda Barbera Lainez [1], Sambou Bacary[3]

[1] International Rescue Committee, New York, New York, USA
[2] International Rescue Committee, Kinshasa, DR Congo
[3] World Health Organization, Kinshasa, DR Congo

Background Integrated community case management (iCCM) is a strategy to train community health workers (*relais communautaires* or *RECOs* in French) in low-resource settings to provide treatment for uncomplicated malaria, pneumonia, and diarrhea for children 2-59 months of age. The package of Ministry of Public Health tools for *RECOs* in the Democratic Republic of Congo that was being used in 2013 included seven data collection tools and job aids which were redundant and difficult to use. As part of the WHO-supported iCCM program, the International Rescue Committee developed and evaluated a simplified set of pictorial tools and curriculum adapted for low-literate *RECOs*.

Methods The revised training curriculum and tools were tested in a quasi-experimental study, with 74 *RECOs* enrolled in the control group and 78 *RECOs* in the intervention group. Three outcomes were assessed during the study period from Sept. 2015-July 2016: 1) quality of care, measured by direct observation and reexamination; 2) workload, measured as the time required for each assessment – including documentation; and 3) costs of rolling out each package. Logistic regression was used to calculate odds ratios for correct treatment by the intervention group compared to the control group, controlling for characteristics of the *RECOs*, the child, and the catchment area.

Results Children managed by the *RECOs* in the intervention group had nearly three times higher odds of receiving correct treatment (adjusted odds ratio aOR = 2.9, 95% confidence interval CI = 1.3-6.3, $P = 0.010$). On average, the time spent by the intervention group was 10.6 minutes less (95% CI = 6.6-14.7, $P < 0.001$), representing 6.2 hours of time saved per month for a *RECO* seeing 35 children. The estimated cost savings amounts to over US$ 300 000 for a four-year program supporting 1500 *RECOs*.

Conclusion This study demonstrates that, at scale, simplified tools and a training package adapted for low-literate *RECOs* could substantially improve health outcomes for under-five children while reducing implementation costs and decreasing their workload. The training curriculum and simplified tools have been adopted nationally based on the results from this study.

While huge strides have been made globally, the under-five mortality rate still remains unacceptably high in many sub-Saharan African countries. According to the World Health Organization [1], children born in sub-Saharan Africa are 14 times more likely to die before their fifth birthday compared to children in developed regions. It is estimated that malaria, diarrhea and pneumonia account for 37% of all under-five deaths in sub-Saharan Africa [2]. To reduce under-five mortality, many low-income countries have implemented integrated community case management (iCCM), a WHO-recommended equity-focused strategy to improve access to care beyond health facilities for children 2-59 months, in which community health workers (*RECOs*) receive training and supplies to treat uncomplicated malaria, pneumonia and diarrhea in their communities and refer complicated cases [3].

Although evidence exists to show that, if well-implemented, iCCM can contribute to saving lives of children under five [4], many recent studies have also revealed the numerous bottlenecks in implementation which may prevent iCCM from having its intended benefit, including poor quality of services [5]. However, there is limited research on factors influencing the quality of care, specifically the impact of training methods, job aids and reporting tools on the quality of care and workload of *RECOs* [6,7]. Many countries have tools and training curricula that are not adapted for low-literate *RECOs*, resulting in errors during assessment of the sick child and long consultation times [8]. In the Democratic Republic of Congo (DRC), the Ministry of Public Health (MoPH) package for *RECOs* included seven highly redundant reporting forms and several job aids which were difficult to use and required a high level of literacy [9,10].

From September 2013 to November 2017 the International Rescue Committee (IRC) facilitated implementation of the Rapid Access Expansion (RAcE) programme in Tanganyika Province with the support of the World Health Organization. Working under the leadership of the MoPH, the program trained and supported approximately 1600 *RECOs*, serving an estimated 360 000 children under five. As part of the RAcE-supported initiative, the IRC developed a curriculum and a simplified set of pictorial tools adapted for low-literate *RECOs*. The purpose of this study was to evaluate the effect of the package on quality of care, *RECO* workload and program implementation costs. Due to resource constraints and scope of work limitations, this study was unable to look at other factors that may have had an impact on quality of care such as supervision.

METHODS

Context and program design

The study was conducted from September 2015 to July 2016 in Tanganyika Province, DRC. It is located in conflict-affected Eastern Congo, covers 150 940 km^2 with a total population estimated at 2 649 317 and a density of 18 inhabitants per square kilometer. Access to health care services is limited by financial and geographic barriers. According to results of the 2013-2014 DRC-DHS, under five-mortality was 121 per 1000 live births and malaria prevalence was 32% among children 6-59 months in Katanga province (which at the time included Tanganyika) [11].

In an effort to address barriers to health services, DRC began implementing iCCM in 2005. As described in the MoPH implementation guide [9], Relais Communautaires, often referred to as *RECOs* in DRC, are unpaid volunteers selected by their communities. They must be literate and have a source of income, limiting the pool of candidates and excluding most women. In the RAcE-supported program, less than 10% of *RECOs* were women. *RECOs* were trained to assess and classify children 2-59 months of age presenting with signs of illness and treat uncomplicated cases of malaria, pneumonia and diarrhea, and refer children with severe illness after giving the first dose of medication. *RECOs* are supervised by the head nurse of the health center located closest to the *RECOs'* catchment area. Additional supervision was provided by the health zone, regional authorities and IRC project staff.

Revised tools

The MoPH package (control) consisted of seven separate tools that must be completed by the *RECOs* (**Table 1**). Due to the complexity of the tools, much of the training was dedicated to teaching *RECOs* how to use them, leaving little time for building skills in assessment and treatment. To address these concerns, the IRC in collaboration with MoPH developed a simplified tool package, henceforth referred to as the intervention. The tools were based on tools that IRC had tested and implemented in Sierra Leone and South Sudan, incorporating best practices for low-literacy communication. The total number of tools used by the *RECOs* decreased from seven to four, limiting the data collected to that used for supervision and program management (**Table 1**). Supervision guidelines, checklists and incentives were not altered by the study.

Table 1. *Summary of tools in control and intervention packages*

Name	MoPH package (control)	Revised package (intervention)
1. Individual Sick Child Form	Takes the *RECO* through steps of sick child management, documenting the findings of the assessment and decisions made. 89 data points.	Replaced with pictorial job aids which provide images and step by step instructions for assessment, classification, treatment, counseling, and referral. Laminated cards given during the training. No data collected.
2. Referral Note	Used for referral of a child with danger signs or another condition the *RECO* is not trained to treat; includes reason for referral and pre-referral treatment provided.	Includes images of danger signs and images of pre-referral treatment that the *RECO* ticks to inform the health center of the reason for referral and treatment given.
3. Register	Includes all cases assessed by the *RECO* during the month and notes whether the child had any danger signs, any procedures carried out during the assessment (malaria testing, middle upper arm circumference (MUAC) measurement, and breath count), the classification of the child, and the treatment received. 30 data points.	Similar to the original register, noting all assessment steps and classifications, but uses images which match job aids as guidance. The register also captures drug management of all medications and supplies that the *RECO* uses monthly. 32 data points.
4. Medication Count Notebook	Notes the number of each medication given out each day by the *RECO*.	Replaced by the register.
5. Medication Stock Register	Notes the medications received by the *RECO* from the health center and the medications used for treatments to children each month. 13 data points.	Replaced by the register.
6. Medication Order Form	Used for requesting medications to the head nurse at the health center each month.	No change.
7. Monthly Report	Summarizes aggregated data on sick children treated and stock management in a reporting month.	No change.

MoPH – Ministry of Public Health, *RECO – relais communautaires*

Training package

The curriculum developed for the intervention was based on best practices of adult learning methodologies and incorporated activities such as role plays and peer discussion. The images from the job aids and registers, along with large format posters, were used throughout to help reinforce learning. Both trainings lasted six days and were guided by a curriculum which provided a detailed training agenda. Because the tools in the intervention were less complicated, the *RECOs* in the intervention group were able to spend more time on practical skills during their training.

Study design and sampling

This was a quasi-experimental study conducted to compare the quality of care and workload between *RECOs* trained and deployed with the current MoPH package and those using the intervention package. Quality of care was evaluated using direct observation and reexamination, a method found in previous research to be the most accurate measure of *RECOs* quality of care [12]. A quality of care evaluation earlier in the program (2014) found that 44% of cases were treated correctly by the *RECOs*. We sought to detect a relative 50% improvement to the earlier assessment (a 66% correct treatment rate), with an alpha of 5% and a power of 80%. With a 10% loss-to-follow-up incorporated, we estimated a sample of 79 *RECOs* for each arm.

Among the health zones covered by the program, Kabalo and Manono were selected for the study because iCCM had not yet been scaled up to those zones. Both health zones are remote, with populations between 66 000 and 67 000, and 100 *RECOs* each. Within the zones, equal numbers of health center catchment areas were selected to participate in the implementation research. Health center catchment areas were used as the unit of assignment to prevent contamination between the two groups. Health center catchment areas that had already begun training *RECOs* with the MoPH package were used as control areas, with about half of the areas in each of the respective health zones assigned to the intervention package. Within each health area, all *RECOs* received the same training and tools.

RECOs in the control group were trained from February to March 2015, and the intervention group was trained from July to September 2015. Trainings were staggered based on the timing of the project scale-up schedule. Both sets of trainings were preceded by a training of trainers facilitated by MoPH personnel with support from RAcE Zonal Supervisors. As per MoPH policy, head nurses from the selected health areas participated in the trainings to support the *RECOs* they would be supervising.

Quality of care evaluations

Among those trained on either package, *RECOs* who had been active for at least six months and had submitted their monthly reports for the preceding two months were included in the evaluation sample.

The quality of care evaluations were conducted six to seven months after each of the trainings — September 2015 for the control group and March 2016 for the intervention group. Because of staff availability and time constraints, a single team performed the first evaluation, while two teams conducted the second. The supervisor from the first evaluation trained all evaluators for both teams. All evaluation teams consisted of one supervisor and two evaluators, a trained IRC clinician and the MoPH zonal focal point. For the second evaluation, a provincial focal point served as one of the evaluators. In total, 154 *RECOs* were evaluated, 75 in the control arm and 79 in the intervention arm. **Table 2** below shows the breakdown of health centers and *RECOs* assigned to each arm per zone. More *RECOs* were trained than evaluated because some *RECOs* did not complete the initial training, were deemed incapable of providing services at the end of the training, or had resigned within the first six months. In addition, our sample size calculations did not require us to evaluate all *RECOs* who had been trained.

The evaluations were conducted at the health facility where the *RECOs* were asked to be present on a prearranged day. The selection of *RECOs* for evaluation was done by zonal project supervisors, and based on availability, possibly resulting in a bias in favor of higher performing *RECOs*, although this would have been equally true for both arms. Evaluations were conducted at the health facility because more time and resources would have been required if each team had to travel to the home of each *RECO* assessed. In addition, there would have been no guarantee of a sick child coming to the *RECO's* home on the day the evaluation team was present. All *RECOs* used an identical kit containing all the necessary drugs, materials, and tools for assessment of a sick child. The children assessed during the evaluation were selected by the head nurse from among the sick children brought to the facility that day. The criteria given to the head nurse was to exclude children who were so ill that a slight delay in treatment would put them at risk.

RECOs were instructed to assess the child using the materials and tools provided, in the same manner as if they were providing care at their home. They were advised that they should present the necessary medications to the mother

Table 2. *Health centers participating in operational research per arm by zone*

Health yone	CONTROL			INTERVENTION		
	No. of health centers	No. of RECOs trained	No. of RECOs observed	No. of health centers	No. of RECOs trained	No. of RECOs observed
Kabalo	14	55	38	10	45	39
Manono	10	51	36	15	49	39
Total	24	106	74	25	94	78

RECO – relais communautaires

during the consultation, but not administer the first dose, as would normally be done. The evaluators observed the assessment and filled out a checklist to document the *RECO's* findings and decisions. All the *RECOs* evaluated were asked to count breaths for the child they were assessing, regardless of the condition. The *RECO's* count was compared to the count of the clinician and considered correct if it was within ± three breaths. Each *RECO* was observed providing case management to one sick child.

After the assessment, the *RECO* was taken to a separate area to complete filling out the rest of their tools (if necessary) and the trained clinician then reassessed and classified the child's condition, giving treatment according to iCCM protocol. The checklists of the two data collectors were cross-examined by the evaluation team for completeness and consistency. Discrepancies were discussed and corrected immediately after the process was completed, before proceeding to the next assessment.

Analysis

Data were entered into Excel (Microsoft Inc, Seattle WA, USA) and cleaned using Excel and Stata 11 (Stata Corp, College Station, TX, USA). Data reconciliation was done in Kalemie, DRC, and New York, USA. Unadjusted and adjusted logistic regression models were run to calculate the odds ratios of correct performance per protocol, comparing *RECOs* trained in the intervention model against the control. The outcome variables of interest are presented in **Table 3**.

The regression models controlled for potential confounders in two categories: *RECO* characteristics (age, sex, education [less than complete secondary/complete secondary or more], occupation [subsistence/professional], the health zone in which the *RECO* worked, the characteristics of the child (age, sex, condition [fever/diarrhea/respiratory symptoms], and the complexity of the child's condition [one condition/multiple conditions/three conditions or a non-iCCM condition/any danger sign]. The analyses were performed in Stata 11 (StataCorp LP, College Station, TX). *P*-value of <0.05 was considered statistically significant.

RECO workload

The total time the *RECO* spent on the assessment and documentation was recorded in minutes and seconds and entered into the study database. Linear regression was used to assess whether there was a difference between the two models, controlling for the same confounders listed above.

Table 3. *Quality of care outcomes*

Outcome	Definition
Correct assessment of danger signs	*RECO* checked for all danger/alert signs as per national protocol, which includes: vomits everything, convulsions, unable to drink/breastfeed, blood in stool, frequently sick, treatment failure, cough for 14 d or more, diarrhea for 14 d or more, fever for 7 d or more, red MUAC, palmar pallor, edema, severe visible wasting, unconscious or lethargic, diarrhea with dehydration, chest in-drawing, fever with generalized skin rash, very weak. MUAC is only taken for children 6 mo or older.
Correct referral decision	*RECO* referred the child for a danger/alert sign that was present or if the child presented with any condition outside of the iCCM conditions.
Correct respiratory count	*RECOs* count of respiratory movements of child was within ±3 of gold standard (trained clinician) after one minute.
Correct classification of individual conditions	Diarrhea: Caregiver reported diarrhea and *RECO* classified as diarrhea.
	Malaria/fever: Caregiver reported fever, RDT was conducted, and *RECO* classified case as malaria if positive and fever if negative.
	Pneumonia/cough: Caregiver reported cough or difficulty breathing, respiratory rate was measured and *RECO* correctly classified case as pneumonia or cough.
Correct treatment of individual conditions	Diarrhea: *RECO* correctly classified diarrhea and gave correct dose of both zinc and ORS according to age
	Malaria: *RECO* correctly classified malaria or fever based on RDT and gave correct dose of ACT and/or paracetamol according to classification and age.
	Pneumonia/cough: *RECO* correctly classified pneumonia or cough and gave correct dose of amoxicillin for age or counselling on home remedies according to classification.
Correct overall management	*RECO* correctly classified all conditions, including referral, and correct treatment for age, including pre-referral treatment when indicated.

RECO – *relais communautaires*

Cost analysis

In assessing the cost difference between the two models, we focused on areas of implementation where costs were expected to be different: printing of tools and training materials, and distribution of tools to *RECOs*. Actual costs and cost estimates from similar activities were used to create a prototype budget for one health zone with 100 active *RECOs* under each of the models. The costs for distribution of tools took into account the gas needed to cover all of the routes in Kabalo health zone, which is similar in size to other health zones in the region, covering a distance of 1706 km to reach all relevant *RECOs*.

Microsoft Excel (Microsoft Inc, Seattle, WA, USA) was used for the workload and cost analyses.

Ethics

Verbal consent was obtained from the *RECO* and each child's caregiver using standard consent forms. Ethical approval was obtained from the Institutional Review Boards of the Lubumbashi School of Public Health and the IRC respectively.

RESULTS

Characteristics of the RECOs

Of the eligible 158 *RECOs*, (79 from each arm), four from the control arm were unable to participate in the assessment due to sickness or a death in the family and were dropped. Additionally, one *RECO* from each arm was dropped because the evaluators did not apply the definition of correct treatment consistently. The two groups of *RECOs* differed significantly in age, sex, and education, as shown in **Table 4**. The intervention group was younger on average (average age 36.3, compared to 43.2 in the control group, $P < 0.000$), included fewer women (18% in the control and 10% in the intervention, $P = 0.192$), and

Table 4. *Demographic characteristics of the RECOs evaluated by health zone and model*

	KABALO		MANONO		COMBINED	
	CONTROL (N = 38)	INTER-VENTION (N = 39)	CONTROL (N = 36)	INTER-VENTION (N = 39)	CON-TROL (N = 74)	INTER-VENTION (N = 78)
Age:						
Mean	41.5	35.2	44.9	37.4	43.2	36.3*
Median (range)	44 (28-70)	33 (22-66)	41 (24-69)	34 (21-58)	43 (24-70)	33 (21-66)
Sex:						
Female	8 (21%)	1 (3%)	5 (14%)	7 (18%)	13 (18%)	8 (10%)
Male	30 (79%)	38 (97%)	31 (86%)	31 (82%)	61 (82%)	70 (90%)
Education:						
Primary or secondary incomplete	18 (47%)	14 (36%)	31 (86%)	22 (56%)	49 (66%)	36 (46%)
Secondary complete or more	20 (53%)	25 (64%)	5 (14%)	17 (44%)	25 (34%)	42 (54%)†
Occupation:						
Subsistence	22 (58%)	25 (64%)	33 (92%)	31 (79%)	55 (74%)	56 (72%)
Professional	16 (42%)	14 (36%)	3 (8%)	8 (21%)	19 (26%)	22 (28%)

RECO – relais communautaires
*$P < 0.001$.
† $P < 0.05$.

had a higher level of education (58% has completed at least secondary school, compared to 34% in the control, $P = 0.013$). All sampled *RECOs* were supervised by the head nurse from their health area. Research personnel had no influence on head nurse work assignments, and policies and procedures were the same across the two groups. However, it is reasonable to expect that the quality of supervision provided would affect quality of care. The only supervision data available was the number of supervisions in the health area, at best a weak proxy for the quality of the supervisor's involvement. In regression analysis, no relationship was found between the average number of supervisions in the health zone and any of the performance indicators, but it was retained in the regression as a control variable.

Characteristics of the children assessed

The characteristics of the children and the mix of presenting conditions were not statistically significantly different between the two groups (**Table 5**). The

Table 5. *Characteristics of the children and presenting symptoms*

	CONTROL (N = 74) N (%)	INTERVENTION (N = 78) N (%)
Sex:		
Male	38 (49)	38 (51)
Female	36 (51)	40 (49)
Age group (months):		
<6	12 (16)	9 (12)
6-11	12 (16)	14 (18)
12-23	16 (22)	29 (37)
24-59	34 (46)	26 (33)
iCCM condition (can have more than one):		
Fever	71 (96)	71 (91)
Cough/difficulty breathing	44 (59)	51 (65)
Diarrhea	20 (27)	17 (22)
Presence of danger signs among children with each condition:		
Fever	11 (15)	20 (28)
Cough/difficulty breathing	3 (7)	12 (24)
Diarrhea	4 (20)	5 (29)
Complexity of the child's condition:		
Single condition	14 (19)	12 (15)
Two conditions	31 (42)	35 (44)
Three conditions or a non-iCCM condition	15 (20)	8 (10)
Danger sign	14 (19)	23 (29)

iCCM – integrated community case management

average age in months was 21.9 for the control group and 20.1 for the intervention group. In regards to the number of children with danger signs, there were 23 (29%) in the intervention group, compared to 14 (19%) in the control group, but the difference was not statistically significant ($P = 0.129$).

QUALITY OF CARE

Assessment and Referral for Danger Signs

Table 6 summarizes the performance of the *RECOs* in identification and referral for danger signs (see **Table 3** for list of danger signs). *RECOs* in the intervention group were more likely to ask about and investigate all relevant danger signs: 63% in the intervention group, compared to 26% in the control group. Controlling for confounders, the *RECOs* in the intervention group were 4.6 more likely to investigate all appropriate danger signs, (aOR = 4.6, 95% CI = 2.1-10.0, $P < 0.001$).

If a child has no danger sign, the *RECOs* are expected to prompt for symptoms and duration of all three iCCM conditions, regardless of the reason for presenting. The intervention group more consistently performed this step correctly: 95% in the intervention group compared to 74% in the control group. After adjusting for confounders, the *RECOs* in the intervention group were 6.7 times more likely to ask for all three conditions and the duration of any condition present (aOR = 6.7, 95% CI = 1.6-28.0, $P = 0.009$) (**Table 7**). There was

Table 6. *RECO – relais communautaire performance on assessment of danger signs and referral*

	CORRECT PERFORMANCE (NO. %)		INTERVENTION PERFORMANCE RELATIVE TO CONTROL		
	Control	Intervention	aOR*	95% CI	P-value
All children	N = 74	N = 78			
All relevant danger signs assessed†	19 (25.7)	49 (62.8)	4.6	(2.1-10.0)	<0.001
Correct referral decision	62 (83.8)	72 (92.3)	4.3	(1.1-16.4)	0.032
Children with danger signs	N = 14	N = 23			
Correctly referred	7 (50.0)	20 (87.0)	24.2	(1.9-300.2)	0.013
Received correct pre-referral treatment	1 (7.1)	10 (43.5)	68.3‡	(1.6-2813.2)	0.026

RECO – relais communautaire, aOR – adjusted odds ratio, CI – confidence interval
*Adjusted for age of the child, the condition and complexity of the child's condition, the age, sex, education and occupation of the *RECO* and the health zone.
†Relevant danger signs here exclude signs obviously absent (lethargy or inability to eat in a child observed breastfeeding) or absent by inference (bloody stools in a child without diarrhea).
‡Adjusted for age of the child, the age, sex, education and occupation of the *RECO* and the health zone.

Table 7. *RECO – relais communautaire performance on assessment of sick children for iCCM conditions*

	CORRECT PERFOR-MANCE (No., %)		INTERVENTION PERFOR-MANCE RELATIVE TO CONTROL		
	Control	Intervention	aOR*	95% CI	*P*-value
All children:	N = 74	N = 78			
Asked for all three conditions	61 (82.4)	74 (94.9)	3.1	(0.8-12.8)	0.103
Asked for all three conditions and duration of each	55 (74.3)	74 (94.9)	6.7	(1.6-28.0)	0.009
Children 6-59 mo:†	N = 62	N = 69			
Performed MUAC measurement	59 (95.2)	60 (87.0)	0.3	(0.1-1.1)	0.068
MUAC measurement correct	51 (82.3)	58 (84.1)	1.1	(0.4-3.0)	0.868
Children with respiratory symptoms:	N = 41	N = 39			
Performed breath count at appropriate indication	33 (80.1)	36 (92.3)	2.0‡	(0.4-10.2)	0.32
Breath count correct (within ±3 breaths of evaluator's count)	22 (53.7)	12 (48.7)	1.0	(0.5-2.2)	0.496

RECO – *relais communautaire,* iCCM – integrated community case management, aOR – adjusted odds ratio, CI – confidence interval, MUAC – mid-upper arm circumference
*Adjusted for age of the child, the condition and complexity of the child's condition, the age, sex, education and occupation of the *RECO,* the health zone and number of supervisions per month in the health area.
†MUAC (mid-upper arm circumference) is not measured on children under 6 mo
‡Condition and complexity of the child's condition dropped.

no significant difference between the two groups in performance of respiratory count when indicated, although accuracy of the counting was consistently low: 55% in the intervention group and 54% in the control group. Both groups performed well on measuring MUAC. All *RECOs* in both groups performed an RDT when the child presented with fever (not shown).

Management of individual iCCM conditions

Both groups of *RECOs* performed well on the classification and treatment of fever, correctly classifying 92% of cases in the control group, vs 94% in the intervention group, and providing correct treatment for the child's age and condition in 63% of cases in the control and 75% in the intervention group **(Table 8)**. The odds ratios for both classification and treatment of fever were not statistically significant. In cases of diarrhea, 19% of the control group and 67% of the intervention group provided correct treatment. The small sample size (n = 37) made interpretation of these results difficult, and the odds ratio

Table 8. *RECO – relais communautaire performance on classification and treatment of individual iCCM conditions among children without danger signs (N = 115)*

	CORRECT PERFORMANCE (No., %)		PERFORMANCE RELATIVE TO CONTROL		
	Control	Intervention	aOR*	95% CI	P-value
Fever/malaria:	N = 60	N = 51			
Correctly classified (RDT done)	55 (91.7)	48 (94.1)	1.2	(0.2-7.2)	0.836
Correctly treated fever with correct dose of ACT and/or paracetamol	38 (63.3)	38 (74.5)	1.7	(0.7-4.1)	0.286
Diarrhea:	N = 16	N = 12			
Correctly classified	14 (87.5)	12 (100)	n/a		
Correctly treated with correct dose of ORS and zinc	3 (18.8)	8 (66.7)	5.8	(0.9-38.5)	0.067
Respiratory conditions:	N = 41	N = 39			
Correctly classified after breath count done	27 (65.9)	26 (66.7)	0.7	(0.3-2.3)	0.606
Correctly treated with correct dose of amoxi or comfort measures for cough/cold	32 (78.1)	26 (66.7)	0.6	(0.2-2.0)	0.418

aOR – adjusted odds ratio, CI – confidence interval, iCCM – integrated community case management, RDT – rapid diagnostic test, ORS –oral rehydration salts, n/a – non applicable, RECO – *relais communautaire*
*Adjusted for age of the child, the condition and complexity of the child's condition, the age, sex, education and occupation of the *RECO* and the health zone.
†Complexity of the child's condition dropped because of co-linearity.

was not statistically significant (aOR = 5.8, 95% CI = 0.9-38.5, P = 0.067). *RECO* performance assessing and treating respiratory conditions was low in both groups: in the control group, 66% correctly classified and 78% correctly treated, while in the intervention group, 67% correctly classified and 67% correctly treated. The odds ratios were not statistically significant. Among cases correctly treated for a respiratory condition in the control group, seven were treated correctly even though they were classified incorrectly.

Management of children with any combination of conditions and/or danger signs

Overall correct treatment of children was 39% in the control group and 55% in the intervention group. Adjusting for confounders, *RECOs* in the intervention group were almost three times more likely to provide care consistent with protocol (aOR = 2.9, 95% CI = 1.3-6.3, P = 0.010) (**Table 9**). With the addition of a higher standard of correct assessment, the aOR = for the intervention group increased to 3.5 (95% CI = 1.6-8.0, P = 0.002). On classification alone, the difference between the two groups was not statistically significant.

Table 9. *RECO – relais communautaire performance on classification and treatment of all children*

	Correct performance (No., %)		Difference		
	Control (N = 74)	Intervention (N = 78)	aOR*	95% CI	P-value
Correctly classified	48 (64.9)	60 (77.0)	2.2	(0.9-5.2)	.084
Correctly classified and treated	29 (39.2)	43 (55.1)	2.9	(1.3-6.3)	.010
Correctly assessed, classified and treated	23 (31.1)	42 (53.9)	3.5	(1.6-8.0)	.002

aOR – adjusted odds ratio, CI – confidence interval
*Adjusted for age of the child, the condition and complexity of the child's condition, the age, sex, education and occupation of the *RECOS* and the health zone.

RECO workload

On average the assessments and documentation lasted 44.6 minutes (range: 17-81) for the control group and 31.7 minutes (range: 5-59) for the intervention group. Controlling for confounding factors, the *RECOs* in the intervention group spent an average of 10.6 minutes less (95% C = 6.6-14.7, $P < 0.001$) per consultation. The difference was related to time spent on documentation, which took the intervention group on average 0.4 (95% CI = 0.2-0.7) minutes compared to 13.1 minutes for the control group (95% CI = 11.7-14.7, $P < 0.001$).

Cost analysis

The cost of tools, distribution and training of 100 *RECOs* in one health zone using the MoPH package would be US$ 34 385 compared to US$ 29 967 for the intervention in the first year of roll-out, a savings of US$ 4418. Tool printing costs for the intervention package would be $29 967, $3632 less than the control group. Printing of the laminated job aids, a non-recurrent cost, represents the greatest part of the cost for the intervention package, reducing costs in subsequent years. The control package requires quarterly distribution of tools, while the intervention package requires distribution only twice a year, halving the cost. Training and supervision costs would be unchanged except for the added cost of US$ 490 to print and laminate large format posters called for in the intervention. At the time of the study, the RAcE project implemented iCCM in 11 health zones with approximately 1500 operational *RECOs*. At this scale, the intervention package represents a savings of US$ 66 270 the first year and US$ 90 825 every subsequent year.

Study limitations

This study has a number of limitations, largely based on the study design. The sample sizes for specific conditions, most notably diarrhea, were small, producing unreliable regression results. The control and intervention areas differed significantly in the age and education of the RECOs. These factors were controlled for in the regression analysis to the best of our ability with limited information about the RECOs. As mentioned in the methods section, the selection of RECOs for the quality of care evaluation was done by zonal project supervisors, and based on availability, possibly resulting in a bias in favor of higher performing RECOs, although this would have been equally true for the two arms. The zonal supervisors were not involved in the research design or analysis and the selection process was done independently for the two arms. RECO performance may have been influenced by direct observation and performing the assessment at the health facility rather than their usual place of work [13]. While this change in setting may have affected their performance, it also means that the children seen were likely more severely ill than those seen in the village. The role of supervision was not explored in this research, though it would be expected to affect RECOs performance [14,15]. The study had no influence on the selection, training, or financial incentives of the supervisors, and was not designed to address supervision. The study design also did not allow differentiation of the effects of the various elements of the intervention package, although this should be included in future studies.

DISCUSSION

It is well understood that quality of care is critical to achieving positive health outcomes and is determined by a range of issues including provider characteristics, motivation, supervision, the complexity of the guidelines and tasks expected, and trainings and job aids. [16] Our study found that with simplified tools and an adapted training curriculum, a group of low-literate RECOs in Tanganyika Province were able to provide higher quality care in less time at lower cost: children treated by RECOs in the intervention group were 2.9 times more likely to receive correct treatment; consultations took 10.6 minutes less time per assessment; and cost savings range from US$ 66 000-91 000 per year for a program supporting approximately 1500 RECOs.

Overall, the level of performance of the RECOs in this study (54% for those in the intervention group) fell within ranges measured in other studies using direct observation and reexamination, ranging from 36% across all three conditions in Burkina Faso [17] to 62% for any uncomplicated condition and 52% for pneumonia alone in Malawi [18] and 64% overall and 72% for pneumonia in Ethiopia [19]. The finding that correct assessment, treatment, and referral, when necessary, of pneumonia cases pose the greatest challenge is consistent with other studies [8,20,21], and has also been found to be true among professional facility based providers [22]. While the results show that the intervention package did not improve quality of care of respiratory conditions, it is possible that the difference in the prevalence of danger signs among those with respiratory conditions (7% in the control vs 24% in the intervention group) skewed the findings. Nonetheless, the low rate of correct treatment overall confirms the importance of developing strategies to improve management of pneumonia.

As in many countries, RECOs in the DRC work as volunteers and are not paid for their services, making workload, motivation and retention an important concern [23]. However, there is still not enough evidence globally that payment of community health workers (CHWs) will resolve the issue of motivation and retention and further research on these areas is needed. In interviews conducted as part of another research study [24] with RECOs in other health zones in the region, many RECOs noted that their work takes up a great deal of time, largely due to the number of tools required to complete, leaving them with limited time for their income-generating activities. Other studies have also found that RECOs are frustrated and confused by complex tools and protocols [8] and Guenther et al. [25] have pointed out that complexity also reduces the quality of data and its utility for program improvement. This study found significant time savings with the intervention tool package, 10.6 minutes on average, which when multiplied by the average caseload adds up to over 6 hours per month per RECO. In addition to improving quality, simplified tools may improve retention rates by reducing workload and opportunity costs [26].

This research adds important evidence about the potential impact of training and tools on RECO performance. Few studies include a control or pre-intervention group [21,27-31]. The only study examining the effect of training or tools looked specifically at the impact of job aids on the correct use of RDTs [32]. Social and gender roles, economic activity, and physical mobility, are all important factors in determining the effectiveness of RECOs [33]. Limiting RECO selection to individuals who are literate may negatively affect the acceptability and availability of services, as well as retention of RECOs. Previous research has found a mixed relationship between characteristics such as literacy, age, and sex and quality of care. Kallander et al [34] found no relationship between these factors and RECO performance. In contrast, Crispin et al [35] found that age and educational factors were associated with correct documentation and adherence to protocol, while less literate individuals were equally capable of counseling and enabling their clients. In one study female sex was associated with improved quality of care [36]. The benefits of a training applying adult learning methodologies, improved job aids and simplified tools might be further enhanced if they allowed a relaxation of the selection criteria such that the *RECOs* better reflect the communities they serve.

CONCLUSION

This study's findings illustrate that simplifying complex iCCM tools and adapting training curricula to meet the needs of low-literate *RECOs* can result in improved services for children and families in their communities. The elimination and replacement of existing job aids and tools, with pictorial job aids and an integrated register resulted in significant improvement in quality of care and reduced workload. This study also shows that the quality of training can influence the quality of care, an obvious statement, yet one that receives little attention in the research literature. Improvements in training and tools, like those undertaken in the RAcE Project, can be made rapidly and have meaningful impact on health outcomes for children. More attention should be focused on how to maximize *RECO* knowledge and skills using insights from educational approaches designed for adult and low-literacy learners, as part of a larger research agenda on improving CHW performance [16]. Key stakeholders implementing iCCM programs in other countries should ensure that tools are fit for purpose, simplified and adapted to the context and educational levels of CHWs. The results of the study have been accepted by the MoPH and the simplified tools and training curriculum have been adopted at the national level. The tools have also been scaled-up across Tanganyika province. Finally, this research illustrates that even in difficult contexts such as Tanganyika Province in DRC, implementation research focused on best practices of iCCM implementation is feasible.

Acknowledgements: *The authors would like to acknowledge the Ministry of Health of DRC, in particular Dr Tutu Kaleme, who provided insight, expertise and collaboration that greatly assisted this research. The authors would also like to acknowledge the contributions of the Provincial Health Office of Tanganyika province and the Zonal Health Offices of Manono and Kabalo Health Zones who supported this research. We would also like to thank the IRC-DRC RAcE project staff whose efforts contributed greatly to this research: particularly Alpha Tambwe, Gilbert Mutchwima, Isaac Muyuma, Constant Nyembo, Innocent Ngongo, and Maxime Bushiri who served as trainers or data collectors for this research. Finally, the authors would like to extend their gratitude to the community health* *workers who were part of this project and worked tirelessly to provide life-saving treatments to children in their communities.*

Funding: *Funding from Global Affairs Canada administered by the World Health Organization under the iCCM Rapid Access Expansion Programme.*

Authorship declaration: *The authors have completed the Unified Competing Interest form at www.icmje.org/coi_disclosure.pdf (available on request from the corresponding author) and declare no conflict of interest.*

References

1 World Health Organization. Children: reducing mortality. Geneva: WHO: 2016.

2 Liu L, Oza S, Hogan D, Chu Y, Perin J, Zhu J, et al. Global, regional, and national causes of under-5 mortality in 2000-15: an updated systematic analysis with implications for the Sustainable Development Goals. Lancet. 2016;388:3027-35. Medline:27839855 doi:10.1016/S0140-6736(16)31593-8

3 WHO, UNICEF. Integrated community case management (iCCM): an equity-focused strategy to improve access to essential treatment services for children. 2012.

4 Amouzou A, Morris S, Moulton LH, Mukanga D. Assessing the impact of integrated community case management (iCCM) programs on child mortality: Review of early results and lessons learned in sub-Saharan Africa. J Glob Health. 2014;4:020411. Medline:25520801 doi:10.7189/jogh.04.020411

5 Hazel E, Bryce J. On Bathwater, Babies, and Designing Programs for Impact: Evaluations of the Integrated Community Case Management Strategy in Burkina Faso, Ethiopia, and Malawi. Am J Trop Med Hyg. 2016;94:568-70. Medline:26936991 doi:10.4269/ajtmh.94-3intro1

6 Kok MC, Dieleman M, Taegtmeyer M, Broerse JE, Kane SS, Ormel H, et al. Which intervention design factors influence performance of community health workers in low- and middle-income countries? A systematic review. Health Policy Plan. 2015;30:1207-27. Medline:25500559 doi:10.1093/heapol/czu126

7 Ballard M, Montgomery P. Systematic review of interventions for improving the performance of community health workers in low-income and middle-income countries. BMJ Open. 2017;7:e014216. Medline:29074507 doi:10.1136/bmjopen-2016-014216

8 Kelly JM, Osamba B, Garg RM, Hamel MJ, Lewis JJ, Rowe SY, et al. Community health worker performance in the management of multiple childhood illnesses: Siaya District, Kenya, 1997-2001. Am J Public Health. 2001;91:1617-24. Medline:11574324 doi:10.2105/AJPH.91.10.1617

9 République Démocratique du Congo Ministère De La Santé Secrétariat General. Prise En Charge Intégrée des Maladies de l'Enfant, Sites des Soins Communautaires, Guide de Mise en Œuvre. 2007.

10 Laìnez YB, Wittcoff A, Mohamud AI, Amendola P, Perry HB, D'Harcourt E. Insights from community case management data in six sub-Saharan African countries. Am J Trop Med Hyg. 2012;87:144-50. Medline:23136290 doi:10.4269/ajtmh.2012.12-0106

11 Ministère du Plan et Suivi de la Mise en œuvre de la Révolution de la Modernité (MPSMRM), Ministère de la Santé Publique (MSP), ICF International. Enquête Démographique et de Santé en République Démocratique du Congo 2013-2014. Rockville, Maryland: 2014.

12 Cardemil CV, Gilroy KE, Callaghan-Koru JA, Nsona H, Bryce J. Comparison of methods for assessing quality of care for community case management of sick children: an application with community health workers in Malawi. Am J Trop Med Hyg. 2012;87:127-36. Medline:23136288 doi:10.4269/ajtmh.2012.12-0389

13 Miller NP, Amouzou A, Hazel E, Degefie T, Legesse H, Tafesse M, et al. Assessing the quality of sick child care provided by Community Health Workers. PLoS One. 2015;10:e0142010. Medline:26551035 doi:10.1371/journal.pone.0142010

14 Hill Z, Dumbaugh M, Benton L, Kallander K, Strachan D, ten Asbroek A, et al. Supervising community health workers in low-income countries–a review of impact and implementation issues. Glob Health Action. 2014;7:24085. Medline:24815075 doi:10.3402/gha.v7.24085

15 Bosch-Capblanch X, Marceau C. Training, supervision and quality of care in selected integrated community case management (iCCM) programmes: A scoping review of programmatic evidence. J Glob Health. 2014;4:020403. Medline:25520793 doi:10.7189/jogh.04.020403

16 Rowe AK, de Savigny D, Lanata CF, Victora CG. How can we achieve and maintain high-quality performance of health workers in low-resource settings? Lancet. 2005;366:1026-35. Medline:16168785 doi:10.1016/S0140-6736(05)67028-6

17 Munos M, Guiella G, Roberton T, Maiga A, Tiendrebeogo A, Tam Y, et al. Independent Evaluation of the Rapid Scale-Up Program to Reduce Under-Five Mortality in Burkina Faso. Am J Trop Med Hyg. 2016;94:584-95. Medline:26787147 doi:10.4269/ajtmh.15-0585

18 Gilroy KE, Callaghan-Koru JA, Cardemil CV, Nsona H, Amouzou A, Mtimuni A, et al. Quality of sick child care delivered by Health Surveillance Assistants in Malawi. Health Policy Plan. 2013;28:573-85. Medline:23065598 doi:10.1093/heapol/czs095

19 Miller NP, Amouzou A, Tafesse M, Hazel E, Legesse H, Degefie T, et al. Integrated community case management of childhood illness in Ethiopia: implementation strength and quality of care. Am J Trop Med Hyg. 2014;91:424-34. Medline:24799369 doi:10.4269/ajtmh.13-0751

20 Druetz T, Siekmans K, Goossens S, Ridde V, Haddad S. The community case management of pneumonia in Africa: a review of the evidence. Health Policy Plan. 2015;30:253-66. Medline:24371218 doi:10.1093/heapol/czt104

21 Kalyango JN, Alfven T, Peterson S, Mugenyi K, Karamagi C, Rutebemberwa E. Integrated community case management of malaria and pneumonia increases prompt and appropriate treatment for pneumonia symptoms in children under five years in Eastern Uganda. Malar J. 2013;12:340. Medline:24053172 doi:10.1186/1475-2875-12-340

22 Horwood C, Vermaak K, Rollins N, Haskins L, Nkosi P, Qazi S. An evaluation of the quality of IMCI assessments among IMCI trained health workers in South Africa. PLoS One. 2009;4:e5937. Medline:19536288 doi:10.1371/journal.pone.0005937

23 Strachan DL, Kallander K, ten Asbroek AH, Kirkwood B, Meek SR, Benton L, et al. Interventions to improve motivation and retention of community health workers delivering integrated community case management (iCCM): stakeholder perceptions and priorities. Am J Trop Med Hyg. 2012;87:111-9. Medline:23136286 doi:10.4269/ajtmh.2012.12-0030

24 van Boetzelaer E, Ho LS, Gutman JR, Steinhardt LC, Wittcoff A, Barbera Y, et al. Universal versus conditional three-day follow up visit for children with uncomplicated fever at the community level: design of a cluster-randomized, community-based, noninferiority trial in Tanganyika, Democratic Republic of Congo. BMC Pediatr. 2017;17:36. Medline:28122542 doi:10.1186/s12887-017-0792-1

25 Guenther T, Lainez YB, Oliphant NP, Dale M, Raharison S, Miller L, et al. Routine monitoring systems for integrated community case management programs: Lessons from 18 countries in sub-Saharan Africa. J Glob Health. 2014;4:020301. Medline:25520787 doi:10.7189/jogh.04.020301

26 Ludwick T, Brenner JL, Kyomuhangi T, Wotton KA, Kabakyenga JK. Poor retention does not have to be the rule: retention of volunteer community health workers in Uganda. Health Policy Plan. 2014;29:388-95. Medline:23650334 doi:10.1093/heapol/czt025

27 Hamer DH, Brooks ET, Semrau K, Pilingana P, MacLeod WB, Siazeele K, et al. Quality and safety of integrated community case management of malaria using rapid diagnostic tests and pneumonia by community health workers. Pathog Glob Health. 2012;106:32-9. Medline:22595272 doi:10.1179/1364859411Y.0000000042

28 Blanas DA, Ndiaye Y, Nichols K, Jensen A, Siddiqui A, Hennig N. Barriers to community case management of malaria in Saraya, Senegal: training, and supply-chains. Malar J. 2013;12:95. Medline:23497188 doi:10.1186/1475-2875-12-95

29 Mengistu B, Karim AM, Eniyew A, Yitabrek A, Eniyew A, Tsegaye S, et al. Effect of performance review and clinical mentoring meetings (PRCMM) on recording of community case management by health extension workers in Ethiopia. Ethiop Med J. 2014;52 Suppl 3:73-81. Medline:25845076

30 Phiri TB, Kaunda-Khangamwa BN, Bauleni A, Chimuna T, Melody D, Kalengamaliro H, et al. Feasibility, acceptability and impact of integrating malaria rapid diagnostic tests and pre-referral rectal artesunate into the integrated community case management programme. A pilot study in Mchinji district, Malawi. Malar J. 2016;15:177. Medline:27000034 doi:10.1186/s12936-016-1237-2

31 Yeboah-Antwi K, Pilingana P, Macleod WB, Semrau K, Siazeele K, Kalesha P, et al. Community case management of fever due to malaria and pneumonia in children under five in Zambia: a cluster randomized controlled trial. PLoS Med. 2010;7:e1000340. Medline:20877714 doi:10.1371/journal.pmed.1000340

32 Harvey SA, Jennings L, Chinyama M, Masaninga F, Mulholland K, Bell DR. Improving community health worker use of malaria rapid diagnostic tests in Zambia: package instructions, job aid and job aid-plus-training. Malar J. 2008;7:160. Medline:18718028 doi:10.1186/1475-2875-7-160

33 Jaskiewicz W, Tulenko K. Increasing community health worker productivity and effectiveness: a review of the influence of the work environment. Hum Resour Health. 2012;10:38. Medline:23017131 doi:10.1186/1478-4491-10-38

34 Källander K, Tomson G, Nsabagasani X, Sabiiti JN, Pariyo G, Peterson S. Can community health workers and caretakers recognise pneumonia in children? Experiences from western Uganda. Trans R Soc Trop Med Hyg. 2006;100:956-63. Medline:16455119 doi:10.1016/j.trstmh.2005.11.004

35 Crispin N, Wamae A, Ndirangu M, Wamalwa D, Wangalwa G, Watako P, et al. Effects of selected socio-demographic characteristics of community health workers on performance of home visits during pregnancy: a cross-sectional study in Busia District, Kenya. Glob J Health Sci. 2012;4:78-90. Medline:22980380 doi:10.5539/gjhs.v4n5p78

36 Bagonza J, Kibira SP, Rutebemberwa E. Performance of community health workers managing malaria, pneumonia and diarrhoea under the community case management programme in central Uganda: a cross sectional study. Malar J. 2014;13:367. Medline:25231247 doi:10.1186/1475-2875-13-367

A mixed-methods quasi-experimental evaluation of a mobile health application and quality of care in the integrated community case management program in Malawi

Simone Peart Boyce[1], Florence Nyangara[2,3], Joy Kamunyori[4,5]

[1] ICF, Atlanta, Georgia, USA
[2] ICF, Rockville, Maryland, USA
[3] US Pharmacopeia, Rockville, Maryland, USA
[4] ICF, Washington, DC, USA
[5] John Snow Inc., Pretoria, South Africa

Background The use of mobile health (mHealth) technology to improve quality of care (QoC) has increased over the last decade; limited evidence exists to espouse mHealth as a decision support tool, especially at the community level. This study presents evaluation findings of using a mobile application for integrated community case management (iCCM) by Malawi's health surveillance assistants (HSAs) in four pilot districts to deliver lifesaving services for children.

Methods A quasi-experimental study design compared adherence to iCCM guidelines between HSAs using mobile application (n = 137) and paper-based tools (n = 113), supplemented with 47 key informant interviews on perceptions about QoC and sustainability of iCCM mobile application. The first four sick children presenting to each HSA for an initial consultation of an illness episode were observed by a Ministry of Health iCCM trainer for assessment, classification, and treatment. Results were compared using logistic regression, controlling for child-, HSA-, and district-level characteristics, with Holm-Bonferroni-adjusted significance levels for multiple comparison.

Results HSAs using the application tended to assess sick children according to iCCM guidelines more often than HSAs using paper-based tools for cough (adjusted proportion, 98% vs 91%; $P < 0.01$) and five physical danger signs - chest in-drawing; alertness; palmar pallor; malnourishment; oedema (80% vs 62%; $P < 0.01$), but not for fever (97% vs 93%; $P = 0.06$), diarrhoea (94% vs 87%; $P = 0.03$), and three danger signs – not able to eat or drink; vomits everything; has convulsions (88% vs 79%; $P = 0.01$). Across illnesses and danger signs, 81% of HSAs using the application correctly classified sick children, compared to 58% of HSAs using paper-based tools ($P < 0.01$). No differences existed for their treatment ($P = 0.27$). Interview respondents corroborated these findings that using iCCM mobile application ensures protocol adherence. Respondents noted barriers to its consistent and wide use including hardware problems and limited resources.

Conclusion Generally, the mobile application is a promising tool for improving adherence to the iCCM protocol for assessing sick children and classifying illness by HSAs. Limited effects on treatments and inconsistent use suggest the need for more studies on mHealth to improve QoC at community level.

Efforts to reduce mortality among children under five years of age have led to endeavors to improve community-level access to life-saving interventions to treat conditions responsible for majority of deaths in this age group [1]. Based on the World Health Organization (WHO) Integrated Management of Childhood Illness (IMCI) guidelines, integrated community case management (iCCM) is a proven, community-based strategy for managing, assessing, classifying, and treating common childhood illnesses (malaria, diarrhoea, and pneumonia) [2]. Under iCCM, community health workers (CHWs) are trained to diagnose illness and treat or refer sick children, thereby extending the reach of the public health system by leveraging these low-skilled front-line workers to populations with limited access to primary health care facilities [1]. Although iCCM can help save lives, reviews are mixed about the quality of care (QoC) provided by CHWs. Some argue that low educational levels and limited clinical background of CHWs decreases QoC, while others observe that better trained, supported, and supervised CHWs advance QoC since they offer timely services and more personalized care [3-7].

The rise in the availability of mobile phones in low- and middle-income countries in the last decade has increased the use of mobile technology to support health workers. Among other uses, mobile technology applications have been developed to provide assistance to health workers as decision support and adherence tools and to improve communication in the health care system—for referrals, medical supplies availability, and client outreach [8-12].

Although electronic health (eHealth) through the use of mobile phones – known as mHealth – is perceived to have great value in increasing efficiencies and reducing the burden of paper-based systems for health workers, not enough evidence from evaluations of eHealth implementations exists to properly guide and make an investment case for scale up; in fact, if improperly used, technology may have minimal impact on improving patient outcomes and only divert valuable resources [13]. The limited evidence available suggests that decision support tools can improve classification of illnesses, promote adherence to the IMCI protocol, and result in treatment with proper drug dosage [10,11]; however, these studies are often small and localized, and have tended to focus on mHealth for health workers in health facilities, with none explicitly addressing case management of childhood illnesses at the community level by CHWs [9,10]. As such, evidence of mHealth technologies improving QoC at the community level is needed in order to make the case for their use and scale up [13].

The iCCM Program in Malawi

The under-five child mortality rate in Malawi has been decreasing steadily, from 234 deaths per 1000 live births in 1992 to 64 deaths per 1000 live births in 2015 [14]. Malaria, diarrhoea, and pneumonia account for approximately half of the under-five childhood deaths [15,16]. In 2008, Malawi introduced iCCM services, delivered by CHWs called health surveillance assistants (HSAs) through village clinics. HSAs are the peripheral cadre of health workers in the Ministry of Health (MOH), providing iCCM services in hard-to-reach areas (defined as more than five kilometers from a health facility or the presence of a physical barrier to a health facility) to children aged 2–59 months [17]. Their responsibilities include assessing, classifying, and treating children who present with common childhood illnesses—uncomplicated cases of fever, cough with fast breathing, diarrhoea, and eye infections. HSAs also identify signs of severe illnesses and refer these children, and children with illness that they cannot treat, to a nearby health facility.

From 2013 to 2017, Save the Children and its partners supported the MOH to implement iCCM in eight districts in Malawi with support from WHO through the Rapid Access Expansion (RAcE) program: Dedza, Likoma, Lilongwe, Mzimba North, Nkhata Bay, Ntcheu, Ntchisi, and Rumphi. In 2014, D-tree International developed a mobile application to help improve QoC provided by HSAs. The application incorporates the national iCCM protocol and guides HSAs through the sick child assessment and classification process and recommends a treatment plan. After registering the sick child in the application, the application guides the HSA through a series of questions for the caregiver; based on the caregiver's responses, the application determines the illness and corresponding treatment and health education advice for the child. As part of the assessment, the application includes a stopwatch to assist the HSA in counting breaths per minute to determine respiratory rate. The iCCM application was piloted in four RAcE districts: Dedza, Mzimba North, Ntcheu, and Ntchisi.

HSAs were trained in iCCM according to national protocols by MOH trainers. HSAs in the iCCM mobile application pilot districts received an additional two-and-a-half days of training by D-tree on using the application as a decision-support tool. A select few HSAs in the intervention group received additional training on the application as "super users" to assist other HSAs with troubleshooting basic user issues.

We report findings from a mixed-methods evaluation of a decision-support mHealth application for HSAs to improve QoC compared to HSAs who use paper-based iCCM tools to manage childhood illnesses among children under five years of age.

METHODS

This was a mixed-method quasi-experimental study with intervention and comparison groups and key informant interviews (KIIs) on stakeholders' perceptions about QoC and the implementation and potential scale-up of the mobile application.

Sample size and selection

The sample size, with an expected 1024 sick child observations, was calculated to detect an 11% point difference in HSA adherence for treatment to the iCCM protocol across the two groups, with 80% power and 5% significance. This difference was estimated from a recent study conducted in Malawi that determined protocol adherence of 73% and 62% among users and non-users of a mobile application, respectively [18]. Sample size was calculated using a design effect of 1.75—calculated from an interclass coefficient of 0.25 with a cluster size of four sick child visits per HSA—and then inflated by 3% for possible nonresponse or low-case load among some HSAs [19-21].

The sampling frame included all trained and active HSAs (493 in the intervention group and 306 in the comparison group) working in the RAcE-supported districts. We anticipated selecting 256 HSAs reporting to randomly selected health facilities located in the RAcE-supported districts using a stratified random sample by size of facility. Large facilities – defined as facilities that supervise at least six HSAs – were sampled disproportionately, with approximately 75% of the selected facilities from this stratum and 25% of the selected facilities from the small stratum. The intervention group included 37 health facilities located in the four RAcE pilot districts (**Figure 1** and **Figure 2**). The comparison

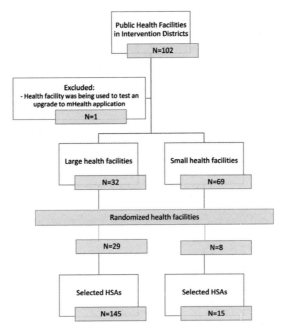

Figure 1. *Sampling strategy for HSAs in intervention districts. mHealth – mobile health, HSA – health surveillance assistant.*

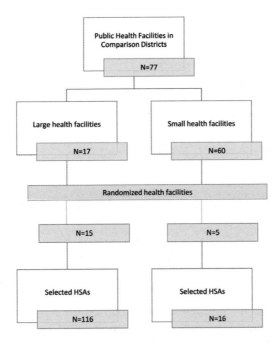

Figure 2. *Sampling strategy for HSAs in the comparison districts. HSA – health surveillance assistant.*

group included 20 health facilities in the three of the remaining RAcE districts – excluding Likoma. Only six HSAs were trained in Likoma, a small island in the middle of Lake Malawi. We excluded Likoma from the study due to the small number of trained HSAs and additional expense of travel. All HSAs from the sampled facilities were included in the comparison group, and only those using the mobile application from the intervention group. During fieldwork, some HSAs were found to be ineligible, away at trainings, or had died or transferred to an out-of-sample village clinic. The study sample included 160 intervention HSAs and 132 comparison HSAs (**Figure 3**).

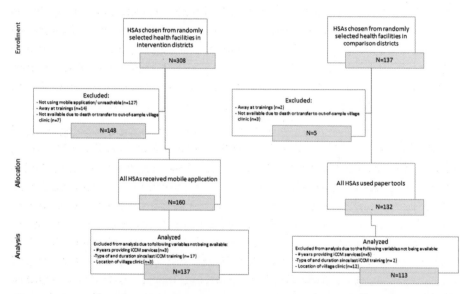

Figure 3. *Participant flow of HSAs in intervention and comparison districts. iCCM – integrated community case management, HSA – health surveillance assistant.*

Data collection

During data collection, teams visited selected village clinics and assessed the first four children 2-59 months of age presenting to the HSA for an initial consultation on their current illness. Severely ill children who needed urgent referral to a health facility were excluded from the study.

Forty-seven KIIs were conducted with stakeholders representing all levels of the iCCM implementation system: the national IMCI coordinator; an IMCI monitoring and evaluation (M&E) officer; two D-tree staff members; a Save the Children M&E staff member; the district IMCI and RAcE program coordinators from all study districts; and two senior HSAs (SHSAs) and caregivers per district. SHSAs and caregivers were selected as follows: in each district, two facilities were randomly selected from which the SHSA reporting to each selected facility and one caregiver from each selected facility were interviewed. If more than one SHSA reported to a selected facility, one was selected at random to interview during the site visit.

All HSAs were interviewed to provide context for study findings. The interview questionnaire included questions regarding the HSA's demographics, last initial or refresher iCCM training, typical data collection, case management and referral processes, as well as comfort with mobile technology and attitude toward the mobile scale-up (intervention group HSAs only). All interview guides were developed in English, with the caregiver guide translated into Chichewa (local language). Study authors conducted all national-level interviews, and the data collection teams conducted interviews with district- and facility-level staff, HSAs, and caregivers during the fieldwork visits.

Fifteen teams consisting of observers – nurses with clinical training in child health and IMCI – and evaluators – MOH iCCM trainers – collected the data, coordinated by the Centre for Agricultural Research and Design of the Lilongwe University of Agriculture and Natural Resources. To observe the assessment, classification, and treatment of children, observers used a case observation checklist based on tools from a previously conducted HSA QoC study in Malawi that used the WHO Heath Facility Survey checklist questionnaire [19]. The tool was updated to match the current iCCM protocol in Malawi and adapted for this study. HSAs were advised to indicate their treatment of the illnesses as if no stockouts of the necessary drugs existed. To ease the burden on sick children and caregivers, the evaluators simultaneously observed the sick child assessment by using an examination form based on caregiver responses to questions from the HSA and then used the assessment and any follow-up questions to independently classify and decide treatment for the child. The evaluator classifications and treatment decisions were used as the gold standard.

All enumerators participated in a five-day training and achieved 80% concordance with evaluators on two iCCM assessments using iCCM training videos that simulated assessment, classification, and treatment of a sick child. Data collection instruments and procedures were pretested and adapted to local conditions. The survey was piloted in village clinics external to the study to practice data collection under conditions that resembled those of the actual survey. Enumerators captured data in the field using tablet computers. All data were uploaded daily and checked for missing values and inconsistencies.

Enumerators did not collect data from village clinics where they normally worked to minimize bias, particularly from influencing HSA behavior and performance. Most HSAs do not open their village clinic every day, consequently they were informed of the site visit date to ensure their availability. In some instances, data collection teams returned to a village clinic if not enough sick children sought care from the HSA on the day of the previous visit. Written consent for participation in the study was obtained from HSAs and caregivers of the sick children.

Data analysis

We conducted statistical analyses using weighted data to account for differential probabilities of selection and adjusted for clustering at the HSA level (Appendix S1 in **Online Supplementary Document**). Analysis was intention to treat. We used descriptive statistics to summarize sample characteristics and reported weighted percentages or means and 95% confidence intervals. We used logistic regression that included child-, HSA-, and district-level characteristics as covariates, and reported predicted probabilities for outcomes. Table S2 in **Online Supplementary Document** describes the outcome variables [19,22]. Covariates included child sex and age, HSA sex and educational level, tenure providing iCCM services as an HSA, type (initial/refresher) and duration since the last iCCM training, case load during the rainy season, village clinic location, access to an improved water source, and the median educational attainment of women. District-level data were derived from the Malawi Millennium Development Goals Endline Survey 2014 and the Malawi Demographic and Health Survey 2010 [23,24]. A Malawi Demographic and Health Survey had been completed in 2016, but district-level data had not yet been released by time of this study.

Access to improved water source was used to control for differences in district-level infrastructure. In retrospect, access to electricity may have been a better control because of the need to charge the mobile phones, but access to electricity varies widely between Lilongwe and the other districts. Our sample included HSAs from Lilongwe that were employed in rural Lilongwe only.

We restricted the overall sample to include only HSAs (n = 137 in the intervention group, n = 113 in the comparison group) and the corresponding sick children seen (n = 987) with non-missing data on the covariates. Characteristics of HSAs and sick children did not differ between the overall and restricted samples (data not shown). One exception was that the HSAs in the restricted sample tended to have completed more schooling (71% in the overall sample, compared to 75% in the restricted sample; $P = 0.002$).We used the Wald test to assess the comparability between the HSAs and children in the intervention and comparison groups. Two-tailed tests with Holm-Bonferroni adjusted significance levels for multiple comparisons indicated statistical significance. All data cleaning and analyses were conducted using Stata, version 14 (Stata Corp., College Station, TX, USA) for the quantitative data and ATLAS.ti (ATLAS.ti Scientific Software Development GmbH, Berlin, Germany) for the qualitative data—to identify themes on perspectives of stakeholders regarding mobile application in Malawi.

Ethical approval was obtained from the Institutional Review Boards of ICF and the Malawi MOH National Health Sciences Research Committee.

RESULTS

HSAs in the intervention and comparison districts tended to be similar, however, more intervention HSAs (34%) had received an initial iCCM training more recently than those in the comparison group (11%) ($P = 0.034$) (**Table 1**). Almost 20% of HSAs in the intervention districts were not using the application on the day of the sick child visit. Reasons for not using the application included the mobile application being time-consuming or a non-functioning, lost, stolen, or out of power phone.

During the sick child visit, HSAs initially asked caregivers for the primary reasons for the visit. Differences existed in care-seeking behavior of caregivers (**Table 2**). Despite these differences, however, no statistically significant differences existed between sick children in the intervention and comparison districts for the majority of illness classifications, based on the gold-standard of the evaluator (**Table 3**).

Assessment, classification, treatment, and counseling

HSAs using the mobile application tended to assess sick children according to the iCCM protocol more often than HSAs using paper-based tools for certain conditions (**Table 4**). In particular, a higher percentage of children seen by intervention HSAs were assessed for cough ($P < 0.001$) and the five danger signs ($P < 0.001$). There were no statistically significant differences between

Table 1. *Comparison of HSA characteristics in districts Using the iCCM mobile application and paper tools*

Characteristics	iCCM Application (N = 137)			Paper Tools (N = 113)			P-value
	N	Weighted %	95% CI	N	Weighted %	95% CI	
Age (years, mean)	137	36.0	33.8, 38.2	110	38.0	37.0, 39.0	0.113
Gender:							
-Female	39	35.1	19.0, 55.5	25	14.7	7.6, 26.6	**0.042**
-Male	98	64.9	44.5, 81.0	88	85.3	73.4, 92.4	
Highest level of education completed:							
-At most two years of secondary school	37	24.4	13.4, 40.4	34	26.5	15.7, 41.1	0.828
-Secondary school or higher	100	75.6	59.6, 86.6	79	73.5	58.9, 84.3	
Years providing iCCM services as HSA (mean)	137	5.4	4.3, 6.6	113	4.7	4.2, 5.2	0.273
Lives in village clinic catchment area	118	76.4	59.3, 87.8	68	77.3	57.2, 89.7	0.930
Sick children seen per day (mean):							
-Rainy season	137	16.3	12.1, 20.6	113	19.1	14.9, 23.2	0.361
-Dry season	137	9.1	6.9, 11.3	113	10.0	7.6, 12.4	0.592
Village clinic located in room not attached or not next to home	55	54.6	38.8, 69.4	85	80.0	70.3, 87.1	**0.007**
Days in past 7 days operate village clinic (mean)	134	3.5	2.7, 4.4	113	3.5	2.5, 4.5	0.930
Hours in past 7 days operate village clinic (mean)	134	30.6	21.6, 39.6	113	32.3	8.2, 56.3	0.896
Primary iCCM protocol used*							
-Sick child recording form	26	16.8	9.6, 27.8	72	46.9	20.6, 75.0	**0.039**
-Village clinic register	69	60.1	39.8, 77.4	113	100.0	100.0, 100.0	**<0.001**
-iCCM mobile application	109	79.1	63.4, 89.2	0	0.0	0.0, 0.0	**<0.001**
Items currently included in drug box†	137	9.2	8.7, 9.6	113	8.9	8.5, 9.3	0.349
Items stockout that lasted 7 days or more‡	137	1.7	1.1, 2.2	113	2.0	1.4, 2.7	0.358

Table 1. *Continued*

Characteristics	iCCM application (N = 137)			Paper tools (N = 113)			P-value
	N	Weighted %	95% CI	N	Weighted %	95% CI	
Training, supervision, and mentoring							
Most recent iCCM training:							**0.034**
-Initial	53	34.0	16.8, 56.9	18	11.7	5.5, 23.1	
-Refresher	84	66.0	43.1, 83.2	95	88.3	76.9, 94.5	
Months since most recent iCCM training (median, interquartile range)	137	4.4	2.4, 18.4	113	2.4	2.4, 15.4	0.508
Tools trained on in most recent iCCM training (mean)§	137	2.9	2.9, 3.0	113	2.9	2.9, 3.0	0.981
Days report to health facility in past month (mean)	137	5.8	4.8, 6.8	113	7.1	5.5, 8.6	0.170
Supervisory visits in past 3 months (mean)	137	1.2	1.0, 1.3	113	1.0	0.8, 1.3	0.330
Most recent supervisory visit by senior HSA (%)	93	69.5	47.4, 85.2	57	60.1	41.0, 76.5	0.494
Tasks conducted during most recent supervisory visit (mean)	137	5.6	5.2, 6.1	113	4.7	3.6, 5.8	0.138
Mentor visits in past 3 months (mean)	136	0.8	0.6, 1.1	113	0.7	0.3, 1.0	0.433
Tasks conducted during most recent mentor visit (mean)¶	137	3.0	2.2, 3.8	113	2.0	1.0, 3.1	0.160

iCCM – integrated community case management, HSA – health surveillance assistant

*Categories are not mutually exclusive because HSA may use multiple guides.

†Drug box should include 11 items: LA (1 × 6 and 2 × 6 blister packets), rapid diagnostic test, rectal artesunate, amoxicillin/cotrimoxazole, oral rehydration solution, zinc, paracetamol, eye antibiotic, timer, and gloves.

‡Nine items included for stockout: LA (1 × 6 and 2 × 6 blister packets), rapid diagnostic test, rectal artesunate, amoxicillin, oral rehydration solution, zinc, paracetamol, and eye antibiotic.

§The tools include sick child recording form, village clinic register, and referral slip.

Seven possible tasks are included: reviewing village clinic register, checking supplies and equipment levels, using a supervision checklist, administering a case scenario, observing management of a sick child, meeting with village committee members, and giving feedback on iCCM activities.

¶Four possible tasks are included: using a mentoring checklist, observing management of a sick child, demonstrating how to care for a sick child or identify danger signs, and giving feedback on case management skills.

Table 2. *Characteristics and presenting complaints of observed sick children seen by HSAs in districts using the iCCM mobile application and paper tools*

CHARACTERISTICS	iCCM MOBILE APPLICATION (N = 535)			PAPER TOOLS (N = 452)			P-VALUE
	N	Weighted %	(95% CI)	N	Weighted %	(95% CI)	
Age (months; mean)	535	23.5	21.1, 25.8	452	23.3	21.5, 25.2	0.943
Gender:							
-Female	275	53.2	46.0, 60.4	237	58.1	51.0, 64.9	0.347
-Male	260	46.8	39.6, 54.0	215	41.9	35.1, 49.0	
Presenting complaint of observed sick children as reported by caregiver*							
Fast or difficult breathing	7	0.7	0.3, 1.5	23	6.4	3.4, 11.8	**<0.001**
Cough	367	69.1	62.4, 75.1	309	62.9	55.7, 69.6	0.200
Pneumonia	1	0.1	0.0, 0.7	21	5.2	2.7, 9.9	**<0.001**
Diarrhoea (loose stools)	126	20.9	15.9, 26.9	107	30.3	23.5, 38.0	0.043
Fever	308	61.5	56.0, 66.8	294	65.2	57.9, 71.9	0.421
Malaria	2	1.0	0.2, 6.0	52	7.6	4.9, 11.5	**0.030**
Convulsions	1	0.1	0.0, 0.7	3	0.3	0.1, 1.0	0.307
Sleepy or unconscious	0	0.0	0.0, 0.0	8	0.9	0.5, 1.6	**0.002**
Difficulty drinking or feeding	11	3.6	1.5, 8.6	14	2.5	1.0, 6.1	0.575
Vomiting	58	12.4	8.2, 18.5	59	13.3	8.4, 20.3	0.837
Red eyes	37	6.2	3.6, 10.5	18	3.9	1.7, 8.6	0.350
Other problem mentioned	46	12.1	7.6, 18.6	50	9.3	5.7, 14.9	0.441

iCCM – integrated community case management, HSA – health surveillance assistant
*Categories are not mutually exclusive as caregivers may report multiple complaints.

the groups for children assessed for diarrhoea (P = 0.026), malaria with rapid diagnostic tests (P = 0.507), fever (P = 0.056), fast breathing through counting of respiratory rates (P = 0.462), and the three general danger signs (P = 0.009).

More than 80% of HSAs using the mobile application classified sick children across the common illnesses and danger signs similarly to the evaluator, compared to 58% of the comparison group (P < 0.001) (**Table 5**). HSAs, especially those using paper-based tools, tended to misclassify non-febrile children as febrile and failed to classify nourished children. No statistically significant differences between the two groups of HSAs for the illnesses were found (P = 0.025).

Overall, children with the common illnesses received the correct treatment for their illnesses, regardless of the tool used to guide treatment (**Table 6**). Investigation by each illness showed that intervention HSAs tended to prescribe an antimalarial drug correctly to children with fever and positive malaria

Table 3. *Classification of observed sick children seen by HSAs in districts using the iCCM Mobile Application and Paper Tools, Based on Gold Standard Re-examination*

CHARACTERISTICS	iCCM MOBILE APPLICATION (N = 535)			PAPER TOOLS (N = 452)			P-VALUE
	N	Weighted %	95% CI	N	Weighted %	95% CI	
Cough with fast breathing	99	21.5	15.7, 28.8	73	21.7	15.3, 29.7	0.980
Fever:							
-Less than 7 days	330	67.1	61.6, 72.1	309	70.8	64.6, 76.3	0.356
-7 days or more	5	1.3	0.3, 5.3	10	3.0	1.3, 6.9	0.319
Diarrhoea:							
-Less than 14 days and no blood in stool	127	21.0	16.2, 26.7	96	28.1	21.7, 35.5	0.108
-14 days or more	7	0.7	0.3, 1.5	1	0.1	0.0, 0.8	0.081
-Blood in stool	13	2.1	0.8, 5.3	8	2.8	0.9, 8.2	0.694
Red eyes:							
-Less than 4 days	26	5.1	2.6, 9.6	18	5.9	2.9, 11.4	0.764
-4 days or more	3	2.3	1.0, 5.3	5	0.5	0.2, 1.2	**0.015**
-Visual problem	0	0.0	0.0, 0.0	1	0.1	0.0, 0.8	0.318
Chest indrawing	11	1.9	0.7, 5.2	7	1.7	0.5, 6.0	0.900
Vomits everything	3	1.1	0.2, 5.7	3	0.3	0.1, 1.0	0.219
Palmar pallor	3	0.3	0.1, 0.9	2	0.2	0.1, 0.9	0.722
MUAC tape:							
-Red	3	0.3	0.1, 0.9	3	0.3	0.1, 1.0	0.921
-Yellow	3	0.3	0.1, 0.9	10	3.0	1.1, 8.2	**0.003**
Convulsions	1	0.1	0.0, 0.7	4	0.4	0.2, 1.2	0.190
Not able to drink or feed anything	1	0.1	0.0, 0.7	3	0.3	0.1, 1.0	0.307
Very sleepy or unconscious	3	0.0	0.0, 0.0	1	0.1	0.0, 0.8	0.318
Swelling of both feet	0	0.0	0.0, 0.0	2	1.2	0.2, 7.0	0.275
Other problems, refer	57	12.3	7.9, 18.7	60	11.4	7.3, 17.4	0.800

CI – confidence interval iCCM – integrated community case management, HSA – health surveillance assistant, MUAC – mid-upper arm circumference

rapid diagnostic test (mRDT) more often (80%) than comparison HSAs (52%) ($P < 0.001$). Further investigation indicated no differences in treatment due to age band mixing. Instead differences were found in whether any treatment was offered for malaria. Of those HSAs incorrectly treating malaria, 67% (62% in comparison and 4% in intervention) failed to offer any treatment despite positive mRDT. Almost 90% of HSAs in the intervention districts correctly referred children with danger signs in need of a referral as compared to 71% of HSAs in comparison districts ($P = 0.010$). The majority of interview respond-

Table 4. *Predicted probabilities of the correct assessment for illnesses of observed sick children seen by HSAs in districts using the iCCM mobile application and paper tools*

Symptoms	N	iCCM mobile application		Paper tools		P-value†
		Weighted %	95% CI	Weighted %	95% CI	
Children checked for presence of cough	987	97.9	96.6, 99.2	90.7	85.5, 95.9	**0.001**
Children checked for presence of diarrhoea	987	93.9	90.8, 96.9	87.4	82.1, 92.6	0.026
Children checked for presence of fever	987	96.7	94.4, 99.0	92.6	87.6, 97.6	0.056
Children with cough assessed for presence of fast breathing through counting of respiratory rates	716	97.1	94.3, 99.8	95.7	92.6, 98.9	0.463
Children with cough assessed for the presence of fast breathing in which HSA counted respiratory rate within ± 3 breaths of gold standard (N = 699)	699	84.8	81.3, 88.3	86.6	82.2, 91.0	0.488
Children with fever assessed for malaria with rapid diagnostic test	652	83.8	73.3, 94.2	88.6	81.9, 95.3	0.507
Children assessed for three general danger signs	987	87.6	83.6, 91.6	78.6	73.3, 84.0	0.009
Children checked if able to drink or eat anything	987	94.9	92.9, 97.0	89.4	86.0, 92.9	<0.001
Children checked if vomit everything	987	94.1	90.7, 97.6	91.1	86.9, 95.4	0.270
Children checked if have convulsions	987	92.8	90.7, 94.8	84.0	80.1, 87.9	<0.001
Children assessed for five physical danger signs	987	79.9	75.9, 84.0	61.7	55.0, 68.4	<0.001
Children checked for chest indrawing	987	94.6	92.8, 96.3	78.2	73.5, 82.9	<0.001
Children checked if sleepy or unconscious	987	98.6	97.0, 100.1	96.5	93.6, 99.5	<0.001
Children checked for palmar pallor	987	99.1	98.5, 99.8	89.6	84.6, 94.6	<0.001
Children checked for malnutrition with MUAC tape	987	86.3	82.9, 89.7	82.6	77.6, 87.6	0.182
Children checked if swelling of both feet	987	96.6	95.0, 98.2	85.9	80.9, 91.0	<0.001

iCCM – integrated community case management, HSA – health surveillance assistant, MUAC – mid-upper arm circumference
*Probabilities adjusted for child characteristics (age and gender), HSA characteristics (gender, highest education level, tenure as an HSA, type and duration since most recent iCCM training, patient case load, and village clinic location), and district characteristics (access to improved water source and median number of years of women's education) using logistic regression with standard errors clustered at the HSA level.
†Compared against Holm-Bonferroni adjusted significance levels.

Table 5. *Predicted probabilities of the correct classification of illnesses of observed sick children seen by HSAs in districts using the iCCM mobile application and paper tools**

CLASSIFICATION		iCCM MOBILE APPLICATION		PAPER TOOLS		
	N	Weighted %	95% CI	Weighted %	95% CI	P-value†
Children whose classifications given by HSA match all classifications given by evaluator‡	987	80.7	76.4, 84.9	57.6	49.6, 65.6	**<0.001**
Children classified by HSA in the three common illnesses (malaria [positive mRDT], diarrhoea, and cough with fast breathing) that match the evaluator classifications	987	91.3	87.6, 95.0	82.5	75.3, 89.8	0.025
Malaria (positive mRDT)	987	99.7	99.1, 100.0	99.9	99.8, 100.0	0.392
Diarrhoea	987	95.7	93.2, 98.2	91.4	86.3, 96.5	0.095
Cough with fast breathing	987	95.6	92.9, 98.4	89.2	82.1, 96.2	0.055

iCCM – integrated community case management, HSA – health surveillance assistant, MUAC – mid-upper arm circumference, mRDT – malaria rapid diagnostic test, CI – confidence interval
*Probabilities are adjusted for child characteristics (age and gender), HSA characteristics (gender, highest education level, tenure as an HSA, type and duration since most recent iCCM training, patient case load, and village clinic location), and district characteristics (access to improved water source and median number of years of women's education) using logistic regression with standard errors clustered at the HSA level.
†Compared against Holm-Bonferroni adjusted significance levels.
‡ Classifications include diarrhoea, cough, fever, fast breathing, blood in stool, chest indrawing, convulsions, not eating or drinking, vomiting everything, red eye, red eye with visual problems, sleepy or unconscious, palmar pallor, foot swelling, and color on the MUAC tape.

ents corroborated these findings that use of the mobile application improves adherence to the protocol. One SHSA said; *"There are no short cuts…not allow HSAs to skip as the phone guides you step by step."* However, one national stakeholder cautioned that adherence varies and the practical effect of the mobile application depended on the HSA's characteristics.

To assess whether caregivers received counseling on the correct administration of drugs, we focused on whether the HSA encouraged the caregiver to give the first dose of treatment to the child in his or her presence. Few children treated by HSAs in either group received their first dose of treatment at the village clinic. This low rate prompted us to explore whether this was remedied by HSAs counseling the caregiver on dosage, frequency, and duration of administering treatments; demonstrating treatment; and requiring caregivers to repeat the instructions for the treatment procedure. Fewer than half of all HSAs in either group, however, provided this support.

Table 6. Predicted probabilities of the correct treatment, referral, and counseling of children seen by HSAs in districts using the iCCM mobile application and paper tools

TREATMENT/ REFERRAL/COUNSELING	iCCM MOBILE APPLICATION			PAPER TOOLS			P-VALUE†
	N	Weighted %	95% CI	N	Weighted %	95% CI	
Treatment:							
Children with cough and fast breathing, positive mRDT, or diarrhoea who are correctly prescribed all medications (antibiotic, antimalarial drug, or ORS and zinc) for their illnesses	223	69.9	62.5, 77.4	186	64.7	58.8, 70.6	0.267
Children with cough and fast breathing who are prescribed an antibiotic correctly	73	70.8	67.9, 73.8	53	74.6	71.1, 78.2	0.147
Children with fever and positive mRDT who are prescribed an antimalarial drug correctly	80	80.0	75.6, 84.5	89	51.8	47.0, 56.7	**<0.001**
Children with diarrhoea who are prescribed ORS and zinc correctly	106	66.8	56.2, 77.5	78	68.7	60.1, 77.3	0.760
Children without cough and fast breathing who would have left the HSA without having received an antibiotic	349	97.3	94.3,100.0	297	98.2	96.2, 100.0	0.561
Referral:							
Children with danger signs needing referral who are referred	96	87.0	83.9, 90.1	88	70.8	57.0, 84.6	**0.010**
Counseling:							
Children who need an antibiotic, ORS and zinc, or antimalarial drug who receive the correct first dose in presence of HSA	223	28.5	18.2, 38.9	186	35.5	25.6, 45.3	0.373
Caregivers of children with cough and fast breathing, positive mRDT, or diarrhoea who are counseled on their illnesses	233	29.0	19.6, 38.4	204	46.4	33.3, 59.6	0.058
Cough and fast breathing	79	58.7	53.1, 64.2	61	65.0	60.2, 69.8	0.155
Diarrhoea	114	5.4	2.4, 8.3	89	23.0	8.0, 38.0	0.014
Fever and positive mRDT	83	57.2	47.2, 67.2	93	64.7	51.3, 78.2	0.374

iCCM – integrated community case management, HSA – health surveillance assistant, MUAC – mid-upper arm circumference, mRDT – malaria rapid diagnostic test, ORS – oral rehydration salts

*HSAs prescribed antimalarial drugs for less than 0.5 percent of children with fever and negative mRDT. Probabilities adjusted for child characteristics (age and gender), HSA characteristics (gender, highest education level, tenure as an HSA, type and duration since most recent iCCM training, patient case load, and village clinic location), and district characteristics (access to improved water source and median number of years of women's education) using logistic regression with standard errors clustered at the HSA level.

†Compared against Holm-Bonferroni adjusted significance levels.

Stakeholder perception of mobile application

Interviews with stakeholders in intervention districts and facilities indicated that HSAs liked the mobile application and generally found it easy to use. They described the mobile application as *"user friendly" "very logical", and "requir(ing) HSAs to complete all steps in proper order."* When asked to identify factors that have facilitated the adoption of the mobile application, respondents described a collaborative process to develop and roll-out the mobile application: D-tree led the development, with input from MOH and Save the Children, and supported all trainings. Other factors noted were recruitment of young HSAs who have higher uptake of technology; simplicity of assessment, classification, and treatment protocols; offering training, supervision, and opportunities to practice using the application; and the availability of "super users" to assist with troubleshooting basic issues.

When asked about problems HSAs encountered when using the mobile application, informants reported that some HSAs were not using the phones consistently because the application was time consuming; hardware and software problems related to malfunctioning phones, inadequate battery power for phones, or problems charging the phone; inadequate airtime and network coverage to sync data from the application; and inability of SHSAs to assist HSAs under their supervision with phone problems. While "super users" were available to assist HSAs, they were not always able to resolve issues, which then required requesting help from D-tree. This was corroborated by approximately 35% of contacted HSAs in intervention districts not using their mobile application or unreachable, resulting in their exclusion from the sample.

DISCUSSION

HSAs who used the iCCM mobile application had higher rates of assessing and classifying sick children correctly, compared to HSAs using the paper-based tool, however, even the differences seen were marginally significant. No statistically significant differences were found between the two groups in classification and treatment of children with the three main iCCM illnesses and in counseling caregivers. Predicted probabilities of correct treatment and counseling were largely similar, which corroborates a previous study finding that there were no differences in treatment rates between CHWs using electronic and paper-based tools [25]. Overall, the results show that the mobile application can help HSAs to adhere to the protocol in terms of conducting assessments of sick children and classifying diseases. A study by Mitchell et al.

found similar results in Tanzania, where adherence to the IMCI protocol used in health facilities was greater for health workers using an electronic IMCI tool than for those using a paper-based tool [10]. Indeed, there is a growing body of evidence that mHealth is a promising tool for shifting some health services tasks that require compliance with guidelines and protocols from clinicians to frontline health workers through the use of algorithm-based decision-support tools [26,27]. However, use of the mobile application was found to be insufficient to improve health outcomes through correct treatment and counseling caregivers.

The majority of stakeholder interviewees liked the mobile application and cited its user-friendliness, despite some challenges using the phones and syncing data. However, some HSAs indicated lack of consistent use of the mobile application because it was time-consuming or hardware or software problems with the phone.

DeRenzi et al., in a study assessing the feasibility of electronic IMCI (eIMCI) tools for improving pediatric care in Tanzania, found that a key factor for acceptability of the eIMCI application by clinicians was speed – a tool seen as taking too long to step through the protocol would be discarded [28]. This corroborates the finding that some HSAs stopped using the application because it was too time-consuming. In designing their application, DeRenzi et al. developed a tool that combined clinicians' use of their experience and prescriptive elements of the protocol, resulting in the application being almost as fast as existing practice – where clinicians rarely consulted the paper tool and instead relied on their memory and training. It is not clear whether such a solution would be suitable in a community setting, where HSAs are generally poorly educated and trained.

Much of the literature refers to "technological" challenges when deploying mHealth interventions in low-resource settings, some of which align with the experiences cited by HSAs: poor mobile network connectivity; lack of or limited electricity to charge phones; lost or damaged phones; costs of handsets; and poor mobile phone maintenance [29]. The literature, however, tends not to expound on how these have been addressed; more attention is generally given to "big picture" issues, such as usability, training, national policies, and technical standards. As mHealth is increasingly considered as an effective tool for improving community health services in resource-constrained settings, additional discussion is warranted on these more mundane challenges of community-level interventions, as they remain important considerations for implementation and scale up [30].

A limitation of this study was the eligibility criteria in the intervention districts that included only HSAs using the mobile application. This provided incidental findings around HSAs' acceptance and use of the mobile application but also potentially biases the results: HSAs who chose not to use the application may be ones who are weaker in the application of iCCM. However, the actual direction of the bias cannot be measured without understanding the characteristics of the HSAs not using the phone. Because this was not the focus of our study, we did not probe this; more qualitative studies should be conducted to determine why HSAs are not using the mobile application, and if there are correlations to any other factors.

The findings of this study should be viewed in light of certain limitations. First, the sick child assessments were conducted simultaneously by the HSA and the evaluator. This approach was strongly recommended by the MOH iCCM trainers during the study training due to concerns about burdening the sick children and caregivers, however it does not follow usual practice (observation followed by separate re-examination) for QoC evaluations. Additionally, the study was not part of the initial program design, so we were not able to randomize the intervention nor have a baseline assessment. Due to the lack of baseline assessment, we were unable to determine if any differences existed between the groups prior to the implementation of the mobile application such as district capacity. We used multivariate regression analysis to control for possible confounding factors related to the district, facility, and HSA observable characteristics that may bias our findings. Also, relying on observation of HSAs as they assess sick children has the potential to introduce bias if HSAs change their assessment habits to satisfy the observer, also referred to as the Hawthorne effect [31]. Since this approach was used for both intervention and comparison HSAs, this should affect both groups and minimize any bias in performance between the groups.

CONCLUSION

Results of the study lend some support to the mobile application as a tool to improve adherence to the iCCM protocol for assessing sick children and classifying illness, especially for less-trained HSAs in hard-to-reach areas with severe shortages of trained health personnel. However, the lack of effect on treatment points to additional support required regarding adherence to the treatment protocol. Additionally, even the significant differences seen in assessment and classification were marginal. It is difficult, therefore, to conclusively say that mHealth for community-level decision support improves QoC; more studies of these technologies at this level are required to develop a solid evidence base.

Acknowledgements: *We would like to thank Gunther Baugh and Salim Sadruddin of World Health Organization (WHO) for their invaluable guidance and suggestions that have enriched this paper as well as Debra Prosnitz and Kirsten Zalisk for their assistance in designing the study and data collection instruments. The Center for Agricultural Research and Development at the Lilongwe University of Agriculture and Natural Resources provided logistical support for the data collection efforts. We are grateful to Save the Children International and D-tree International for their partnership in this effort. Most of all, we wish to thank the staff members from the Malawi Ministry of Health at the national, district, facility, and village clinic levels, and caregivers who endured long interviews and shared their perspectives with us for this research.*

Funding: *The authors acknowledge support from the WHO Rapid Access Expansion program funded by Global Affairs Canada.*

Authorship declaration: *SPB, FN, and JK conceptualized the study and analysis plan and led the data collection and management. SPB and FN led the data analysis. SPB wrote the first draft of paper. FN, and JK reviewed, revised, and contributed writing to the paper. All authors read and approved final manuscript.*

Conflict of interest: *All authors completed the Unified Competing Interest form at www. icmje.org/coi_disclosure.pdf (available upon request from the corresponding author), and declare no conflicts of interest.*

Additional material
Online Supplementary Document

References

1 World Health Organization, United Nations International Children's Emergency Fund. Joint Statement: Integrated Community Case Management. New York, NY: UNICEF: 2012.

2 World Health Organization. Integrated Management of Childhood Illness: Chart Booklet. Switzerland: World Health Organization, 2014.

3 Amouzou A, Morris S, Moulton LH, Mukanga D. Assessing the impact of integrated community case management (iCCM) programs on child mortality: Review of early results and lessons learned in sub-Saharan Africa. J Glob Health. 2014;4:020411. Medline:25520801 doi:10.7189/jogh.04.020411

4 Najjemba R, Kiapi L, Demissie SD, Gossaye T, Engida M, Ratnayake R, et al. Integrated community case management: quality of care and adherence to medication in Beneshangul-Gumuz Region, Ethiopia. Ethiop Med J. 2014;52 Suppl 3:83-90. Medline:25845077

5 Kalyango JN, Rutebemberwa E, Alfven T, Ssali S, Peterson S, Karamagi C. Performance of community health workers under integrated community case management of childhood illnesses in eastern Uganda. Malar J. 2012;11:282. Medline:22905758 doi:10.1186/1475-2875-11-282

6 Bosch-Capblanch X, Marceau C. Training, supervision and quality of care in selected integrated community case management (iCCM) programmes: A scoping review of programmatic evidence. J Glob Health. 2014;4:020403. Medline:25520793 doi:10.7189/jogh.04.020403

7   Callaghan Koru JA, Hyder AA, Geroge A, Gilroy KE, Humphreys N, Mtimuni A, et al. Health Workers' and managers' perceptions of the integrated Community Case Management Program for childhood illness in Malawi: The importance of expanding access to child health services. Am J Trop Med Hyg. 2012;87:61-8. Medline:23136279 doi:10.4269/ajtmh.2012.11-0665

8   Mobile Technology Strengthens Behavior Change Communication and Referrals by Community Healt Workers for Maternal, Newborn, and Child Health in Rural Afghanistan. 2014. Available: https://www.usaid.gov/sites/default/files/documents/1864/WorldVisionORBrief.pdf. Accessed:22 December 2018.

9   Peters DH, Kohli M, Mascarenhas M, Rao K. Can computers improve patient care by primary health care workers in India? Int J Qual Health Care. 2006;18:437-45. Medline:17041232 doi:10.1093/intqhc/mzl053

10 Mitchell M, Lesh N, Cranmer H, Fraser H, Haivas I, Wolf K. Improving care – improving access: the use of electronic decision support with AIDS patients in South Africa. Int J Healthc Technol Manag. 2009;10:156-68. doi:10.1504/IJHTM.2009.025819

11 Mitchell M, Hedt-Gauthier BL, Msellemu D, Nkaka M, Lesh N. Using electronic technology to improve clinical care - results from a before-after cluster trial to evaluate assessment and classification of sick children according to Integrated Management of Childhood Illness (IMCI) protocol in Tanzania. BMC Med Inform Decis Mak. 2013;13:95. Medline:23981292 doi:10.1186/1472-6947-13-95

12 Zurovac D, Sudoi RK, Akhwale WS, Ndiritu M, Hamer DH, Rowe AK, et al. The effect of mobile phone text-message reminders on Kenyan health workers' adherence to malaria treatment guidelines: a cluster randomised trial. Lancet. 2011;378:795-803. Medline:21820166 doi:10.1016/S0140-6736(11)60783-6

13 The Bellagio eHealth Evaluation Group. Call to action on global eHealth evaluation: consensus statement of the WHO Global eHealth Evaluation Meeting. 2011.

14 United Nations International Children's Emergency Fund, World Health Organization. Countdown to 2015: Maternal, newborn & child survival; A decade of tracking progress for maternal, newborn and child survival: The 2015 report. Geneva, Switzerland: World Health Organization, 2015.

15 World Health Organization. Malawi neonatal and child health country profile. Available: https://www.who.int/countries/mwi/en/. Accessed: 2 February 2019.

16 Bjornstad E, Preidis GA, Lufesi N, Olson D, Kamthunzi P, Hosseinipour MC, et al. Determining the quality of IMCI pneumonia care in Malawian children. Paediatr Int Child Health. 2014;34:29-36. Medline:24091151 doi:10.1179/2046905513Y.0000000070

17 Nsona H, Mtimuni A, Daelmans B, Callaghan-Koru JA, Gilroy K, Mgalula L, et al. Scaling up integrated community case management of childhood illness: update from Malawi. Am J Trop Med Hyg. 2012;87:54-60. Medline:23136278 doi:10.4269/ajtmh.2012.11-0759

18 Evaluation Report of the Barr Foundation eCCM Project. D-tree International, 2015.

19 World Health Organization. Health Facility Survey Tool to Evaluate the Quality of Care Delivered to Sick Children Attending Outpatient Facilities: Using the Integrated Mangement of Childhood Illness Clinical Guidelines as Best Practices. Geneva, Switzerland: World Health Organization, 2001.

20 Gilroy K, Winch PJ, Diawara A, Swedberg E, Thiero F, Kane M, et al. Impact of IMCI training and language used by provider on quality of counseling provided to parents of sick children in Bougouni District, Mali. Patient Educ Couns. 2004;54:35-44. Medline:15210258 doi:10.1016/S0738-3991(03)00189-7

21 Rowe AK, Lama M, Onikpo F, Deming MS. Design effects and intraclass correlation coefficients from a health facility cluster survey in Benin. Int J Qual Health Care. 2002;14:521-3. Medline:12515339 doi:10.1093/intqhc/14.6.521

22 Johns Hopkins University. Quality of Care Provided to Sick Children by Health Surveillance Assistants in Malawi: Final Report. 2009.

23 Malawi MDG Endline Survey 2014. Zomba, Malawi: National Statistical Office, 2015.

24 Malawi Demographic and Health Survey 2010. Zomba, Malawi & Calverton, Maryland, USA: National Statistical Office &ICF Macro, 2011.

25 Rambaud-Althaus C, Shao A, Samaka J, Swai N, Perri S, Kahama-Maro J, et al. Performance of Health Workers Using an Electronic Algorithm for the Management of Childhood Illness in Tanzania: A Pilot Implementation Study. Am J Trop Med Hyg. 2017;96:249-57. Medline:28077751 doi:10.4269/ajtmh.15-0395

26 Agarwal S, Perry HB, Long LA, Labrique AB. Evidence on feasibility and effective use of mHealth strategies by frontline health workers in developing countries: systematic review. Trop Med Int Health. 2015;20:1003-14. Medline:25881735 doi:10.1111/tmi.12525

27 Labrique AB, Vasudevan L, Kochi E, Fabricant R, Mehl G. mHealth innovations as health system strengthening tools: 12 common applications and a visual framework. Glob Health Sci Pract. 2013;1:160-71. Medline:25276529 doi:10.9745/GHSP-D-13-00031

28 DeRenzi B, Gajos KZ, Parikh TS, Lesh N, Mitchell M, Borriello G. Opportunities for Intelligent Interfaces Aiding Healthcare in Low-Income Countries. 2008. Available: http://aiweb.cs.washington.edu/ai/puirg/papers/derenzi-iui4dr08.pdf. Accessed: 20 December 2018.

29 Amoakoh-Coleman M, Borgstein AB, Sondaal SF, Grobbee DE, Miltenburg AS, Verwijs M, et al. Effectiveness of mHealth interventions targeting health care workers to improve pregnancy outcomes in low- and middle-income countries: A systematic review. J Med Internet Res. 2016;18:e226. Medline:27543152 doi:10.2196/jmir.5533

30 Braun R, Catalani C, Wimbush J, Israelski D. Community Health Workers and Mobile Technology: A Systematic Review of the Literature. PLoS One. 2013;8:e65772. Medline:23776544 doi:10.1371/journal.pone.0065772

31 Leonard K, Masatu MC. Outpatient process quality evaluation and the Hawthorne Effect. Soc Sci Med. 2006;63:2330-40. Medline:16887245 doi:10.1016/j.socscimed.2006.06.003

Clinical evaluation of the use of an mHealth intervention on quality of care provided by Community Health Workers in southwest Niger

David Zakus[1], Moise Moussa[2], Mahamane Ezechiel[3], Joannes Paulus Yimbesalu[4], Patsy Orkar[5], Caroline Damecour[6], Annette E Ghee[7], Matthew MacFarlane[7], Grace Nganga[3]

[1] University of Toronto, Toronto, Canada
[2] Ministry of Public Health, Niamey, Niger
[3] World Vision International, Niamey, Niger
[4] York University, Toronto, Canada
[5] World Vision Canada, Mississauga, Canada
[6] Independent Consultant, Aurora, Canada
[7] World Vision International, London, UK

Background Under the World Health Organization's (WHO) integrated community case management (iCCM) Rapid Access Expansion Program (RAcE), World Vision Niger and Canada supported the Niger Ministry of Public Health to implement iCCM in four health districts in Niger in 2013. Community health workers (CHWs), known as *Relais Communautaire* (RCom), were deployed in their communities to diagnose and treat children under five years of age presenting with diarrhea, malaria and pneumonia symptoms and refer children with severe illness to the higher-level facilities. Two of the districts in southwest Niger piloted RCom using smartphones equipped with an application to support quality case management and provide good timely clinical data. A two-arm cluster randomized trial assessed the impact of use of the mHealth application mainly on quality of care (QoC), but also on motivation, retention and supervision.

Methods A two-arm cluster randomized trial was conducted from March to October 2016 in Dosso and Doutchi districts. The intervention arm comprised 66 RComs equipped with a smartphone and 64 in the paper-based control arm. Trained expert clinicians observed each RCom assessing sick children presenting to them (264 in intervention group; 256 in control group), re-assessed each child on the same set of parameters, and made further observations regarding perceptions of motivation, retention, supervision, drug management and caregiver satisfaction. The primary outcome was a QoC score composed of diagnostic and treatment variables.

Results On average, the mHealth equipped RComs showed a 3.4% higher QoC score (mean difference of 0.83 points). They were more likely to ask about the main danger signs: convulsions (69.7% vs 50.4%, $P < 0.001$); incapacity to drink or eat (79.2% vs 59.4%, $P < 0.001$); vomiting (81.4% vs 69.9%, $P < 0.01$); and lethargy or unconsciousness (92.4% vs 84.8%, $P < 0.01$). Specifically, they consistently asked one more screening question. They were also significantly better at examining for swelling feet (40.2% vs 13.3%, $P < 0.01$) and advising caretakers on diarrhea, drug dosage and administration, and performed (though non-significantly) better when examining cough and breathing rates, referring all conditions, getting children to take prescribed treatments immediately and having caregivers understand treatment continuation. The control group was significantly better at diagnosing fast breathing, bloody diarrhea and severe acute malnutrition; and was somewhat better (non-significant) at treating fever and malaria. With treatment in general of the three diseases, there was no significant difference between the groups. Further analysis showed that 83% of the intervention group had a QoC score greater than 80% (25 out of 31), whereas only 67% of the control group had comparable performance. With respect to referrals, the intervention group performed better, mostly based on their better assessment of danger signs, with more correct (85% vs 29%) and fewer missed, plus a lower proportion of incorrect referrals, with the reverse being true for the controls ($P = 0.012$). There were no statistically significant differences in motivation, retention and supervision between the two groups, yet intervention RCom reported double the rate of no supervision in the last three months (31.8% vs 15.6%).

Conclusions Results suggest that use of the mHealth application led to modestly improved QoC through better assessment of the sick children and better referral decisions by RComs, but not to improvement in treatment of malaria, pneumonia and diarrhea. Considering mHealth's additional costs and logistics, questions around its viability remain. Further implementation could be improved by investing in RComs' capacity building, building organization culture and strengthened supervision, all essential areas for improving any CHW program. In this real-world setting, in poor and remote communities in rural Niger, this study did not support the overall value of the mHealth intervention.

Niger, a large arid landlocked country in West Africa on the southern edge of the Sahara Desert, is one of the poorest and least developed in the world, ranking 187 of 188 countries on the United Nations' Human Development Index [1]. Its economy is mainly dependent on subsistence agriculture and livestock and suffers from threats of frequent droughts, insurgency and displaced people. It has the highest global fertility rate of 7.2 children per woman and equally high rates of infant and child disease and death [2]. In 2016, Niger's under-five mortality rate was 129 deaths per 1000 live births, or 121 225 deaths of children under age five [3]. Three of the most prevalent childhood illnesses – malaria, pneumonia and diarrhea – account for over 60 per cent of deaths in Nigerien children aged 2 to 59 months [4].

The Integrated Community Case Management (iCCM) strategy, based on the deployment of local community health workers (CHWs), aims to increase access to effective case management for children under five years of age suffering from malaria, pneumonia and diarrhea, by bringing services closer to people living in the hard-to-reach communities and among the most vulnerable populations [5]. Studies demonstrate that iCCM, in general, is highly cost-effective if well utilized and it has been widely used as a major public health strategy for early diagnosis, treatment and referral of preventable childhood illnesses, especially in malaria-endemic countries in sub-Saharan Africa [6].

Globally, the first implementation of iCCM and similar programs was encouraging. In Ghana, 92% of carers of sick children sought treatment from CHWs trained to manage pneumonia and malaria; 77% sought care within 24 hours of onset. In Zambia, a study of iCCM for pneumonia and malaria found 68% of children with pneumonia received early and appropriate treatment from CHWs, and overtreatment of malaria significantly declined [7]. This was also the case with Ethiopia's Health Extension Worker Program, whereby CHWs became actual employees of the state health system. Similarly, in countries like South Africa, Nigeria, Malawi and Rwanda, national programs integrate CHWs into health care systems and provide sustainable career paths [8].

Studies on CHW performance have demonstrated that they had the necessary knowledge and skills to successfully carry out treatment of childhood diseases [9-14], including the use of rapid diagnostic tests (RDTs) and timers in the assessment and management of malaria and pneumonia, respectively, in children [15], and in the delivery of immunization [16]. Others have highlighted challenges CHWs encounter with less education [17] and with diagnosis in the absence of proper supervision and follow-up [18,19]. Training CHWs but not providing adequate supervision has been found to be a key bottleneck in effective iCCM implementation, motivation and retention [20].

Increased phone use by over 420 million unique mobile subscribers in sub-Saharan Africa today, accounting for 43% penetration rate, has greatly revolutionized the health sector [21]. There is an emerging body of evidence demonstrating how use of mobile phones in health programming – mobile Health or mHealth – improves and reduces the cost of patient monitoring, medication adherence, and health care worker communication, especially in rural areas.

In Malawi, mHealth applications were designed to increase CHW access to health information, decision-making and logistical support. Research, using a mixed-method approach, provided understanding of the frequency of use of text messaging (SMS), the reasons for use and CHW feedback on the quality of medical care and disease management [22]. Promising mHealth interventions have also been developed around medication adherence for HIV/AIDS and tuberculosis (TB) patients; including the SIMpill, a pill dispensing system with an SIM card embedded in a small bottle. Each time the bottle is opened, an SMS text is sent to a central server uniquely linked to the patient's mobile number. As a result, drug adherence increased between 86 to 92% with a treatment success rate of 94% within the ten months of SIMpill use. In addition to improving treatment adherence, the SIMpill freed up time for CHWs from their routine daily observations of patients taking their medications [23]. In Kenya, a mobile directly observed therapy model, using video and text messaging to enhance medication adherence for TB patients in rural settings, was preferred by 73% of users [24]. In another study in Rwanda, CHWs used RapidSMS, a mobile phone-based system designed to track pregnancy and reduce existing bottlenecks associated communication with health facilities, including emergency transportation. This led to a 27% increase in facility-based delivery [25].

Several reviews on mHealth projects and their overall impact on public health outcomes reveal that while mHealth interventions may positively influence CHW performances in low- and middle-income countries very few studies demonstrate impact on clinical outcomes [26]. Other systematic studies on the use of mobile mHealth tools by CHWs in the area of maternal and child health [27], HIV/AIDS and sexual and reproductive health provide some evidence on the importance of mHealth in improving quality of care, service efficiency and increasing capacity for program monitoring [28].

In 2013, the World Health Organization (WHO), under the Rapid Access and Expansion (RAcE) iCCM program, funded World Vision Canada and the Nigerien Ministère de Santé Publique (hereafter referred to as the Ministry of Public Health or MPH) to implement iCCM delivered through CHWs in four districts of southwestern Niger. The RAcE program supported MPH to introduce iCCM-delivered services through trained volunteers, known as *Relais Communautaire* or RCom. RComs differ from the regular MPH CHW program in Niger, in which the paid Community Health Agents (*Agents de Santé Communautaire* or ASC) are based at Health Posts and trained to a higher level. The iCCM approach used in Niger also focused on supervision – through inventory management, data collection review, clinical mentoring and problem solving – and a delivery approach, which included monthly community and health facility meetings.

An mHealth intervention was introduced among a sub-set of RComs. Samsung smartphones, equipped with a dedicated application, training and regular supervision were provided to 100 RComs. The mHealth intervention complemented the standard use by all RComs of advanced yet appropriate therapeutic tools, including artemisinin-based combination therapy (ACT), rapid diagnostic tests for malaria, amoxicillin, paracetamol, oral rehydration salts (ORS), zinc supplementation and referral to a higher level of care as needed. The value of mobile technology in delivering iCCM services by the RCom was assessed. The objective was to contribute to the body of quality research on mHealth in iCCM and inform and influence iCCM program implementation and policy in Niger. The study was conducted in two administrative regions of southwestern Niger, Dosso and Doutchi, located 120 and 150 km east of the capital city, Niamey and bordering upper northwest Nigeria (**Figure 1**); all as part of the larger iCCM RAcE project in four regions of Niger with approximately 1200 RCom in total.

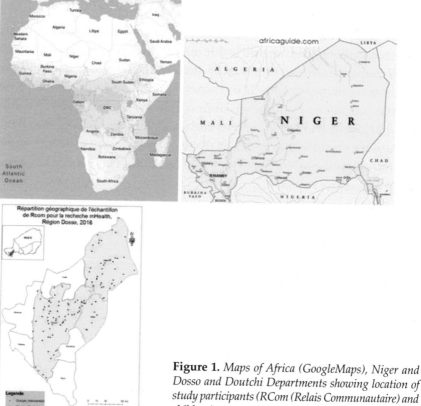

Figure 1. *Maps of Africa (GoogleMaps), Niger and Dosso and Doutchi Departments showing location of study participants (RCom (Relais Communautaire) and children).*

The primary research question focused on whether the use of a specially equipped smartphone (or mHealth intervention) could make a difference in the diagnosis and treatment by RComs of malaria, pneumonia and diarrhea in children aged 2 to 59 months. In addition, we assessed the effects of mHealth on RCom motivation and retention.

METHODS

Sampling

This was a controlled randomized cluster trial with two arms, taking into consideration an intra-group coefficient of 0.1, a significance level of 5%, a power of 80% and a cluster size of four (or four patients seen by each RCom). The Hayes and Bennett sample size calculation formula [29] was used to calculate the sample size: 252 cases in 63 intervention and control groups (where one group is one RCom) each. By applying a dropout rate of 10%, a final sample of 554 patients needed for this study (or 227 in each of the intervention and control groups) was obtained.

A total of 130 RCom from 129 villages were selected randomly for the study: 66 in the intervention group (mHealth; out of a total of 95) and 64 in the control group (paper based; out of a total of 463). Ultimately, 65 community health centres were involved with 32 in Dosso District and 33 in Doutchi District. These two districts, were chosen from within the overall larger programme for their closer proximity to Niamey and for their better security situation. The intervention group RCom had used the smart phone application for about six months prior to the beginning of the study. See **Table 1** for a socio-demographic description of the RCom.

All RCom, including those in the intervention and control groups, received ten days of standard MPH iCCM training in their local languages (Hausa mainly in Doutchi and Zarma in Dosso). They were then deployed in their respective communities to diagnose and treat uncomplicated malaria, pneumonia and diarrhea and refer children with severe illnesses. The intervention group RCom were provided Samsung smartphones loaded with a contextualized French version of the CommCare application (Dimagi Inc, Cambridge, MA, USA) which World Vision had prepared for multi-country use [30].

The smartphone/application-supported RComs enabled to follow standard diagnosis and treatment protocols during their encounter with the caregiver and sick child.The application also contained a module for drug and supplies

Table 1. *RCom (Relais Communautaire) socio-demographic and work context characteristics (Dosso and Doutchi Districts combined)*

CHARACTERISTIC	INTERVENTION GROUP		CONTROL GROUP	
	Number (n = 66)	Proportion (%)	Number (n = 64)	Proportion (%)
Age (years):				
<20	2	3.0	2	3.1
20-29	9	13.6	17	26.6
30-39	27	40.9	20	31.3
40-49	23	34.8	16	25.0
>50	5	7.6	9	14.1
Sex:				
Male	54	81.8	35	54.7
Female	12	18.2	29	45.3
Education:				
Some primary	11	16.7	15	23.4
Primary	11	16.7	15	23.4
Some middle	41	62.1	32	50.0
Middle	2	3.0	1	1.6
Some high school	1	1.5	0	0.0
More than high school	0	0.0	1	1.6
Marital status:				
Married	64	97.0	60	93.8
Single	2	3.0	4	6.3
Distance from health centre (km):				
1-5	7	10.6	4	6.3
6-10	12	18.2	16	25.0
11-15	12	18.2	9	14.1
16-20	5	7.6	4	6.3
21-25	6	9.1	3	4.7
26-30	7	10.6	3	4.7
>30	17	25.8	25	39.1
Number of supervisory visits:				
0	21	31.8	10	15.6
1 or 2	18	27.3	23	35.9
3 or more	27	40.9	31	48.4

management. All intervention RComs were trained for five days on the use of smartphone and application by the local senior research staff.

A team with a trained clinician and assistant per district (Medical Doctor/ Nurse; Medical Doctor/Master of Public Health) visited each RCom during normal service hours to assess QoC and levels of motivation and retention. They were trained for five days under the supervision of two MPH trainers with the support of the MPH Directorate of Statistics. Specifically-designed survey tools included RCom observational assessments and questionnaire surveys, clinical reassessments of the sick children, and questions designed to assess learning levels based on four presented case studies on diarrhea, cough, fever and referral. All 130 RCom were observed managing four children each, followed by re-examination by the clinicians. A total of 520 sick children (aged 2 to 59 months) were diagnosed and treated by the RComs (264 intervention group and 256 control group).

The children were selected on a first-come basis on the days that the trained clinicians presented themselves in the communities with the RCom. Informed consent was obtained from the children's caregivers. Ethical clearance was obtained from Ryerson University, Toronto, Canada and MPH Niger.

Quality of care definition and measurement

Three dependent variables were measured: QoC provided by RCom, RCom motivation and retention. Quality assurance was achieved by a random audit of 20% of the overall sample. Using SPSS software (IBM Corporation, Armonk NY, USA), univariate and multivariate logistic regression analyses were performed to determine the relationship between the three variables and the potential explanatory effect of using CommCare-equipped smartphones in the context of community-based primary health care.

Since no standard measure of QoC for this purpose existed, a composite overall QoC score was developed specific to the diagnosis and treatment job responsibilities of the RCom. It included aspects of health screening, danger sign identification, and treatment which included referral, medication use and advising caregivers.

The QoC score was developed such that a 100% score could be achieved for each child so as to consider illness identification and delivery of care equally important to ruling out illness and avoiding unnecessary treatment or referral. A perfect score was achieved when the RCom asked all ten health screening questions (including mid-upper arm circumference, or MUAC) and correctly classified (ie, present or absent) the four major danger signs and six additional serious symptoms, made an immediate referral according to the presence of the four major danger signs and/or red MUAC, administered medication appropriately, and provided advice to caregivers. Scoring non-events was done to avoid distortion of results when there was no evidence of serious illness or need for medication.

The four referable danger signs included: convulsions; incapacity to drink or eat; vomiting; and lethargy or unconsciousness. A fifth serious danger sign was severe acute malnutrition, assessed by MUAC tape showing red, although this was not considered a referral condition in Niger. The six additional serious conditions were: chest indrawing; swelling of feet; fast breathing; diarrhea; blood in stool; and fever. These comprised the 11 conditions checked for by the RCom.

The maximum QoC score was 31 points; the score was weighted with two-thirds of the score allocated to screening questions and correct identification of the danger signs and signs/symptoms of serious conditions (**Table 2**).

A QoC score was first computed for each child; the mean score for the four children seen by each RCom was then used for comparison to determine the effect of mHealth intervention on QOC. An independent-samples two-tailed test using bootstrap to normalize the data was used to compare QoC scores for intervention and comparison groups. Statistical tests were completed using SPSS v.22.0 (IBM Corp, Armonk NY, USA). For further comparison between experimental groups, a Chi Square test was used, with calculations completed in Excel (Microsoft Corporation, Redmond WA, USA). An alpha level of 0.05 was used for all statistical testing as the minimum level of significance.

RESULTS

There were no significant demographic differences between intervention and control groups at baseline, except that the intervention group was comprised of fewer female RComs (**Table 1**). A total of 520 sick children (264 intervention group and 256 control group) presenting to the RCom were diagnosed and treated. Overall, the symptom profiles of the children presenting were quite similar between the intervention and control groups with about 45% presenting with cough, 10% with diarrhea, and very few with vomiting. Approximately 70% of the children assessed showed signs of a fever with 40 to 50% of these children showing only signs of a fever with no co-existing cough, diarrhea or vomiting, depending on the group. Statistical comparison showed no significant difference in the mix between experimental groups based on the above symptoms ($P = 0.10$).

Small differences were observed between experimental groups in relation to signs and symptoms of serious illness and complexity. No significant difference between groups was seen for children diagnosed with the four immediately referable danger signs and red MUAC ($P = 0.49$); but a difference emerged between groups when all the danger signs were considered including referral signs ($P = 0.000$; data not shown). The differences in the latter were seen for fast breathing (73% vs 69% for intervention and control group, respectively), chest indrawing (47% vs 56%, respectively) and fever (9.3% vs 12.5%, respectively).

Table 2. *Components and criteria of the quality of care score*

Component	Description	Score Criteria	Score
Assessment			
Health screening	RComs are expected to complete a full health screen which consists of 10 questions; one point was awarded for each question asked. The health screen addresses respiratory, gastro-intestinal, neurological, and systemic conditions including fever, swelling, cough, vomiting, etc.	1 point for every question asked	10
Identification of danger signs and other serious conditions/ symptoms	Based on the response to health screening questions, RComs are expected to further assess, looking for four danger signs for immediate referral and seven other serious health conditions including red MUAC. One point was awarded for each of the 11 possible signs that were correctly confirmed by the clinician; the point was awarded whether the flag was correctly identified as positive (being present) or negative (not present).	1 point for every sign correctly identified	11
Treatment			
Referral	RComs are expected to refer sick children to a health centre when a child presented with at least one major danger sign (convulsions, lethargy/ unconsciousness, feeding/drinking incapacity and vomiting).	3 points were awarded when a correct referral or non-referral occurred.	3
Medication administration	RComs are expected to administer four types of medications when appropriate. RComs are able to administer: ORS/Zinc for gastrointestinal /, ACT for malarial symptoms, Paracetemol for fever, and Amoxicillin for respiratory illness/pneumonia.	One point was awarded for each of the 4 medications that were administered or not administered correctly.	4
	The criteria for administering a medication were based on positive symptoms, rather than positive danger signs. Children presenting with diarrhea required ORS/zinc; with fever, they required Paracetemol; with vomiting or diarrhea combined with a fever, they required ACT; and with cough combined with a fever, they required Amoxicillin. Children that were referred to a health clinic were considered to have been treated appropriately regardless of whether medication had been administered or not.		
Advice given	RComs are expected to advise caregivers regarding the need for referral. If a referral occurs, for those returning home, one point was awarded for advice when it was given in each of the following three topics: home care, immunizations, and follow up.	3 points awarded if reason for referral was made; or,	3
		1 point awarded for each of the following: advice on home care, immunizations, and follow-up	
Total score			31

ACT – artemisinin-based combination therapy, ORS – oral rehydration solution, RCom – *Relais Communautaire*

Small differences between groups were seen for case complexity. The experimental group had approximately 10% more cases presenting with multiple symptoms; however, the control group tended towards more complex, serious cases: 43% vs 45% cases had at least 1 of the 11 signs of serious illness, respectively; and 15% vs 17% for two or more of these signs.

Quality of care

The average QoC score for all 130 RCom was 25.77, SD 1.83, (or 83.1%), indicating satisfactory QoC overall. Identification and classification of danger signs and serious conditions/symptoms, medication administration and providing advice were all done well. The QoC per RCom was significantly higher for the intervention group than the control group ($P = 0.009$) indicating that use of the smart phone and mHealth application improved QoC, and this was attributable to better assessment. The effect, though, was small with a mean difference of 0.9 points (or 3.6% higher; $P < 0.01$) (**Table 3**). However, upon further analysis, 83.3% of the intervention group had a QoC score greater than 80% (25 out of 31), whereas only 67.2% of the control group had a score of 80% or higher (**Figure 2**), thus demonstrating that the average QoC values somewhat understate the intervention group's effectiveness. QoC was calculated for each RCom by using the data collected for each of the four children seen (a cluster analysis). Individual per child scores were also compared and were very similar to the cluster calculation.

Clinical assessment (screening)

Analysis of various components comprising the QoC score showed the difference between the two study groups was driven by differences in health assessment, with the intervention RComs consistently asking one

Table 3. *Mean (standard deviation) quality of care score per RCom for key outcomes*

	INTERVENTION GROUP	CONTROL GROUP
	26.2 (2.1)	**25.3 (1.4)**
Health screen*	7.4 (1.6)	6.4 (1.2)
Danger signs	10.5 (0.5)	10.6 (0.4)
Treatment:	8.3 (1.0)	8.4 (0.8)
-Referral	2.7 (0.6)	2.8 (0.4)
-Medications	3.1 (0.5)	3.0 (0.4)
-Advice	2.8 (0.4)	2.6 (0.5)

RCom – *Relais Communautaire*
*Significant difference between intervention and control arms, $P < 0.001$.

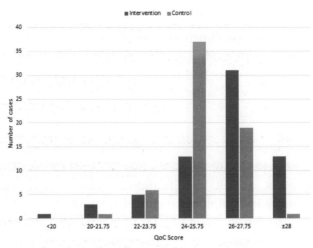

Figure 2. *Distribution of quality of care score by study group (Intervention n = 66, Control n = 64).*

more assessment question on average than the control group. The mHealth-enabled RComs trended towards a more complete health assessment with a higher proportion asking each of the ten assessment questions (**Figure 3**). This difference was significant ($P < 0.01$) for all four major danger signs (convulsions, incapacity of feeding, vomiting, and lethargy/unconsciousness) meaning that a significantly greater proportion of children were assessed for the important factors among RCom with the mobile phones (data not shown).

The intervention group was also significantly more likely (40.2% vs 13.3%, $P < 0.01$) to look for swelling of the feet (nutritional edema) and more likely (non-significant) to ask about blood in stool (data not shown). Conversely, the control group was significantly more likely to assess for severe acute malnutrition using MUAC tape measurement showing red ($P < 0.05$). Cough and diarrhea were almost always equally assessed and the control group had considerably more cases with fever (73 vs 51 cases).

Classification (diagnosis)

The QoC subscores for correct classification of 4 danger signs and 7 serious conditions were similar between the intervention (10.5, SD 0.5) and control groups (10.6, SD 0.4) (**Table 3**). Of the four main danger signs, there was no significant difference in correct classification between groups (**Table 4**). The intervention group had a lower rate of missing a danger sign compared to the control group (29.2% vs 32.3%) but a higher rate of being incorrect (56.5% vs 28.3%). The most frequently missed signs across both groups were

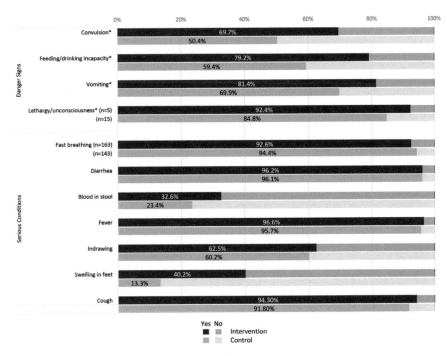

Figure 3. *Percentage of cases examined by RCom (Relais Communautaire) for all danger signs and conditions, by study group (Intervention n = 264; Control n = 256). Asterisk – P < 0.010 for difference between study arms.*

chest indrawing (54.5%), fever greater than 7 days (20.5%), and fast breathing (19.3%). All RComs generally used RDT well, but answered assessment questions related to the four case studies poorly.

The control group was significantly more likely to correctly classify chest indrawing (P = 0.021) and blood in the stool (P = 0.027) (**Table 4**). Otherwise, there was no significant difference in the identification and classification of conditions between groups of RCom, including diarrhea and fever (P > 0.05 for both).

However, difficulty for RCom to correctly identify the danger signs and serious conditions was not apparent in the QoC score since the average sub-score for identifying danger signs was 10.55 out of 11, or 96%, for the whole group. When this was reviewed more closely, it was apparent that the assessment score was strongly influenced by the ability to recognize when a danger sign was absent (**Table 4**). This effect was not surprising given that 58% and 56% of the children seen in the intervention and control groups, respectively, had no danger signs or other serious conditions or symptoms of illness.

Table 4. Proportion of RCom classifications for general danger signs which corresponded to clinician observer's classifications by study group

	Intervention (n = 264)				Control (n = 256)				P-value comparing intervention with control
	% correct		% missed	% incorrect	% Correct		% missed	% incorrect	
	Positive	Negative			Positive	Negative			
Danger signs:									
Convulsions	0.0	99.2	0.0	0.8	0.0	100.0	0.0	0.0	NS
Incapacity of feeding	0.4	97.7	0.8	1.1	0.4	98.4	0.4	0.8	NS
Vomiting	1.1	98.5	0.4	0.0	0.0	98.8	0.8	0.4	NS
Lethargy	0.4	98.1	0.4	1.1	0.0	98.8	0.0	1.2	NS
Other conditions:									
Fast breathing	25.4	60.6	4.5	9.5	26.6	62.9	3.5	7.0	NS
Diarrhea >14 d	0.4	97.7	0.0	1.9	0.4	98.8	0.0	0.8	NS
Blood in stool	0.4	96.6	0.4	2.7	0.4	99.2	0.0	0.4	0.021
Fever >7 days	0.4	91.3	3.4	4.9	2.0	93.0	3.5	1.6	NS
Chest indrawing	12.5	72.0	6.8	8.7	12.9	71.1	11.7	4.3	0.027
Swelling of feet	0.4	97.0	0.4	2.3	0.0	99.2	0.4	0.4	NS
Red MUAC	3.0	95.8	0.4	0.8	0.4	98.0	1.2	0.4	NS

RCom – Relais Communautaire, MUAC – mid-upper arm circumference

Treatment and counselling

The QoC subscores for treatment were similar between the intervention (8.3, SD 1.0) and the control group (8.4, SD 0.8) (**Table 3**). However, a significant difference was observed between the intervention and control groups for malaria treatment, with the intervention group more correctly administering ACT as indicated (72.3%) compared to the control group (66.4%) ($P = 0.012$), including being less likely to administer the drug when it was not required (**Figure 4**).

Among the most important conditions, RComs in the control group had significantly fewer errors when treating fast breathing ($P = 0.022$) (**Figure 4**) and were significantly better at giving advice about the use of either the antibiotic, ORS, zinc or anti-malarial ($P < 0.05$). There was no significant difference between groups in the use of amoxicillin to treat pneumonia (cough and fast breathing) which together with good RDT use contributed to good overall QoC in both groups. Regarding other conditions or symptoms, the control RCom had significantly fewer errors when addressing cases of blood in the stool ($P = 0.035$).

Medications were administered similarly by all RCom [**Figure 4**];

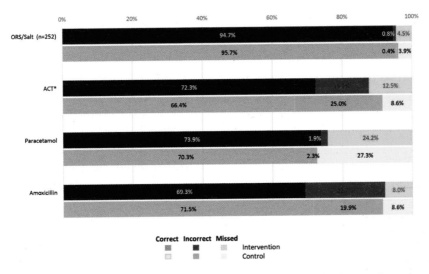

Figure 4. *Correct RCom (Relais Communautaire) administration of medication to each case, by study group (Intervention n = 264; Control n = 256). Asterisk – P = 0.023 for difference between study arms.*

however, of concern was the relatively high number of incorrect and missed administrations of medication. ACT treatment was missed or prescribed incorrectly in 27.9% of cases by intervention RCom and 33.6% of cases by control group RCom, with similar numbers also seen for paracetamol (26.1% and 29.7%) and amoxicillin (30.6% and 28.5%). Use of drugs (correct diagnosis and prescription) was appropriate, therefore, about 70% of the time.

The proportion of caregivers who were counselled by the RComs to give more fluids and continue to feed their child in cases of diarrhea was significantly higher in the intervention group (64.9% vs 46.0%, *P* = 0.049). On the other hand, intervention group RComs gave significantly less advice to mothers/caregivers on the dosage of medication, (*P* = 0.028), but were somewhat more likely to have caregivers properly explain back drug dose and administration on site.

There was little to no difference in caregiver satisfaction with the RCom's work and the willingness of caregivers to return for more services in the future, which were all generally high.

Referrals

There was no difference in QOC scores between the RCom groups with respect to referral, when considering correct, missed and wrong referrals (*P* = 0.33). Both groups did relatively well, scoring just over 90% correct, though mainly on the strength of not referring when not needed. The mHealth-enabled RComs, however, did significantly better ($P = 0.012$) in referring to a higher level of care when needed, ie, when danger signs were present. Using a restricted sample of referrals (referrals confirmed and needed and referrals made), statistical differences were observed based on correct, missed and wrong referrals ($P = 0.044$): the intervention group was more likely to correctly refer (11/13 vs 2/7 for intervention and control groups, respectively), and less likely to miss the referral (2/13 vs 5/7). Furthermore, the intervention group was less likely to make referral when a referral was not required (21/32 vs 15/17 for intervention and control groups, respectively).

To better understand these referral results, a similar comparison of referrals was completed based on the RCom identifying a referral sign and making the referral; this analysis showed no significant difference in results between groups ($P = 0.240$) thus suggesting that missed referral signs were the main reason. Surprisingly, wrong referrals (20/32 vs 14/17 for intervention and control groups, respectively) suggests that RCom based their decision to refer on other criteria in addition to the established referral criteria.

Incorrect referrals, where the clinician did not agree with the RComs' decisions to refer, were not a large problem, as only 36 such referrals occurred (21 and 15 in intervention and control, respectively).

Supervision, retention and motivation

RCom in the control group received more supervision in terms of numbers of supervisory visits (**Table 1**), including complete lack of supervision in the last three months at about half the rate (15.6% vs 31.8%) as well as a somewhat better quality of supervision as reflected by supervisor actions (**Figure 5**). In general, regardless of smart phone use, RComs located less than 15 km from their supervisor provided better QoC compared to those located more than 15 km from their supervisor (data not shown).

RComs in the intervention group reported being slightly less likely to be retained compared to RComs in the control group (21.2% vs 17.2%) and reported poor working conditions more often (24.2% vs 15.6%). RCom retention also depended on education level across both groups: those at the secondary level (first cycle not completed) were 13.9 times more likely to be retained compared to those with a primary level not completed. Both groups were equally satisfied with their work environment (60% positive, with 20% non-response rate).

There were no statistically significant differences between both groups of RCom in their answers to 15 questions on motivational factors; though with

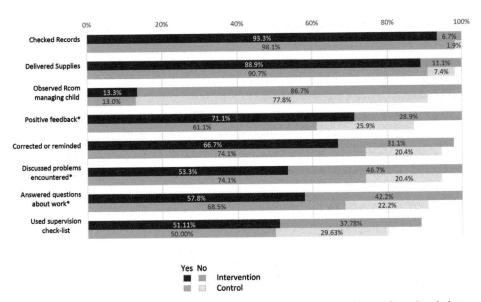

Figure 5. *Proportion of RComs (Relais Communautaire) whose supervisor performed each duty during visit, by study group (Intervention n = 45; Control n = 54). Asterisk – P < 0.050 for difference between study arms.*

the direct question about job satisfaction, RComs in the intervention group were slightly more satisfied than those of the control group (93.9% vs 85.9%; *P* = 0.256). Almost all RComs reported feeling respected, proud of their work and committed to it. The distance separating the RComs from her or his supervisor constituted a major factor in RComs motivation. RComs who were located less than 15 km from their supervisor were more motivated than those located more than 15 km from their supervisor. Academic training levels also had an effect on RComs motivation regardless of mHealth group assignment; those who completed primary school level were 3.6 times more likely to be motivated compared to those who had not completed primary education.

A summary overview of all the key study findings is found in **Table 5**, indicating where the mHealth intervention had a positive effect, but also several instances where the control group RComs did better than the mHealth intervention group.

DISCUSSION

The QoC delivered by RComs was dependent on their ability to complete a full screening assessment, accurately assess the child's health status and deliver appropriate care, whether administering medication, advising on home care

Table 5. *Summary of key findings of differences when comparing RCom intervention and control groups*

Level of differences	Summary of findings
1. Statistically significant findings in favour of mHealth equipped RCom	• Greater proportion of children examined for the four major danger signs by the RComs
	• Greater proportion of children examined for swelling of both feet by the RCom amongst additional danger signs
	• Greater proportion of children with diarrhea whose caretakers got advice to give more fluids and to continue feeding
	• Greater proportion of children in need of an antibiotic, ORS, zinc and/or anti-malarial whose caregivers received at least one advice about drug dosage and administration
	• Greater proportion of RComs whose supervisor provided positive feedback about doing a good job
	• More suggested that World Vision can increase RCom job satisfaction by providing a salary and financial support (as they find their RCom work difficult to balance with the need to have income generating work)
	• More showed less appreciation of motivation statements
	• More suggested that cell phones could be used for other functions, like calculator and timer
2. Not statistically significant findings but which showed a higher positive difference in favour of mHealth equipped RCom	• Greater proportion of children examined for cough and diarrhea by the RCom
	• Greater proportion of children correctly referred for the all danger signs/classified diseases by the RComs
	• Greater proportion of children in need of antibiotic, ORS, zinc and/or anti-malarial who received the first dose of the treatment right away
	• Greater proportion of children whose breathing rate had been evaluated and compared favourably within a gap of ±3 between measures by RComs and clinicians
	• Proportion of children given an antibiotic, ORS, zinc and/or anti-malarial whose caregiver could explain how to administer the treatment (further complementing the statistically significant finding above)
	• Received fewer supervisory visits in the last three months than the control group
	• Had a more negative perception of their working conditions (worse than control)
	• Suggested that World Vision could increase their job satisfaction by working to improve transportation (complementing that of financial resources above)
3. Statistically significant findings in favour of the RCom control group, those not equipped with the mHealth intervention	• Greater proportion of children assessed for severe acute malnutrition by MUAC tape colour reading by the RComs (as one of the other danger signs)
	• Greater proportion of children whose classifications given by the RComs corresponded to the clinicians' in two major areas (diarrhea with blood in stool and fast breathing)
	• Greater proportion whose supervisor discussed problems and answered questions during the most recent visit
	• More control group RComs were women

Level of differences	Summary of findings
4. Not statistically significant findings but which showed a high positive difference in favour of the RCom control group not using the mHealth intervention	• Greater proportion of children with confirmed fever and positive RDT who received an anti-malarial from the RComs
	• Greater proportion of children with fever confirmed by high temperature who received Paracetamol from the RComs
	• Greater number of times the RComs received a supervisory visit in the last 3 months; the control group RComs received more supervisory visits overall
	• Greater proportion of RComs whose supervisor corrected or reminded them of things during the most recent visit
	• More satisfaction with their work environment
	• Have a better perception of their working conditions
	• More suggested that World Vision can increase their job satisfaction by providing them materials, medications and food support
5. No difference between RCom groups	• Proportion of children examined for fever
	• Proportion of children whose breathing rate had been evaluated and compared favourably within a gap of ±3 between measures by RComs and clinicians
	• General treatment of children
	• Proportion of children with cough and fast breathing who were prescribed Amoxicillin by the RComs
	• Correct classifications (as verified by the clinicians) for: diarrhea less than 14 days and no blood in the stool; diarrhea for 14 days or more; blood in the stool; fever for last 7 days; fever for less than 7 days; and chest indrawing
	• Caregiver satisfaction of the RCom's work and their willingness to return for more services in the future (but was all generally high)
	• Most poorly answered the questions related to the four case studies.

RCom – *Relais Communautaire*

and follow up, and referral to a nearby health centre if appropriate. Overall, QoC by RComs was high, with the intervention group having a small but significant better score (3.4%). This small difference appears to be related to the assessment process, with the mHealth-enabled group asking one more question on average than the control group, suggesting slightly improved protocol adherence in this area attributable to mHealth use.

Irrespective of the considered general danger signs, the proportion of children examined for danger signs was significantly higher among the smartphone equipped RComs than those who did not use smartphones for case management. This could be attributed to the intervention RComs being more attentive and following the protocol when looking for general danger signs than the control group RComs. The higher proportion of children presenting with multiple symptoms to the intervention group may have biased them towards a better assessment, shifting their QoC score upwards.

Most RComs performed well in correctly identifying the presence or absence of danger signs, with the most frequently missed serious conditions being chest indrawing, fast breathing and fever. The intervention group was more likely to incorrectly identify chest indrawing; while the control group was more likely to miss this sign. Additionally, results showed that the three screening questions indicating systemic involvement were not being asked; the extent of screening for illness severity appeared to be limited. The intervention group missed classifying a much smaller percentage of the four main iCCM danger signs including red MUAC (30.8% vs 71.4%), with missing the danger signs attributed to inadequate screening or low skill level.

There was a relatively high number of incorrect and missed administrations of medications that, when combined, were greater than the number of correctly administered medications; this being of great concern and an area where supervision should be focused. The use of the mHealth application in correctly administering medications only had a significant effect for ACT medication with the intervention group prescribing it better and being less likely to prescribe when the drug was not required, a positive finding that might contribute to lessening the development of drug resistance. The availability and use by all of the RDT also contributed to ensuring a better QoC. In general, amongst all RCom, the correct use of drugs, including amoxicillin, was similar at about 70%, and over 90% for ORS.

Consideration should also be given to factors related to the child's family. For example, a caregiver who has prior experience with sick children may delay seeking medical help or encourage the RCom to administer a medication they consider helpful. In our study, mHealth RCom showed better communication skill with caregivers, suggesting a potentially useful strategy to counter such influences on treatment and referral.

While referral in general was poor, intervention group RComs did better, with much fewer missed referrals when needed compared to the control group (2/13 or 15% vs 5/7 or 71%, respectively), and fewer incorrect referrals (21/32 or 66% and 15/17 or 88%, respectively). Better referral performance in the mHealth group can potentially build community-wide confidence in the health system, so important in such remote and isolated settings. Amongst both groups, though, referrals were more likely to occur when the distance from a clinic was farther and RComs did not delay referral because of a long distance to further medical assistance. Since RComs in the control group tended to be further from a health clinic (**Table 1**), distance from a health centre may have masked an mHealth effect.

In general, the use of the CommCare mHealth application contributed to a slight improvement in QoC given to sick children by RComs. As can be deduced from the data, RComs in both groups performed well in their work, providing needed health services to children in their communities, though many areas were identified for improvement, including better training, continuing education and better supervision. RComs in the intervention group were slightly more satisfied and more likely not to be retained than those of the control group, which may have been related to sex (there were many more male RComs in the intervention group) and to using an mHealth-enabled smartphone in a village clinical setting, potentially having the perceived added community status and potential career mobility that it confers, possibly more so to males vs females. This potential set of impacts on social dynamics following mHealth introduction merits further investigation.

It should also be noted that carrying out such a study in one of the poorest areas of the world was a challenge, but constant progress was made and plans were mostly attained by the diligent staff. Accessing cloud services, having constant access to electricity, having reliable transport (mostly small motorcycles), distances, and lack of maps and travel landmarks were further challenges. Carrying out one of the first ever clinical randomized controlled trials at community level on mHealth was a great learning experience by all; and progress, even meagre, was a commendable achievement and should continue.

Limitations

The scope of this study was focused on detecting differences in case management of children by CHWs using smartphone equipped with a special application. The findings have several limitations. First is the possibility that the initial and subsequent training on using the smartphone could have been better, along with closer and more specific supervision to use the technology to maximum effect to leverage effectiveness of the iCCM program. Subsequently, the results are applicable to settings where World Vision's version of the CommCare application in support of iCCM programming is deployed. Our definition of QoC could have been faulty, yet it was composed of logical variables that were adequately measured. Finally, the study was not designed to assess efficiency gain in RCom work patterns or in the potential cost-benefit or cost-effectiveness of the mHealth intervention, nor was it designed to evaluate various other possible smartphone applications [13,15,17,18].

CONCLUSIONS

The positive impact of mHealth on RComs diagnosis and treatment of the three diseases responsible for majority of deaths among children under five years of age, although encouraging, was relatively small and therefore the results of this study do not lead to a definitive recommendation to scale up mHealth in this setting, especially considering trade-offs related to associated costs and logistics. It would be essential to address identified gaps in the use of the mHealth intervention. While it is likely that the mHealth program could evolve into a more effective one, especially if supervision and training were enhanced, the cost-benefit remains poorly understood and the potential to improve overall RCom performance through other strategies, including better overall supervision, continuing education and building organization culture [31], should remain a priority for iCCM.

Acknowledgements: *We acknowledge the Niger Ministry of Public Health and World Vision program managers and clinician assistants in Doutchi and Dosso who very competently monitored the field research and carried out the data collection, Issoufu Saidu who worked hard on the initial data analysis, research assistant Idé Seydou, Jaren Eriksen and Agnes Mukamana who contributed greatly in the initial stages with research design and implementation, and the WHO RAcE team in both Geneva and Niamey. The contributions of many other individuals and institutions in supporting the implementation and evaluation of the Niger Integrated Community Case Management/Rapid Access Expansion program are also gratefully acknowledged, including the community participants who volunteered their time to be interviewed and provided valuable feedback, and our funders. Insightful reviews by Loria Kulathungam and Barbara Main contributed to the completion of the final manuscript.*

Disclaimer: *The opinions expressed in this manuscript are those of the authors and do not necessarily reflect the views of the World Health Organization, World Vision or Global Affairs Canada.*

Ethics: *Ethical clearance and research permission were obtained from Ministère de la Santé Publique (MSP) in Niger and Ryerson University, Toronto, Canada.*

Funding: *This study was supported by the World Health Organization's Rapid Access Expansion program funded by Global Affairs Canada along with various contributions from World Vision Niger, Canada and International.*

Authorship contributions: *DZ, with assistance from WHO, conceptualized the study and analysis plan and oversaw the data collection and management. GN and EM managed the data collection and helped lead the data analysis. DZ, together with JPY, wrote the first draft of the manuscript, with significant contributions from all authors. CD provided excellent statistical input and manuscript reviews. AEG and MM contributed* *data visualization support and provided critical reviews and content edits on manuscript drafts. All authors read and approved the final manuscript.*

Competing interests: *The authors completed the Unified Competing Interest form www. icmje.org/coi_disclosure.pdf (available upon request from the corresponding author), and declare no conflicts of interest.*

References

1 United Nations Development Programme. Human Development Report 2016: Human development for everyone, p. 25. Available: http://hdr.undp.org/sites/default/files/HDR2016_EN_Overview_Web.pdf. Accessed: 28 February 2019.

2 The World Bank Data. Fertility rate, total (births per woman). Available: https://data.worldbank.org/indicator/SP.DYN.TFRT.IN. Accessed: 28 February 2019.

3 UNICEF Data. Monitoring the situation of children and women. United Nations Interagency Group for Child Mortality Estimation (UN IGME), 2017. Available: https://data.unicef.org. Accessed: 28 February 2019.

4 UNICEF Data. Child Survival, Under-five mortality, March 2018. Available: https://data.unicef.org/topic/child-survival/under-five-mortality/. Accessed: 28 February 2019.

5 World Health Organization /UNICEF Joint Statement on Integrated Community Case Management: An equity-focused strategy to improve access to essential treatment services for children, June 2012. Available: https://www.unicef.org/health/files/iCCM_Joint_Statement_2012.pdf. Accessed: 28 February 2019.

6 UNICEF and World Health Organization. Overview and latest update on integrated community case management: Potential for benefit to malaria programs, February 2015. Available: https://www.unicef.org/health/files/WHO-UNICEF_iCCM_Overview_and_Update_(FINAL).pdf. Accessed: 28 February 2019.

7 World Health Organization. Integrated community case management of malaria, updated 12 July 2016. Available: http://www.who.int/malaria/areas/community_case_management/overview/en/. Accessed: 28 February 2019.

8 Chandani Y, Andersson S, Heaton A, Noel M, Shieshia M, Mwirotsi A, et al. Making products available among community health workers: Evidence for improving community health supply chains from Ethiopia, Malawi, and Rwanda. J Glob Health. 2014;4:020405. Medline:25520795 doi:10.7189/jogh.04.020405

9 Biemba G, Yeboah-Antwi K, Vosburg KB, Prust ML, Keller B, Worku Y, et al. Effect of deploying community health assistants on appropriate treatment for diarrhoea, malaria and pneumonia: Quasi-experimental study in two districts of Zambia. Trop Med Int Health. 2016;21:985-94. Medline:27224652 doi:10.1111/tmi.12730

10 Hamer DH, Brooks ET, Semrau K, Pilingana P, MacLeod WB, Siazeele K, et al. Quality and safety of integrated community case management of malaria using rapid diagnostic tests and pneumonia by community health workers. Pathog Glob Health. 2012;106:32-9. Medline:22595272 doi:10.1179/1364859411Y.0000000042

11 Mukanga D, Tibenderana JK, Peterson S, Pariyo GW, Kiguli J, Waiswa P, et al. Access, acceptability and utilization of community health workers using diagnostics for case management of fever in Ugandan children: a cross-sectional study. Malar J. 2012;11:121. Medline:22521034 doi:10.1186/1475-2875-11-121

12 Johnson AD, Thomson DR, Atwood S, Alley I, Beckerman JL, Koné I, et al. Assessing early access to care and child survival during a health system strengthening intervention in Mali: a repeated cross sectional survey. PLoS One. 2013;8:e81304. Medline:24349053 doi:10.1371/journal.pone.0081304

13 Perry H, Zulliger R. How effective are community health workers? An overview of current evidence with recommendations for strengthening community health worker programs to accelerate progress in achieving the health-related Millennium Development Goals. Johns Hopkins Bloomberg School of Public Health, September 2012. Available: http://www.everywomaneverychild.org/wp-content/uploads/2016/11/review-of-chw-effectiveness-for-mdgs-sept2012.pdf. Accessed: 28 February 2019.

14 Sirima SB, Konaté A, Tiono AB, Convelbo N, Cousens S, Pagnoni F. Early treatment of childhood fevers with pre-packaged antimalarial drugs in the home reduces severe malaria morbidity in Burkina Faso. Trop Med Int Health. 2003;8:133-9. Medline:12581438 doi:10.1046/j.1365-3156.2003.00997.x

15 Mukanga D, Babirye R, Peterson S, Pariyo GW, Ojiambo G, Tibenderana JK, et al. Can lay community health workers be trained to use diagnostics to distinguish and treat malaria and pneumonia in children? Lessons from rural Uganda. Trop Med Int Health. 2011;16:1234-42. Medline:21752163 doi:10.1111/j.1365-3156.2011.02831.x

16 Haines A, Sanders D, Lehmann U, Rowe AK, Lawn JE, Jan S, et al. Achieving child survival goals: potential contribution of community health workers. Lancet. 2007;369:2121-31. Medline:17586307 doi:10.1016/S0140-6736(07)60325-0

17 Wanduru P, Tetui M, Tuhebwe D, Ediau M, Okuga M, Nalwadda C, et al. The performance of community health workers in the management of multiple childhood infectious diseases in Lira, northern Uganda – a mixed methods cross-sectional study. Glob Health Action. 2016;9:33194. Medline:27882866 doi:10.3402/gha.v9.33194

18 Kelly JM, Osamba B, Garg RM, Hamel MJ, Lewis JJ, Rowe SY, et al. Community health worker performance in the management of multiple childhood illnesses: Siaya District, Kenya, 1997–2001. Am J Public Health. 2001;91:1617-24. Medline:11574324 doi:10.2105/AJPH.91.10.1617

19 UNICEF. Review of systematic challenges to the scale-up of integrated community case management: Emerging lessons and recommendations from the catalytic initiative (CI/IHSS). UNICEF Health Section, Program Division: Maternal, Newborn and Child Health Working Paper, New York, 2012. Available: https://www.unicef.org/health/files/Analysis_of_Systematic_Barriers_cover_1163.pdf. Accessed: 28 February 2019.

20 UNICEF. Access to healthcare through community health workers in east and southern Africa. UNICEF Health Section, Program Division: Maternal, Newborn and Child Health Working Paper, New York, 2014. Available: https://www.unicef.org/health/files/Access_to_healthcare_through_community_health_workers_in_East_and_Southern_Africa.pdf. Accessed: 28 February 2019.

21 Maila DN, Fenny C. Sub-Saharan Africa to surpass half a billion mobile subscribers by end of decade, finds new GSMA study. Press Release, July 11, 2017. Available: https://www.gsma.com/newsroom/press-release/sub-sarahan-africa-surpass-half-billion-mobile-subscribers-end-decade/. Accessed: 28 February 2019.

22 Lemay NV, Sullivan T, Jumbe B, Perry CP. Reaching remote health workers in Malawi: baseline assessment of a pilot mHealth intervention. J Health Commun. 2012;17(suppl1):105-17. Medline:22548604 doi:10.1080/10810730.2011.649106

23 Barclay E. Text messages could hasten tuberculosis drug compliance. Lancet. 2009;373:15-6. Medline:19125443 doi:10.1016/S0140-6736(08)61938-8

24 Hoffman JA, Cunningham JR, Suleh AJ, Sundsmo A, Dekker D, Vago F, et al. Mobile direct observation treatment for tuberculosis patients: A technical feasibility pilot using mobile phones in Nairobi, Kenya. Am J Prev Med. 2010;39:78-80. Medline:20537846 doi:10.1016/j.amepre.2010.02.018

25   Ngabo F, Nguimfack J, Nwaigwe F, Mugeni C, Muhoza D, Wilson DR, et al. Designing and implementing an innovative SMS-based alert system (RapidSMS-MCH) to monitor pregnancy and reduce maternal and child deaths in Rwanda. Pan Afr Med J. 2012;13:31. Medline:23330022

26   Källander K, Tibenderana JK, Akpogheneta OJ, Strachan DL, Hill Z, ten Asbroek AH, et al. Mobile health (mHealth) approaches and lessons for increased performance and retention of community health workers in low- and middle-income countries: a review. J Med Internet Res. 2013;15:e17. Medline:23353680 doi:10.2196/jmir.2130

27   Lee SH, Nurmatov UB, Nwaru BI, Mukherjee M, Grant L, Pagliari C. Effectiveness of mHealth interventions for maternal, newborn and child health in low- and middle-income countries: Systematic review and meta-analysis. J Glob Health. 2016;6:010401. Medline:26649177 doi:10.7189/jogh.06.010401

28   Braun R, Catalani C, Wimbush J, Israelski D. Community health workers and mobile technology: a systematic review of the literature. PLoS One. 2013;8:e65772. Medline:23776544 doi:10.1371/journal.pone.0065772

29   Hayes RJ, Bennett S. Simple sample size calculation for cluster-randomized trials. Int J Epidemiol. 1999;28:319-26. Medline:10342698 doi:10.1093/ije/28.2.319

30   Studies DC. World Vision: Deploying MOTECH suite to support global MNCH and nutrition programs. Available: https://www.dimagi.com/case-studies/mhealth-world-vision-motech/. Accessed: 28 February 2019.

31   Deal TE, Kennedy AA. Corporate Cultures: The Rites and Rituals of Corporate Life. Harmondsworth, UK: Penguin Books; 1982, reissue New York, USA: Perseus Books; 2000.

Appendix 1.

Links to online supplementary documents

Online supplementary materials for chapter: Evidence of Impact: iCCM as a strategy to save lives of children aged under five.
http://jogh.org/documents/issue201901/jogh-09-010801-s001.pdf

Online supplementary materials for chapter: Integrated community case management: Planning for sustainability in five African countries.
http://jogh.org/documents/issue201901/jogh-09-010802-s001.pdf

Online supplementary materials for chapter: Home visits by community health workers for pregnant mothers and newborns: coverage plateau in Malawi.
http://jogh.org/documents/issue201901/jogh-09-010808-s001.pdf

Online supplementary materials for chapter: A mixed-methods quasi-experimental evaluation of a mobile health application and quality of care in the integrated community case management program in Malawi.
http://jogh.org/documents/issue201901/jogh-09-010811-s001.pdf